CONTENTS

1 THE FASHION WORLD   1

2 A BRIEF HISTORY OF FASHION   11

3 THE MATERIALS OF FASHION

4 THE CREATING OF FASHIONS

5 ACCESSORIES IN FASHION

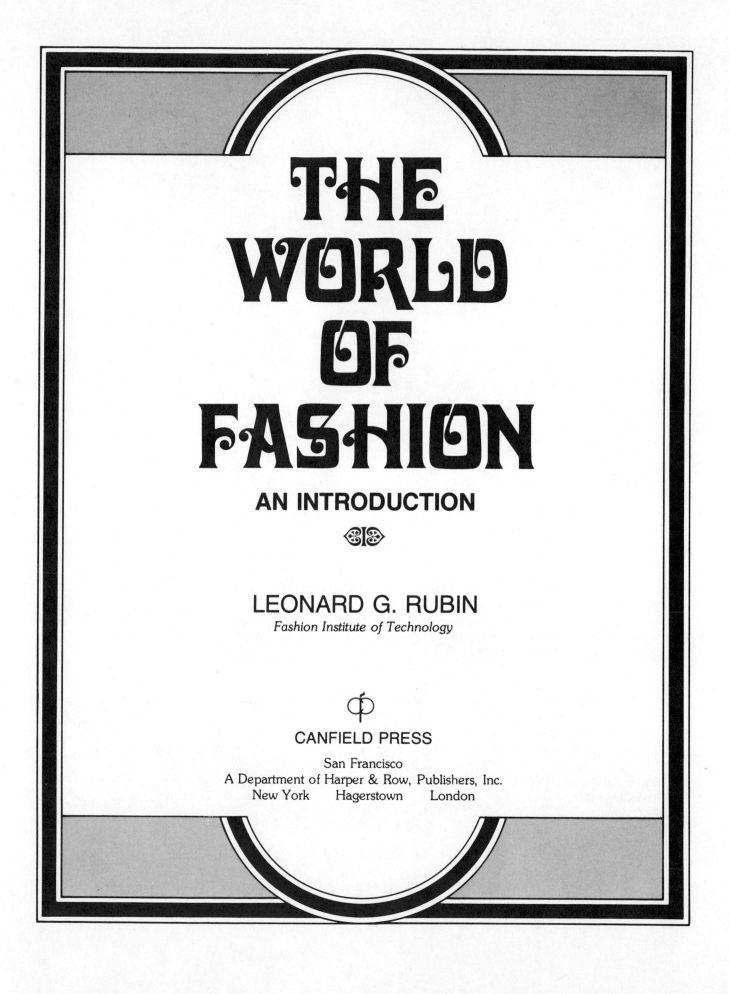

THE WORLD OF FASHION

AN INTRODUCTION

LEONARD G. RUBIN

Fashion Institute of Technology

CANFIELD PRESS

San Francisco
A Department of Harper & Row, Publishers, Inc.
New York   Hagerstown   London

For EWR, CLR,
CH, AH, CR

Cover and interior design by Geri Davis

The World of Fashion: An Introduction
Copyright © 1976 by Leonard G. Rubin

Library of Congress Cataloging in Publication Data

Rubin, Leonard G
    The world of fashion.

    Bibliography: p.
    Includes index.
    1. Clothing trade. 2. Fashion. I. Title
TT497.R75   338.4'7'687   76-4078
ISBN 0-06-453500-2

76 77 78 79   10 9 8 7 6 5 4 3 2 1

6 FASHIONS FOR CHILDREN 79

7 MEN'S AND BOYS' FASHIONS 93

8 FASHION IN HOME FURNISHINGS 107

9 FASHION CENTERS AND THEIR INFLUENCE

127

10 UNIONS AND THE FASHION INDUSTRY

149

11 THE MARKETING AND RETAILING OF FASHION

171

12   ADVERTISING, PROMOTION, AND PUBLICITY   193

13   HOME SEWING   219

14 FASHION AND CHANGE 237

15 FASHION CAREERS 259

THE WORLD OF FASHION

GEOFFREY BEENE attended Tulane University in his native state of Louisiana. While continuing his studies at the University of Southern California, he took a part-time job in the display department of a department store. When his fashion sketches were brought to the attention of store executives, they were so impressed that they advised him to "go East," where the fashion industry is centered. Instead of New York, he went to Paris, where he studied painting at the Académie Julien during the day and worked with a retired tailor from the House of Molyneux in the evenings. When he returned to the United States, he determined to make a success in the fashion business.

Now in his twelfth year in his own firm, Geoffrey Beene is increasingly influential, as his simple, elegant designs have become a hallmark of innovation and quality. His ideas are now making themselves felt in the field of sportswear through his "Beene Bag" division. He also designs collections of furs, jewelry, watches, scarves, and men's wear.

Among the many citations he has received for his contribution to fashion are the Coty American Fashion Critics Hall of Fame Award, two National Cotton Awards, the Neiman-Marcus Award, and the great honor of having his designs displayed in the Costume Institute of the Metropolitan Museum of Art.

FOREWORD

In recent years American fashions have achieved growing importance and leadership in the fashion world. Our more casual approach and the world's interest in imitating our life styles have put emphasis on fashions created by American designers. Many of these fashions have been translated and popularized, and are currently worn by millions of men and women throughout the world.

I believe Leonard Rubin has caught the spirit of these trends and ideas. In *The World of Fashion,* he has done an outstanding job in sorting out the various complicated aspects of fashion and the apparel business. He tells the reader in plain language and in an interesting manner how the fashion industry operates. His choices of illustrations are illuminating.

As one whose entire adult life has been involved in fashion and who believes strongly that the American influence will continue to grow, I welcome you to what I consider an immensely stimulating business—the business and art of fashion.

New York, 1976   *Geoffrey Beene*

PREFACE

Fashion is specific and vague, timeless and changing, chic and gaudy, yesterday and tomorrow, young and old. Fashion affects every aspect of our lives—from apparel to home furnishings to automobiles. Some of the world's top apparel designers are now creating imaginative automobile interiors.

Each year, each season, new fashions appear on the scene. Some catch on, most don't. Who can predict which fashions will and which won't? Perhaps you will be able to, after reading this book and learning about some of the basic facets of the fashion world. You may be reading this book for your own enlightenment or because it is the text for a fashion course. In either case, *The World of Fashion* will introduce you to an exciting, ever-changing scene.

To make order out of the industry, the book begins with an overview of the fashion business, followed by a capsule history of fashion. The purpose of the history chapter is to reveal some of the roots and to trace how they have run through the world of fashion over the years.

The third chapter launches into the fashion manufacturing process by discussing the materials of fashion—fibers, fabrics, furs. The next chapter focuses on fashion design and manufacturing. Subsequent chapters are devoted to accessories, children's wear, men's and boys' wear, and home furnishings. The chapter on fashion centers includes international, as well as United States, centers. The impact of labor unions on the fashion industry is discussed in a historical context. The marketing and the retailing of fashion are important topics given ample treatment, as are advertising, promotion, and publicity. A separate chapter concerns the recent revival of home sewing as an indicator of the contemporary emphasis on individualism and creativity. The chapter on fashion change encompasses the new consumerism movement and varying life styles, both of which have far-reaching effects on the fashion world. The concluding chapter describes representative careers in this diverse, challenging business of fashion.

The approach of the book reflects an effort to introduce the reader to the social, cultural, and business aspects of fashion. The story is told largely through the use of visual materials drawn from all phases of the industry, from all periods, from all over the globe. Statistics are used sparingly, for they change as quickly as they are gathered. To travel with the moving panorama of fashion, one must turn to the trade media for up-to-the-minute information.

I appreciate the helpful comments of my colleagues in the education field who helped in the writing and revising process: Marty Diviak (Los Angeles),

Karen Zwissler (Milwaukee Area Technical Institute), Larry Wright (Fashion Institute of America, Atlanta), and Joann Driggers (Mt. San Antonio College, California). Many of their suggestions have been incorporated in the book.

I welcome you to the world of fashion. May you enjoy it and profit by your association with it.

New York, 1976   *Leonard G. Rubin*

1
THE FASHION WORLD

ome humorously say fashion began when Eve selected a fig leaf in the Garden of Eden. The history of fashion is probably as old as the history of apparel itself. Soon after man discovered that clothes served as a protection against nature, he probably considered their esthetic and status aspects. From the days of the cave men, a tiger skin, when worn, was probably a greater status symbol than that of a less fierce animal, as it indicated that the wearer had more hunting prowess. And, of course, the mate of a great hunter would have a fine skin to cover her body.

BACKGROUNDING FASHION

At first, historians regarded the covering of the human body as mainly a symbol of chastity and modesty. This interpretation is obviously too limited; warmth and comfort were important. Accessories had other values. The first types of jewelry worn were not to cover the body but to bring good luck and ward off evil spirits.

In ancient Egypt, there were strict rules governing what everyone wore. We can identify to this day, when we examine Egyptian art and statues, the status of nearly every person depicted. Only the pharaoh could carry certain symbols and wear a beard. Only members of his court could adorn themselves with certain robes and signets. This same concept applied to early Romans and their society. A senator's robes distinguished him from other men. Various ranks in the military service were denoted by colors and symbols. Spanish monarchs and the nobility of medieval times distinguished themselves by special costumes and adornment. In fact, the shields and coats of arms that have come down through the ages are marks worn by feudal barons and lords. Some of the names of famous families are taken from their shields or emblems. For example, the name Rothschild, still famous in the world of finance today, derives from the German *Rothschild,* meaning "red shield."

Before the French Revolution, one way of determining a man's position was by his wig. The nobility wore wigs; the proletariat did not. Through the years, clothing has often been the symbol of groups or segments of society other than military. The word "sabotage" comes from the French word for a wooden clog shoe—*sabot.* The sabot was thrown into machinery to keep it from working when the laborers at plants thought that the machines might contribute to their unemployment.

The sabot was a symbol of the French laborer, while leather shoes or boots were worn by the aristocracy. The military wear distinguishing dress to indicate branch of service—for example, the Army wears brown and the Navy, blue. Different nations have selected different colors as well to distinguish their troops on the field. Certain military leaders have assigned themselves unique dress, recognizable anywhere—Napoleon with his bicorne black hat, General MacArthur with his gold-encrusted visored officer's hat, Field Marshal Montgomery with his beret, and Eisenhower with the jacket that still bears his name. Fashion ideas are often borrowed from these famous symbols.

Rothschild

Today a symbol of youth, and those imitating youth, might be blue jeans. Clothes have meaning as symbols—the blue jean speaks of casualness, informality, being down-to-earth. While clothes, in a sense, are among the most individual creations, fashion is also closely related to mass psychology. Fashions are meant to be copied by everyone. There is a contradiction in this: people want to stand out and be individuals; yet at the same time they want to be "in fashion," which means looking the same as many others.

People usually adapt themselves to their surroundings, and, if the adaptation is successful, others copy them and a fashion is born. Prominent personalities often create fashion by dressing in a certain manner. Many rush to imitate them. Such famous figures as Jacqueline Kennedy Onassis, the Duchess of Windsor, or a movie or television star can create a new look instantly.

Fashion-conscious people give a great deal of thought to how they "put themselves together." More and more, they individualize themselves by taking a thought from a fashion magazine, something else they saw on television or at the movies, a clipping from a newspaper, and putting all these ideas together to create a unique combination. They are fashionable, but in their own particular way—they are, in the vernacular, "doing their own thing."

Each period in history has had its own fashions, determined by the people living at that time. At one time there was much more conformity than there is now due to scarcity of materials and lack of fashion knowledge from other places. With better communication and the visual impact of magazines and television, what is worn anywhere in the world is now quickly transmitted everywhere. Today women in New York, Paris, London, or elsewhere may be wearing ponchos from South America over "mod" shirts from London and blue jeans from the American West, accented by beads from India and bracelets from Africa.

The same can be said of how we furnish our homes. A typical living room may have an Oriental rug, lamps from England, furniture from America and Spain, draperies from the Philippines, and objets d'art and accents from Scandinavia, Italy, Mexico, Portugal, Japan, Hong Kong, and Bolivia.

Generally it is agreed that clothing and furnishings through the centuries began by being functional in the sense of providing protection and comfort for the wearer. As time went by, however, many fashions and furnishings that were practical and functional became chiefly decorative.

For example, head coverings that at one time protected the wearer from rain, sun, cold, or wind later became mostly ornamental, particularly in the case of women. Hats were often designed, feathered, and decorated in such a way that wind, rain, or too much sun would actually destroy the headpiece instead of protecting the person wearing it.

In the case of home furnishings, simple benches became upholstered pieces and, ultimately, elaborately constructed chairs. Fabric hung on walls in chilly castles or manor houses to make the rooms warmer became beautiful tapestries and, later, paintings and murals.

Men's vests filled in the space over a shirt, protecting the wearer from the cold. Boots protected mounted horsemen from the chafing caused by saddle and stirrups. Armor shielded the knight against assaults from spears and arrows. Scarves protected the neck and later became decorative ties or cravats. Sandals and later shoes guarded the feet against stones, rough earth, and sharp underbrush. In warmer climates loose robes and hoods sheltered against the bright, hot sun.

In the house, curtains and draperies kept some of the drafts from blowing through windows and into rooms.

Fireside chairs protected the sitter's back against the cold while the fire warmed him from the front. Footstools kept a person's feet off the chilly floor. At night, blankets, robes, and furs would insulate the sleeper, sunk in a feather mattress, against the cold.

Most apparel and home furnishings solved a problem for the wearer or user at some period in history. In an air-conditioned or heated-room society, we can dispense with many of the articles of apparel earlier societies found necessary.

Apparel has become light-weight and simplified. Even transportation vehicles have controlled temperatures, so that apparel for traveling need not be much different from what is worn every day.

Anatole France, the great French writer, once said,

If I were allowed to choose from the pile of books which will be published one hundred years after my death, do you know which one I would take? No, by no means would I select a novel from that future library—I would simply take a fashion magazine so that I could see how women dress one century after my departure. And these rags would tell me more about the humanity of the future than all the philosophers, prophets, and scholars.

In a sense, the history of fashion is the history of society coping with the environment and at the same time trying to add beauty and charm both to the home and to one's personal self.

THE VOCABULARY OF FASHION

The world of fashion is exciting and stimulating. Fashion connotes change—something new and different from what existed before. Those involved in the fashion world must be genuinely aware of what is going on around them. Top fashion people have definite ideas about what is right for their times.

Fashion is an important part of environment—in fact, it helps create environment as well as being a product of environment. Is it any wonder that those who make fashion their business are among the most creative, alert, interesting people?

Like most professions, fashion has its own vocabulary. Law, medicine, architecture, and the other professions have developed specialized vocabularies in order to transmit ideas easily and to better define specific concepts. Fashion, too, has many words that communicate its special ideas.

If you are a woman, you are probably familiar with many words in the fashion vocabulary. Most women have heard or used such terms as "empire waist" (fitted below the bust) or "princess style" (fitted at the waist with a flared skirt). Men, on the other hand, may have to learn many new terms. The fashion vocabulary is extensive, including such terms as "turtleneck," "scoop neck," "mini," "maxi," "longuette," and "bikini." Printed fabrics may be called "paisley," "madras," "geometric," or "houndstooth." Men's fashions may incorporate such terms as "ascot," "lapels," "herringbone," and the "safari" look. Since these words often have different meanings, it is important to understand how we intend to use the words for our purposes.

Lapels or reveres

Longuette and mini

Turtleneck

Safari or bush coat

Let's begin with the word *fashion* itself, which has a number of meanings:

Fashion (1) The current style or custom as in dress or behavior; the mode for the present: "in or out of fashion." (2) Something that is in the current mode: "latest fashion." (3) Fashionable or style-conscious people in general; the social elite: "the fashion set."

Other uses of the word are:

Fashion (4) The way in which something is formed: "and wilt thou have me fashion into speech the love I bear thee" (Elizabeth Barrett Browning). (5) Kind of variety or sort: "What fashion of a man is he?" (6) Manner of performing: "Do it in this fashion."

Fashion, then, in the broadest sense denotes customs or practices that prevail among any group of persons—a way of life. For our purposes, we will define fashion in this sense: *The prevailing or preferred practice in dress, manners, and behavior at given times.* This covers home furnishings and artifacts of societies as well as apparel. Fashion comprises all outward manifestations of civilized behavior which receive general acceptance for limited periods of time. These may include moral standards, table manners, and even automobile designs. However, our primary interest is in *apparel,* the first thing that comes to mind at the mention of the word *fashion.*

The word *style* is closely related to fashion. Does it mean the same thing? Let's go to the dictionary:

Style (1) The way in which something is said or done, distinguishing it from its substance: "style of dress." (2) The combination of distinctive features of expression or performance characterizing a particular person, people, school, or area: "Afro style." (3) The fashions of the moment, especially of dress; the vogue: "in or out of style." (4) Sort, kind, or type: "a style of furniture." (5) A particular fashion design: "style number 18." (6) A customary manner of presenting material, printed or oral: "his style." (7) To design: "to style one's hair."

Other uses of the word include:

Style (8) A quality of imagination and individuality expressed in one's actions and tastes: "she has style." (9) A comfortable, elegant way of existence: "living in style."

In some cases *style* and *fashion* are interchangeable: for example, "latest style" and "latest fashion."

In the ready-to-wear business a particular garment is given a "style number" for identification. From *style,* of course, also come *stylist* and *styling.* A stylist is the person who arranges garments and accessories. Styling is the work of creating a fashion—sometimes interchangeable with designing.

Another word often mentioned in a fashion context is *mode.* Let us see how this word is used:

Mode (1) Short for French *à la mode;* in the fashion or according to the fashion; the current or customary fashion or style: "it's the mode."

Other uses of the word:

Mode (2) Manner, way, or method of doing or acting: "the modern mode of traveling is by air." (3) A particular form or variety or manner: "He had a different mode of acting for every occasion."

The word *model* is derived from the same origin—a person employed to display clothing by wearing it. *Model* is also used interchangeably with *style* on occasion: "model number."

Another word in this family is *vogue.*

> *Vogue*   (1) The prevailing fashion, practice, or style. Often used with the word *in:* "Recently, pants for women have been in vogue." (2) Popular acceptance or favor; popularity: "It's the vogue now to dress casually."

It is interesting to note that the word *vogue* derives from the French word *voguer,* which means "to row," as a boat—or in other words, to go along smoothly.

Couture comes from the French "to sew" and refers to the product of a dressmaker. *Couturier* refers to the business of dressmaking, as well as to the person who designs, makes, and sells fashionable (usually custom-made) clothing. For example, the house of St. Laurent is a couturier, and St. Laurent himself is a couturier.

"French couture" collectively describes the better French designers. *Haute couture* is French for "high fashion" and refers to the better-designed, custom-made, and more expensive apparel—the apparel of Dior, St. Laurent, Chanel, and others of their caliber.

A phrase that constantly crops up in fashion talk is "the fashion cycle." Fashion cycles, like business cycles, come and go. One hears of a cycle of long skirts for women or double-breasted suits for men. Generally this refers to a period of years, usually from five to seven, when a particular look or style is in vogue. In recent years we have adapted many of the styles from past years, so we speak of going through fashion cycles of the 1930s or 1940s. Such cycles almost always refer to broad looks in apparel rather than to specific, individual styles.

Many other words will be explained as they are mentioned. The key words defined above are enough to help us start exploring the stimulating world of fashion.

THE SCOPE OF FASHION

As we have seen from our definitions, fashion covers a wide scope of human activity—manners, styles of living, modes of dress, the way we furnish our homes, and the way we live in and create our environment. Let us begin by an overview of fashion with particular respect to apparel.

Fashions in dress have played an important role in civilized society, to say nothing of their importance in the economies of those societies. Every fashion change holds the promise of the ultimate ideal of beauty. Consumers are usually willing to believe in the possibility of achieving that goal and feel obligated again and again to accede to the dictates of the newest fashions.

Each period in history develops its own concepts of beauty, taste, and manners. One has only to examine paintings, drawings, and artifacts through the ages to see how ideals change. About one hundred to one hundred fifty years ago, the plump, buxom woman was the ideal. Today the concept of the more perfect beauty is tall and slim, with elegant lines.

When fabrics were expensive, the importance and social standing of a woman might be determined by the length and fullness of her costume. Ladies of the monarchs' courts often wore enormous skirts with yards and yards of fabric to indicate their social position and importance. The queen at times even prescribed rules for her ladies-in-waiting so that none would be more elaborately dressed than she.

500 B.C.   1750   1920   1970

Clothes can accentuate or play down the physical proportions of the human body to help the wearer achieve the current ideal. Apparel can correct "faults" and create illusions. If, for example, small waists are a desirable look, fashions can cinch them in. If well-developed bosoms are wanted, fashion apparel can be made to accentuate this part of the body.

Generally men want to look taller and stronger. Therefore, most men's apparel through the ages has tended to "build them up" and increase their stature. Men in the court of Louis XVI of France wore high heels. Much of the armor of knights of old was considerably larger than the wearer to make him seem more formidable and was padded out underneath to make it fit and to make the wearer more comfortable.

Only relatively recently have the natural body and normal lines of the human figure become important in fashion. There were times when the human body was tortured and distorted to be "fashionable." Women wore corsets so tightly laced that they fainted from restricted breathing. Oriental women had their feet tightly bound from infancy. Some tribes in Africa still distend lips or earlobes with huge discs as a mark of beauty.

Ideas of modesty also vary with the ages and societies. Many Moslem women even today cover their bodies completely with layers of cloth and veil their faces, leaving only the eyes uncovered so they can see.

In other societies there have been periods when exposure of various parts of the body was stylish. Bosoms, necks, backs, and arms, at one time or other, have all been exposed. When such changes first took place, they were considered revolutionary. Exposure may have reached its peak in the late 1960s with the advent of the "micro-mini" dress and the 1970s with the brief bikini and topless swim suit. There are some anthropologists and cultural experts who can't understand what all the fashion fuss is about: they point out that a woman's leg is the same when she goes bathing in a bikini as when she wears a dress. This is probably a good example of how manners, morals, and customs all play an important role in determining fashions.

Erotic appeal is without question a major factor influencing fashion in both male and female attire. There have been times in the history of fashion when this approach was represented in a variety of ways—low-cut dresses, transparent materials, tight pants. Many fashion experts claim that sexuality is a major influence on fashion. It is, according to them, one of the important factors which consciously or unconsciously affect the way in which clothes are designed, worn, and judged.

There has been much speculation, both in and out of the fashion world, about whether men and women dress to please themselves, members of their own sex, or members of the opposite sex. The most likely answer is that they do all three.

THIS BUSINESS OF FASHION

The fashion business covers a wide area. It includes all manufacturers of apparel and accessories, as well as most manufacturers of home furnishings. It incorporates the manufacturers of the fibers and fabrics that are the materials of fashion.

The advertising agencies and public relations firms involved with fashion-related accounts are part of the fashion world. It also includes the photographers and artists who make fashion their business. The business of fashion must communicate, so many connected with women's and men's magazines, newspapers, radio, and television are also involved. Then there is the fashion trade press, with separate publications for each category of merchandise.

Not to be forgotten are the apparel designers and decorators for the theater and films. Naturally, the schools involved in the fashion business and the apparel labor unions must also be included.

Finally, and by far the largest area in terms of scope and numbers of people involved, are the wholesalers and retailers of apparel and home furnishings and the buying offices and retail consultants related to them.

The world of fashion is large and many-faceted. In *Ready-Made Miracle* Jessica Daves, former Editor-in-Chief of *Vogue* magazine, described the scope of the fashion industry in America along these lines:

> In the broad view, it is a sturdy part of the American economic structure, accounting for nearly $15,000,000,000 in 1970. In its individual application it is satisfying, gettable, flattering, soothing, or exciting and, most women think, absolutely essential. It is something wonderful not only for the 70,000,000 American women but for the other millions who live by its products, profit by its taxes, or who find a large part of their pleasure in looking at, talking with, dancing with, and marrying its wearers. American ready-made fashion is a phenomenon unique in the world. In its beginnings it could only have happened here; today other countries are beginning to ride the ready-made fashion wave, too.*

CONCLUSION

What is fashion? What makes fashion? Perhaps, like beauty, it is in the eye of the beholder. And the beholder is conditioned by hundreds of factors—where you live; the schools you attended; the kind of work you do; how your associates dress at work and play; the movies and television shows you see; your sports

*(New York: Putnam, 1967). Figures have been updated.—L. G. R.

and hobbies; the life styles of your parents, relatives, neighbors, and friends; your personal tastes and preferences; and many other factors. We will discuss these ideas more fully in later chapters. Suffice it to state here that perhaps fashion is a form of art personally expressed; perhaps it's what you and others say it is. Assuredly, fashion is newness, fashion is change, fashion is excitement!

REVIEW QUESTIONS AND DISCUSSION

1. Name three or four currently prominent women who are "fashion symbols."
2. What industries are included in the fashion business?
3. Name five articles of clothing or home furnishing that began for a functional reason and later became decorative. What were their original functions?
4. Define *vogue, style, mode,* and *couture.*

2

A BRIEF HISTORY OF FASHION

Greek   Ionic   Doric   Roman

Because fashion is constantly borrowing ideas from the past, a knowledge of fashion through the years is essential. Here is a brief historical and pictorial résumé.

In prehistoric times men wore animal skins. Probably the first cloth was tree bark beaten into a reasonably soft, pliable covering.

At least 3,000 to 4,000 years ago, we know men wore apparel made of cotton, and perhaps wool or hair of other animals. Pictorial records of early Egyptian, Assyrian, Babylonian, and Persian civilizations show simple garments of fabric, and translated writings talk of cotton and fabrics. Let us begin our historical summary.

EARLY CIVILIZATIONS

In the Old Kingdom in Egypt, about 4,500 to 5,000 years ago, garments were few in number. Of course, the climate was mild. The king of the Fifth Dynasty wore a loin cloth with a lion's tail fixed at the back. As the climate was warm, most fabric was of light-weight cotton or linen. The king's loin cloth was decorated with gold material. All men wore loin cloths—the peasants plain ones, the kings and their courts more elaborate ones. When worn by dignitaries, the loin cloth was often pleated. Women wore sheaths of the same fabrics, covering the entire body, supported by shoulder straps.

Women of rank in later periods had embroidered garments. Working women often wore short garments from waist to knee which left the breasts bare.

The later dynasties in Egypt were ones of extravagance and elaborate apparel. Men and women wore earrings, pendants, necklaces, bracelets, jeweled girdles, and amulets. Signet rings, colorful stones, and pearls were lavishly used.

The Asiatic costumes of this time were more elaborate. As far back as the nineteenth or twentieth century B.C. there are representations showing close-fitting tunics and cloaks, richly patterned or ornamented. The Bible talks of Joseph's "coat of many colors," which dated from this period.

Babylonian, Persian, and Assyrian attire of this time generally consisted of two garments. A straight tunic, long or short, edged with fringe called a *kandys,* was worn with a fringed shawl of various sizes. While linen was used, wool was the principal fabric. Both men and women wore the same costume, but with variations. They, too, used embroidery, which became known as "Babylonian work." These were brilliantly colored fabrics; royalty trimmed their garments with gold.

GREECE AND ROME
700 B.C. to 600 A.D.

The elaborate culture of the Cretans preceded the Greek culture. Their clothes were beautifully cut and fitted and often patterned. In the Mycenaean period—contemporary with the Egyptian civilization—women wore corsets and sewn and fitted dresses of bright colors. The flaring skirt was tight at the hips and ankle-length, perhaps with rows of ruffles or flounces. A garment called a *chiton* was worn long by Greek women and to the knees by the men. It was rectangular—made of wool or linen partly sewn up the sides, with a *fibula,* a clasp that looked

like our safety pin, holding the garment at the shoulders. Another rectangular garment was worn by Greek women over their chiton, while some men wore the chiton as their only garment. In Rome the *tunic* was common to both sexes, often worn under the *palla* or *toga.* Over the tunic women wore a *stola,* a long, straight garment, to the ankle. It was worn bloused over a girdle.

Many of our fashion ideas come from these graceful, simple garments with classic lines.

THE MEDIEVAL PERIOD
700 to 1299

Often the dates of certain periods are not precise or exact. The period between the fall of Rome in 476 A.D. and the fall of Constantinople in 1453 is called by many historians the Medieval period. Apparel did not change much from the pre-Christian and early Christian era until about 1000 to 1200 A.D. The period between the tenth and fourteenth centuries is generally called the Gothic period.

When the Romans arrived in England, they found the people fully clothed and well protected against the cold climate. With the end of the Dark Ages, which preceded the Medieval period, men and women were still wearing Greco-Roman apparel with a Byzantine Turkish influence. Christianity influenced both the style and color of clothes, advocating modesty and concealment of the body.

In northern climates people had added tightly fitting leather garments and furs for winter wear. Women's ankle-length gowns were covered by a short outer tunic. Because the English people were dyers and weavers, they often wore colorful garments. They decorated themselves with massive gold armbands, rings, brooches, and pins. Armor was not yet introduced for men, but their heavy felt covering was almost sword-proof.

In France and other parts of Europe women's long gowns covered their feet and the sleeves were loose and sometimes extended as low as the knee. Over the gown a shorter tunic was worn. Mantles covering the head were either short or long. Gloves and handkerchiefs were used, and stockings were first worn by the men. These stockings, or tights, were close-fitting and held up by a belt around the waist. By the eleventh century the *bliaud,* or tunic, and mantle were worn by men and women. The bliaud was worn long by both men and women and either hung straight or was belted with plain or decorated girdles. The *chainse,* an undertunic, was made of wool, linen, or silk. It was fastened at the neck and wrists by buttons or tie-strings. Later this garment became lingerie, made of light, workable fabric and embroidered at the edges. Silk was coming more into use and was worn by the affluent.

The period of the early Crusades acquainted Europeans for the first time with the East. It is not surprising that many Oriental influences were felt—the use of silks, unusual dyes, loops instead of buttonholes, and turban head covering. In the twelfth century men wore not only long, loose-skirted outer and undertunics with tightly fitted lace bodices, but also undershirts of linen, to which long hose were attached. A woman's tunic was similar but longer. Under this tunic was a linen or silk undergarment, the *chemise.* In cold climates a large, fur-lined overgarment called the *pelisson* was worn by both sexes. Hoods were popular, lengthened at the back to a long point.

By the thirteenth century the full overtunic of the men had shortened to the knee. A comparatively simple cloak became the dominant dress form. Hip-length stockings or tights were worn with jeweled garters and soft leather shoes. Among the upper classes furs, silk, or gold cloth served as linings for the cloaks. Women often draped their hair with a piece of fabric that fell to the shoulder.

Dress was now varied, colorful, and interesting. Furs, jewels, silks, embroidery, gold cloth, bias-cut hosiery, fine shoes, leather belts, and tunics had all made their appearance.

THE GOTHIC PERIOD
1300 to 1399

The principal head covering for women of this period was a square, oblong, or circular-shaped fabric hanging to the shoulder. It was a continuation of the palla—the headrail, wimple, or couvrechef. The affluent often placed crowns over the head covering, but these did not become a symbol of rank until the sixteenth century.

The basic dress remained simple and rectangular until the late fourteenth and early fifteenth centuries, when society grew more sophisticated and complex and clothing began to assume the fantastic richness and elaborateness associated with the later Medieval period. A tailored doublet for men was developed, and a low-necked, laced, or buttoned outergarment called the cote-hardie was introduced from Germany. A large, loose tunic, usually belted with fitted shoulders, high collar, and flowing sleeves, was also worn.

Women of rank wore loose, trailing gowns, borrowing from the men. The women's version was a short-waisted bodice and a belted and gored skirt trailing behind. This snug-fitting, bodiced gown required a slim figure, and both lacing and dieting were necessary to acquire the desired silhouette. The hair was dressed close to the head, often parted in the middle, sometimes with a coronet braid. Small caps, nets, and curls—some with fine filigree work—were popular, covered with veils of silk or linen. The hennin, a long, conical, pointed headdress, appeared in its variations in Italy at this time and lasted for more than a hundred years.

The Crusades continued to influence fashion—the Persian art of appliqué was introduced and copied. There was much demand for decoration and embroidery. Shoes, bags, pouches, girdles, and gloves were richly embroidered by the women, who were proud of their accomplishment.

During the fourteenth century there appeared particolored clothes for men which later were copied by the women. Garments were divided into halves or quarters, with each section in a different contrasting color. This was carried to extremes with each shoe and stocking of a different color. Later particolored garments included diagonal sectors. Nobility with coats-of-arms often placed motifs of both families in these diagonal sectors.

Both men and women wore soft, pliable shoes with pointed toes, covering the foot to the ankle. They were beautifully colored, made of velvet or gold cloth, ornamented with embroidery, or even encrusted with gems. This type of shoe was called poulaine, and pattens were the clogs of wood made to protect these soft, beautiful shoes. A novel foot covering introduced in Venice was the chopine, a stilted, wooden affair, painted or gilded.

This was a period of massive chains and jeweled belts with a purse or pouch attached. Men often wore jeweled daggers suspended from these belts. Other accessories included embroidered and decorated gloves, the women's being scented. The wealthy had handkerchiefs and fans of feathers or of Oriental import, sometimes set with precious stones.

It is interesting to note that at this time in Venice, glass mirrors were made for the first time on a commercial scale. From this time until the seventeenth century, when for the first time large mirrors were made, these small glass mirrors were carried by both men and women. Who can say how much this little invention influenced fashion? When you could see yourself, did it influence your desire for change?

During the Middle Ages, a person's costume was, of course, determined by wealth and position in society. When discussing fashion, we are describing the apparel of the affluent, as the peasants and poor wore much the same shapeless, uninteresting garments for centuries. This unfortunate state of affairs was not modified until feudalism was eliminated in the sixteenth and seventeenth centuries.

THE AGE OF EXPLORATION
1400 to 1499

At the beginning of the fifteenth century men wore loose, pleated tunics, often lined or edged with fur in the northern countries. Long, full sleeves were worn, drawn tightly at the wrist. Underneath was another tunic or doublet with close-fitting, long sleeves also fastened at the wrists. A cloak, often hooded, was worn as an outergarment over all. Shoes were still pointed, but grew shorter toward the end of this period.

There are many references at this time to silks and fine fabrics from the East, as well as spices and foods new to the West. This interchange of ideas and products stimulated the Renaissance, which reached full flower in the next century. However, the groundwork and beginnings of the great emergence of culture, dress, and growing awareness of other peoples began during the fifteenth century. The Renaissance began during this century in both France and Italy. Venice was the center of the Renaissance, so the fashions worn there influenced the entire Western world.

Women adopted men's fur-trimmed tunics, but they wore them as long gowns. These gowns were worn with skin-tight bodices, girdled high under the breasts. Some sleeves were long and extended below the hands; others were buttoned at the wrists. Long, plain cloaks were worn closed at the neck by a long cord. Hair was often arranged in an elaborate manner with cambric veiling or a wimple floating out behind like a trailing veil.

Slashings in tunics appeared in the last quarter of the fifteenth century and lasted until the middle of the seventeenth century. This style was adopted from the Swiss soldiers and appeared all over Western society. These slashes often revealed shirts of rich material. Panes or strips of fabric were used vertically over puffings. Scallops and tassels, as well as fur, trimmed both men's and women's garments.

The turban in various forms was worn as a head covering by both men and women. This was just one of the many Oriental influences resulting from the Crusades and the growing trade between East and West. This trade led to a wider assortment of fabrics, and many ideas from the East were copied by Western craftsmen. Feathers of various types adorned some of the head coverings of both sexes, and long pieces of cloth hung to the waist or lower in some headdresses.

As travel and communication continued to improve, the dress and manners of the court or an influential group had effects throughout the Continent. This was the period of Joan of Arc, the famous Medici family in Florence, and Gutenberg, who, with movable type, printed the first Bible. At the very end of this period, in 1492, Columbus landed in America. However, before this famous voyage, other ships had sailed around Africa and to India and the East, bringing back many new ideas for apparel and home furnishings.

We should mention that men wore armor of various types throughout the period from the ninth to the sixteenth centuries. While all apparel is a part of fashion, we are overlooking this category, as well as military uniforms, because they are not of particular interest to us in the fashion framework.

THE RENAISSANCE
1500 to 1599

During this period, style centers and influences shifted from country to country. In the first part of this century the Swiss-German influence dominated. The Swiss-Germans had previously been influenced by the Venetian and Italian fashions. Now, Spain was to have its turn as a major influence. The English followed all these trends with interest and pleasure.

Women had scented themselves and their clothing from biblical times by placing their clothing in flower petals and certain spices. They had also bathed themselves in sweet smelling baths created from crushed flowers and saps from trees and shrubs. They used cosmetics and perfumes and whitened their bare chests. Perfume making originated in Italy during the Renaissance. Rene, an Italian perfumer, opened the first shop in Paris about 1500. Perfumes were made from formulas brought from the Orient by returning Crusaders. Feudalism was disappearing; craft guilds were formed. There was a growing middle class of tradesmen, craftsmen, and those who served the affluent. This middle class wore apparel similar to that of royalty, but not as elaborate or expensive. Among the upper classes, both men and women demanded color and splendor in their dress.

Sixteenth-century England broke with the past in matters of dress and social customs. Men's clothing changed almost completely. Doublet and jerkin were very tailored with high necks, while the shirt began its change into the ruff. Breeches were puffed and slashed, worn over stockings. Shoes were also slashed and decorated with pointed toes, later giving way to the shovel type. Long cloaks were worn as outer garments, with small toques or berets crowned with jewels or plumes.

The women of the Renaissance in Italy wore artistic gowns of rich fabrics, including brocades, velvets, satins, and damasks, often embroidered and even pearl-sewn on a cloth of gold. In reference to apparel, the Renaissance is called the "Pearl Age." Rare stones, gems, and gold or silver cloths came from the East. From the North and Russia came fine furs—sable, ermine, fox, lynx, and lambskin. From Germany came rich brocades, and from Venice elaborate silks and velvets. The spectacular headdresses of the preceding period were discarded for the hood with gabled front, edged with needlework. During this period lace was invented. However, it was used sparingly, as it was in short supply. Lace was widely used during the next century. Gowns had tight-fitting bodices and were long-waisted. The long skirts flared at the hips. Sleeves were wide and turned back to form a cuff, often of fur. A loose girdle encircled the waist, with pendants dangling to the floor. Over this, long cloaks were worn, tied at the neck with long dangling cords.

This was the period of Henry VIII in England. His luxurious tastes and love of finery influenced the tastes and styles all over Europe. Men wore beards and mustaches. Swords and daggers were everyday accessories.

Under Mary Tudor (1553–1558) apparel lost its ornate and elaborate character. There were religious and moral laws forbidding rich apparel for the middle class. Clothing was rather plain. Among the affluent, the skirts of women's gowns spread out stiffly from a tight waist opened in the front in an inverted U, showing heavily embroidered or decorated petticoats beneath.

Then came the Elizabethan period (1558–1603) when everything changed again. Women's clothing set the style and men's followed it. False hair and wigs were worn decorated with jewels, glass ornaments, or feathers. Red and blonde were the most popular. Powder and rouge were used. Corsets were worn, first of metal, later bone. Elizabeth, like Catherine de Medici of France, wore high-heeled slippers, or "pumps." In general, the fashions of this period were elaborate and artificial.

THE RISE AND DECLINE OF ROYALTY
1600 to 1699

The Elizabethan influence continued into the seventeenth century under the rule of James I of England and Louis XIII of France. This is an important era in costume because it was during this period that France definitely established herself as the leader and arbiter of fashion. The richness of costume was curtailed when Cardinal Richelieu banned imports of gold and silver cloth as well as elaborate velvets and brocades.

Men wore a tight, one-piece doublet with short skirts and tightly-cut sleeves; padded and puffed breeches were still the style. Fabrics included plain but heavy satins and velvets in more neutral tones. About this time ribbons came into vogue. Lace as a trimming became important, especially for flat collars. It was during this period that "Cavalier fashions" appeared. The corseted shape

gave way to the waistcoat with sleeves; the ruff gave way to a turned-down collar with a falling band of lace or cambric. The skirt gained importance.

The cravat originated during this period and was to last a long time. It started in 1636 as long, folded, white linen or lawn, tied loosely around the neck. It derives its name from the Cravates or Croats who were serving with the French army and wore these scarves. Ever since, men have worn some form of this fashion.

Short leather boots with falling tops of Spanish origin became the fashion in about 1625. Spurs were worn with these boots even indoors. Longer capes with square collars were worn with cords under the collar to fasten them at the neck. A loose greatcoat was also worn, with big sleeves and turned-back cuffs. Both usually had rich, colorful linings.

Both men and women began wearing silk stockings which, by this time, were being woven mechanically. The women of this period wore a chemise, a corset, then several petticoats over the hoop, which continued in fashion until 1630. The gown consisted of a skirt and bodice or stomacher with sleeves of light-colored fabric. Over all this was worn a redingote, or robe, of darker, contrasting material opened the full length of the front. The sleeves were often slashed, showing the undersleeves.

There were two distinct influences at this time, widely dissimilar and irreconcilable. On the one hand was the Puritan dissenter, who was fanatically religious and dressed severely. The men wore black, wide-brimmed hats with high crowns over short-clipped hair. A plain coat with a simple white collar was worn over loose breeches, to the knee, with plain woolen stockings and square-toed shoes finishing the costume. The Puritan women wore simple gowns in dark colors over stiff underskirts. These were usually topped by simple white bonnets.

The second influence derived from the cavaliers and their ladies, known for their sumptuous magnificence!

Toward the end of this period women abandoned paddings and slashings, and their apparel became loose and casual. Series of lace collars were worn with a vest that revealed a good deal of the bosom. Sleeves were wide and elbow-length with lace-trimmed cuffs. Skirts were full, worn over petticoats. Hair was casual—often deliberately rumpled. The headdress introduced by Anne of Austria, wife of Louis XIII, was a fringe of hair across the forehead with the hair at the sides cut short and hanging in ringlets over the ears. The remainder was drawn in a knot at the back of the head. Veils and kerchiefs were worn, occasionally tied under the chin. Shoes were of leather or satin and high-heeled, worn over flesh-colored or rose stockings. Capes were worn in cooler climates with long gloves and muffs. The folding fan was popular and was used by some men as well as women. Women often wore a small mirror and perfume box suspended from their belts. The umbrella of Italian origin was fashionable in Italy and was later adopted in France.

This was also the age of contrasts in royalty and courts. Oliver Cromwell (1649–1660) came to power in England, making the Puritan views dominate its dress and thinking. Meanwhile, in France, the Court of Louis XIV reached its height. It was one of the most sumptuous and elaborate periods in the history of France. The bans by Richelieu and his successor, Cardinal Mazarin, were dropped after the latter's death. Venetian lacemakers were brought to France and the wearing of lace was encouraged. Wig-making reached its height, with elaborate wigs for both sexes.

It was an age of ruffles, laces, feathers, and trim for both men and women, in France and Italy, Germany and Spain, but not England—because of Cromwell and his impact.

THE AGE OF REVOLUTION
1700 to 1799

Possibly the most distinguishing aspects of fashion in the eighteenth century were women's headdresses and men's head coverings. In the early part of this period, women wore modest powdered wigs covered by hoods. By mid-century they wore exaggerated styles that have never been equaled.

During the period 1750 to 1770, French costume is thought to have reached its acme. There are really two periods—the first from 1724 to 1750, known as the "Rococo Period," with headdresses following a basic shell motif combined with curls, curves, flowers, feathers, and bowknot ribbons. The second period, from 1750 to 1770, was more dignified. The manners and customs of the French court still influenced the entire Western world.

Men's costume still consisted of coat, vest, and breeches from the reign of Louis XIV. Perfected during the Regency, these became the attire for European men and lasted a century. The coat was still slit up the outer back to the waist, made necessary originally for horseback riding. The skirt of the coat reached the knees. The vest was buttoned over a lingerie-like shirt with cravat or jabot attached. Later the coat was shortened and cut away from the hips, and the neck cut down showing more of the jabot or cravat. The sleeve became smaller and tighter. The breeches first were buttoned above the knees, then later buttoned below the knee and fitted fairly close to the body.

For women, the hoop returned, circular and made of whalebone, gradually widening from waist to ankle. Gowns became so large and cumbersome that often doorways, stairways, and carriages had to be modified or adapted to allow women of fashion to pass.

This fashion did not last the entire century. The "Watteau gown," a loose sack or dress over a tight bodice and full underskirt came into vogue—the loose folds falling from the back and shoulders became part of the skirt. The front of the women's costume was varied, either hanging loose or fitting at the waist, worn open or closed and, if open, showing an underskirt and bodice. The sleeves were elbow-length with vertical pleats and soft, wide cuffs. After 1746 the pagoda sleeve took over. It was tight from elbow to shoulder. Below the elbow it spread into flared ruffles decorated with ribbons and bows. The neck of the costume was low in front, with the stomacher ornamented with ribbon loops or lacings of narrow ribbons.

This was a most important period in terms of world events, literature, and personalities, all of which affected the fashions of this century. Jonathan Swift wrote *Gulliver's Travels* in 1726; Daniel Defoe, *Robinson Crusoe,* 1719; Bach his B Minor Mass, 1738; Henry Fielding, *Tom Jones,* 1740; Samuel Johnson, *Dictionary of the English Language,* 1755; and Voltaire, *Candide,* 1759. The spinning jenny was invented by James Hargreaves in England in 1770, speeding up the process of making fiber.

In 1776 came the American Revolution, followed in 1789 by the French Revolution, both of which had far-reaching effects on the social and political customs of the world, as well as on fashion.

Fabrics during this period changed to light, crisp textiles. Flowered, striped, or plain taffetas, lustrous satins and damasks, and flowered lawns or dimities in pastels were all in style. Fine, soft laces with many ribbons and artificial flowers added to this new lighter, brighter look. Aprons continued to be in fashion, as did petticoats in silk or satin. The vogue of the shawl is thought to have begun in the 1770s. Shawls were worn short in summer, long in winter, with armholes and perhaps a hood. Collarettes or chokers of ribbon and lace were sometimes worn around the neck.

The hair was worn more simply at the end of the century, close to the head, off the forehead, and up in the back. From about 1750, the front hair, cut short, was dressed off the forehead, the ends set in curls over the head from ear to ear. A pomade dressing for the hair held the ringlets in place, with a tiny cushion supporting the center with false hair and flowers attached. Powder was added to the hair for formal occasions by both men and women. It is estimated that by 1769 there were over twelve hundred hairdressers in Paris! Madame DuBarry, mistress of Louis XV of France, was virtual dictator of fashion at the court and, as the court influenced fashion everywhere, of the Western world.

It was a period of drastic change in politics, fashions, and world outlook. The revolutions in America and France had changed the attitudes of people, and the class structure was undergoing vast changes. By the end of the century the influence of the French court had disappeared, and royalty of every land had been diminished. The court of England had modified its posture, commensurate with its loss of the colonies and the more democratic attitudes adopted by most of Western society.

THE INDUSTRIAL REVOLUTION
1800 to 1899

The first years of the nineteenth century marked the beginning of a radical change in apparel. It might be characterized as a reversion to the classical simplicity of the Greek and Roman eras. Prior to becoming emperor, Napoleon ruled with two others for a short time. This was known as the Directoire Period. This trend was encouraged by Napoleon both during the Directoire and particularly the Empire period, 1804 to 1814.

This was an age of romance. Lord Bryon wrote his famous poetry; Walter Scott wrote *Ivanhoe;* Shelley wrote "Ode to the West Wind" and other romantic poems, while Keats was writing "Ode on a Grecian Urn." Beethoven composed his Ninth Symphony, the *Choral,* and Alexis de Tocqueville wrote his great book *Democracy in America.* In 1837 Victoria became queen of England, and soon began the Victorian era, which influenced the rest of the century.

Women abandoned their corsets and wore simple, sheath gowns girdled just under the bosom and falling straight to the ground. The Grecian effect was carried out by square necklines and short, puffed sleeves. With this were worn white, clocked stockings, pumps with low heels, and hair in the simple style of classical times. Head covering consisted of tremendous scoop bonnets, while the arms were covered by long gloves reaching to the upper arms. The "spencer," a short, close-fitting jacket, came into style along with cashmere shawls. The fashions were no longer dictated by Versailles but were launched at public winter balls and summer garden affairs.

With the advent of the nineteenth century, trousers or pantaloons became the feature of masculine dress. At the beginning of the century breeches still ended below the knee. The full-length trouser made its impact during the Empire period. Trousers and breeches were tight-fitting, of elastic fabrics such as stockinet, finely stripped cotton, or buckskin. The most popular material for informal and formal wear for all seasons was buff or yellow nankeen imported from Nanking, China. Between 1810 and 1815 trousers and garters were made in one piece. The Directoire influence was still present, at first, in the bulky-necked coats of dark cloth. The English wore jockey boots with tight cuffs at the top. Also popular was the hussar boot, cut lower in the back than in the front, where it was ornamented with a tassle. Napoleon wore a (Wellington!) boot, which was high over the knee, cut below the knee in the back.

There were continuous changes in both men's and women's clothing as the French Empire was succeeded by the Restoration. A man named Mackintosh invented a practical process for waterproofing, and elastic cloth with rubber in it was first produced. In the United States in 1827, Samuel Williston patented a machine to produce cloth-covered buttons.

It was during this period that the groundwork was laid for present apparel. Men began wearing jackets, pants, vests, and shirts with ties or cravats. Top hats, capes, and overcoats were common.

While women's skirts were long until well into the twentieth century, many styles were forerunners of today's fashions.

As the century drew to an end, France was still the fashion leader of the western world. By 1890 the bustle, which had been in vogue up to this time, was out of the picture, and the hourglass figure in style. Tailored suits were the most important fashion for men.

Some men were more interested in clothes, some in ideas—it was the age of Charles Darwin, H. G. Wells, Toulouse-Lautrec, Cezanne, Gauguin, Henrik Ibsen, Richard Wagner, Gladstone, Disraeli, and Karl Marx. Many of these men had great influence on the thinking, times, fashion, and customs. The specialization of costume for specific occasions began to take shape. There were clothes for sports—tennis, boating, bicycling, and golf.

New concepts were in the air, and the world of fashion responded with new ideas, new looks, and new freedom—modern shoes, accessories, and bathing suits were born. Women's spheres of activities broadened into sports and office work. It was the beginning of a new age.

THE AGE OF SCIENCE
1900 to the PRESENT

This period must be divided into three parts: the period between 1900 and World War I; the period between World War I and World War II; and the period after World War II to the present. Different forces and influences were at work during each of these times. In the period preceding World War I, rather plain and severe outer daytime clothes were worn.

A doctor in Vienna named Sigmund Freud was to begin his work that would influence the entire world in its thinking about sex. Painters such as Matisse, Roualt, Derain, Dufy, Braque, and Picasso began to exhibit their "wild" paintings. These would influence ideas about color and fashions for years to come. It was an age of new literature as well: Marcel Proust, D. H. Lawrence, James Joyce, Shaw, Gide, and Oscar Wilde. It was an age of new music: Ravel, Stravinsky, Mahler, and Gershwin.

And there were the Wright brothers who, in 1903, made the first successful flight with a motor-powered airplane. It was indeed the beginning of an age that would see more rapid changes take place in fifty years than had taken place in the last two hundred years. Then came the cinemas, or movies, as they were called, in the United States, followed by the radio and later television, all of which had vast influences on fashion.

In America, during the first part of the twentieth century, there was little excitement or elegance in clothing. The "genuine" American—the now great middle class which included a large part of the population—followed the styles set by Paris.

Men's stand-up, starched collars and cuffs, straw hats in the summer and fedoras in the winter, with the English-type suits and raincoats, all came to stay. Seldom was upper-class clothing so widely worn—affluent, respectable, and completely impractical.

During World War I, women's skirts rose rather quickly—an indication of the exaggerated fashions that were to come. Belts were lowered considerably below the normal waistline.

The rebellion in both men's and women's fashions occurred in a period immediately after the war, called the Jazz Age, the turbulent 1920s. Women's skirts were above the knee, hair was "bobbed"—cut short—and the "flapper" was born.

Men's clothes accentuated the chest and straight-line shoulder and a high waistline, which necessitated high-rise trousers. The double-breasted vest from London made its appearance. A little later, the lines were softened, and the drape suit was in style. With good tailoring, a man's figure could be improved. The growth of sports clothes was a marked trend. These styles persisted with modifications through the thirties, when they became more modest and practical.

With the advent of the early 1940s and World War II came modifications which demanded less fabric for both men's and women's apparel. Skirts were short; men's vests disappeared. Men's lapels shrunk; women's pleats and full skirts disappeared. The jumpsuit appeared, and military clothes dominated the news. The "Eisenhower jacket" was adapted for both men and women for casual wear.

After the war in 1947 came the "New Look" with long, full skirts, and tight, small waists. Bare shoulders for women were now common for summer, daytime, and playclothes. Women began discarding the all-in-one corset and began to wear brassieres and girdles. America became a greater and greater influence with its casual and sport clothes. By 1950 the American influence began to shape the fashion ideas in London and Paris. American men and women wanted less formal, more functional clothes, and they got them. As the 1960s arrived, the American style became a world style. Blue jeans became

1910

a worldwide fad. Men's and women's sport clothes were copied everywhere. Trousers and pants gave way to slacks, and women began to wear pants of all lengths and descriptions. By the 1970s, these new concepts were an accepted fact.

It is interesting to note that in the United States there has always been "democracy" in apparel. Visitors from Europe always remarked that in America you could not tell a person's class by the way he or she dressed. In Europe "gentlemen" and "ladies" dressed as such, while servants and tradesmen dressed in such a manner that they could be identified occupationally.

Apparel from now on will probably continue to be practical and functional, fitted to the needs of active people with multiple interests. Apparel will be more and more end-use-oriented as we approach the twenty-first century.

Prehistory and Early Civilizations (Egypt)

Early Civilizations (Babylonia and Persia)

Greece and the Byzantine Empire: 700 B.C. to 299 A.D.

The Roman Empire: 300 to 600

The Medieval Period: 800 to 1099

The Medieval Period: 1100 to 1299

The Gothic Period: 1300 to 1399

The Age of Exploration: 1400 to 1499

The Renaissance: 1500 to 1599

The Rise and Decline of Royalty: 1600 to 1699

The Age of Revolution: 1700 to 1799

The Industrial Revolution: 1800 to 1899

30

1900 to 1929

1930 to 1939

1940 to 1949

1950 to 1959

1960 to 1969

1970s

CONCLUSION

Fashion history is important to those involved, because again and again fashion borrows from its past to create the contemporary. We have seen this recently as designers have "updated" the fashions of the 1920s, 1930s, 1940s, and 1950s. Fashion ideas not only come from the past, but from all over the world. New ideas may have a Chinese, Spanish, Greek, or Egyptian influence that may go back thousands of years. To those who would create fashion, its history is indispensable.

REVIEW QUESTIONS AND DISCUSSION

1. Point out five recent fashion trends that derived their ideas from previous fashion history.
2. Take one period of history, or a particular century and place, and describe the apparel worn by men and women in that period. Find out the major influences on fashions in that period—rulers, leaders, historical events, art, plays, books, or any other influences affecting fashion.
3. Discuss how you might go about doing research on fashion trends. Clip from daily newspaper or a fashion magazine some current fashions and point out their fashion inspiration.

3

THE MATERIALS OF FASHION

All apparel and much of home furnishings begin with fibers. Fibers are fine filaments or hair-like substances, as in the fiber of wool, cotton, flax, or synthetics.

There are two main classifications of fibers—natural and synthetic. Almost all textiles are made from these two classifications or combinations of them.

The entire field of fibers and textiles is so large that it is a subject in itself. However, in this chapter we will cover only the main points and explain how fibers and fabrics fit into the fashion framework.

Where does fashion start? It starts with threads or fibers which are woven into cloth. The first step is to define and explain the natural and synthetic fibers and then proceed to the actual yarns which can be woven or knitted into fabric. The process of covering the body with fabric existed long before written history, when cave men decided that animal skins were practical but didn't serve every need. A multibillion-dollar industry has evolved from these simple beginnings, and today there are many different fibers used in creating fashion.

In order to understand these fibers and their uses, we might first examine the United States textile industry to determine its scope.

In colonial days there were many small operations for making yarn and fabric. The first successful textile mill opened in Pawtucket, Rhode Island, in 1793. The Slater Mill, as it was called, has been restored and today houses a textile museum.

In the United States the industry first thrived in New England and, during the industrialization period in the nineteenth century, spread to the South.

Today there are over 7,000 textile manufacturing plants in 42 states employing about 950,000 persons. They produce approximately 18 billion square yards of fabric annually, or enough to wrap a yard-wide strip nearly 400 times around the earth! This is in addition to the millions of pounds of yarn or thread produced. Each year sales of this industry's products amount to over 21 billion dollars. Most of the plants are located along the Atlantic seaboard, primarily in the southeast. However, there are textile plants as far west as California. The clothing industry, a major consumer of textile company products, employs about 1.4 million people. Altogether, about 15 million people directly or indirectly derive their income from textiles.

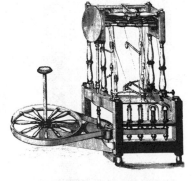

Arkwright's first spinning machine

Textile making in ancient Egypt

The textile industry uses natural fibers such as cotton, wool, linen, and silk, as well as dozens of synthetic fibers. Cotton and wool producers depend on the textile industry to use the bulk of their products. At the same time, chemical companies turn out several billion pounds of synthetic fibers which textile plants transform into fabrics for apparel, the home, or industrial uses.

Many industries and people have indirect interest in textiles and the textile industry. For instance, the textile industry uses a great deal of starch which is made from corn or potatoes. The industry also uses chemicals made from minerals, oil, gas, wood, air, and water. It is a big customer for electricity, machinery, paper, transportation facilities, and many other forms of materials and services. Many skills are used in the process before an attractive fabric comes alive.

NATURAL FIBERS

The natural fibers known to man are flax, wool, cotton, and silk. All have been in use for thousands of years.

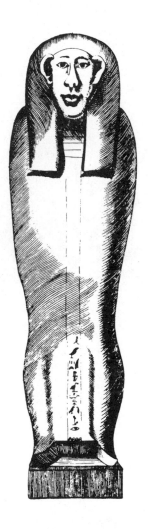

LINEN

Flax is the inner bark of the flax plant and is legally the only fiber that can be used in the manufacture of linen. Ireland is a major source of flax and, therefore, "Irish linen." Flax is generally considered to be one of the most ancient of textile fibers. The archaeological remains of Stone Age man in the lake dwellings of Switzerland show bundles of flax fibers, spun linen yarn, and even fragments of linen fabric. The ancient peoples who lived in Mesopotamia, Assyria, and Egypt some 5,000 years ago learned to cultivate flax and weave linen fabrics. Mummies were carefully wrapped in linen, as were the Dead Sea Scrolls.

Linen has again been popular in more recent times, finding use in both apparel and bedding. In the eighteenth and nineteenth centuries, a linen suit or dress for summer was considered the best, since it was relatively cool, light-weight, and porous. Even today, sheets, pillow cases, and toweling are called "linens," and the section that sells these items in a department store is often still called the "linen department."

Linen has a fresh clean hand, or feel, and attractive appearance after laundering. It is absorbent and has good resistance to bacteria and mildew.

With the increased use of synthetic, permanent-press fabrics, linen fell out of favor for some time, because it wrinkled and had to be ironed. Currently linen is staging a revival in apparel, although it has long since ceased to be used widely for sheets, which are now generally a blend of cotton and synthetic fiber. Linen fabrics have improved and are now even lighter in weight and less easy to wrinkle.

WOOL

Wool fiber comes from the fleece of sheep and similar animals. Together with cotton, it is the world's most important natural fiber. Wool is elastic, resilient, and warmer when made into fabrics because its fibers do not conduct heat. It is highly absorbent and releases moisture slowly, yet its tensile strength is greater than that of cotton.

According to pictures scratched by primitive people on cave walls, wool was probably woven into textiles as early as 4000 B.C. The people of Babylonia, which, incidentally, means "the land of wool," wore woven-wool garments.

Pieces of woolen fabrics have also been found in the tombs and ruins of Egypt, Nineveh, and Babylon, in the lake dwellers' huts, in barrows of the early Britons, and among the relics of the Peruvians.

The Britons kept sheep and wore wool long before the Roman invasion. But in 55 B.C. the Romans introduced the manufacture of wool textile, and a factory was built at Winchester.

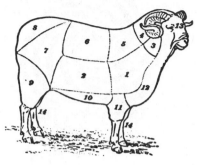

Although sheep were introduced into the Western Hemisphere by Columbus in Cuba and Santo Domingo, and by Cortez and Francisco de Coronado in Mexico, the Dutch settlers probably brought the first sheep to the eastern part of the New World. By 1698 the sheep population had grown so rapidly that there was considerable trade in wool and fabric among the colonies.

After the American Revolution the United States became aware of the lack of fine-apparel wool. George Washington, long a sheep breeder at Mount Vernon, imported rams from Spain to improve his stock. Weavers and other woolcraftsmen from abroad were offered immediate citizenship, and the industry began to grow.

Until very recent times, sheep walked from the desert areas of New Mexico and Utah into the lush meadows of the Wyoming and Colorado mountains each summer and then returned to the low country for the winter. Today sheep ride from coast to coast on fast trucks, express rail cars, and even airplanes. Sheep are found in each of our 50 states, and they provide 200 million pounds of wool as raw material for an industry which supports thousands of people employed in creating wool textiles—textiles that are beautiful in the ballroom, warm in the Antarctic, resilient in rugs, elegant and durable in drapes and upholstery, and perfect for blankets. Australia and New Zealand are also important sources of wool.

While on the topic of wool, we must also mention the alpaca, a domesticated llama in Peru, and the vicuna, a wild species of llama found in the Andes from

PURE WOOL ®

Ecuador to Bolivia. Both these animals provide soft, warm, and light-weight fleece for coats and other garments.

Woolen fabric is most important in coats and outerwear apparel. It has also been woven into lightweight fabrics that can be worn comfortably in warmer climates. In addition to being used in its pure form, it is often blended with synthetic fibers to make fabrics combining the best features of both natural and synthetic fibers.

Wool, because of the ability of its fibers to interlock, is an ideal fiber for felt, a heavy fabric that is made by pressing fibers together. Felt is widely used for hats and upholstery covering. Because of its versatility, wool is used to make many fine fabrics of different weights and textures. Among the most popular wool fabrics are flannel, melton (a heavy cloth used for coats), challis (a light-weight cloth widely used for dresses), wool crepe, and most important yarns that make sweaters and knit garments of all types.

COTTON

Cotton has been the companion of civilization for many centuries. Its earliest origins have been fixed at about 5000 B.C. in the Tehuacan Valley of Mexico. Scientists have determined that fragments of cotton fiber and boll found in that valley are about 7,000 years old.

Cotton is the most important of the vegetable fibers. It has been spun, woven, and dyed since prehistoric times. It was used for the staple clothing worn in India, Egypt, and China. Thousands of years before the Christian era, cotton textiles were woven with great skill in these civilizations and eventually spread to the Mediterranean. Cotton fabrics and garments dating hundreds of years before western man arrived in North and South America have been found in Peru and Mexico. Cotton was also known to the Zuni and Hopi Indians of North America and used in their ceremonies about 500 B.C.

When Columbus landed in the Bahamas in 1492, he discovered cotton growing there. Over 100 years later the colonists planted cotton in Virginia. A few years afterward a cargo of slaves and cotton seed arrived in Jamestown Colony in Virginia to begin the cotton industry in the United States. Cotton is grown in some 500,000 farms in a 19-state area referred to as the "Cotton Belt," stretching across the southern United States from lower Virginia to California. It is a major crop in some 14 states where it averages a third of all crop marketings. Cotton is big business for the nation as a whole, since it forms the basis of a $25-billion industry in terms of investment. Cotton and cotton-seed marketings add up to about $2.5 billion per year. More than nine million Americans depend directly or indirectly on cotton as their source of income.

Cotton has long been the world's major textile fiber, as its serviceability and relative low cost are difficult to match. Cotton is versatile, dependable, durable, and strong. It does not irritate sensitive skin. Laboratory tests prove it to have the highest abrasion resistance of any fiber suitable for apparel. Some fibers lose their strength when wet; others can't be tumble-dried, or glaze and melt under the iron. Some shrink as much as 20 percent or lose hand and texture. Cotton launders beautifully because of its high wet-strength and wet-abrasion resistance, dimensional stability, fast dye-acceptance, resistance to heat, and refusal to melt.

To explain what this means to the consumer: Abrasion resistance means the ability to take rubbing without weakening. Dimensional stability means little expansion or contraction after being wet and dry. Wet-strength means it does not grow weak and tear easily when wet. It keeps the wearer cool because its porosity allows it to "breathe," taking air in and moisture out.

Many persons in different walks of life are indebted to cotton, which keeps them comfortable and appropriately dressed. From the time you dry your face on a soft, terry cotton towel in the morning until you slide between the fresh cotton or cotton and synthetic sheets at night, this fabric contributes to your well-being.

Cotton and cotton-blended fabrics are most popular for cool, lightweight clothing. For this reason, they have always been popular for summer wear. However, since our environment is becoming more temperature-controlled through air conditioning, lighter-weight apparel is being worn throughout the year, boosting cotton into even greater prominence. The future of cotton looks particularly bright due to the fact that many synthetic fibers are petrochemically based. As oil becomes shorter in supply and its price increases, the cost of synthetic fibers will go up, making cotton more attractively priced by comparison.

Some of the better-known cotton fabrics are: broadcloth, used in shirts, blouses, and home decorating; corduroy and denim, used mostly in sportswear; organdy and dotted Swiss, sheer fabrics that are popular for summer dresses, children's wear, and curtains; gabardine, used in slacks, riding clothes, uniforms, suits, and dresses; velvet and velveteen; seersucker; pique and gingham; sailcloth and tapestry; terry cloth, for toweling; flannel and knit. Cotton is everywhere.

SILK

Silk is a natural filament made of protein, which a silkworm spins for its cocoon. The worm is actually the caterpillar of the silk moth, and the cocoon is the shell it constructs to protect itself during its growth from caterpillar to moth. Once the cocoon has been formed it is necessary to destroy the worm inside so that it will not break the continuous filament spun in the formation of the shell, which is then unwound from the cocoon onto silk reels.

Silk traces its origin to the antiquities of China more than 4,000 years ago, when it is chronicled that a young bride of a Chinese emperor discovered the gleaming thread by dropping a cocoon into hot water and noticing a slender filament unwind.

Whether fable or fact, for many centuries until the fall of the Chinese empire one day was set aside each year for the empress of China to feed the silkworms and pay homage to the "goddess of the silkworms." Silk became an important factor in Chinese economic life around 2640 B.C. The Chinese guarded the secret of silk for 3,000 years, until approximately 300 A.D., when Japan penetrated the mystery. Silk was found in the ancient courts of Persia and, through trade with the Mediterranean, was brought to Greece and Rome.

It was not until 550 A.D. that the West saw the worm. The Emperor Justinian of Byzantine ordered two Nestorian monks to bring back the precious worm and mulberry seeds to grow the bushes to feed it. They returned with their precious cargo secreted in walking staffs, consequently ending the Chinese and Persian silk monopolies.

As conquest followed conquest, the culture of silk moved with the conqueror. When Islam armies swept into Sicily and Spain, they brought the silkworm, and by the twelfth and thirteenth centuries Italy had become the silk center of the West. By the seventeenth century, France challenged Italy's leadership with luxurious fabrics woven in Lyons.

Hugenot weavers from France introduced the industry to England. Since the English climate was too chilly for the silkworm to flourish, the kings of England determined to encourage the culture of the worm in their American colonies. However, it was not until 1810 that the first silk mill was created in America. Because of the relatively small quantity of silk produced in the United States and the patience and hand work necessary for successful silk production, it never thrived in this country. Today the United States imports more raw silk than any other country and weaves some of the most beautiful silk fabrics in the world.

The most rare and costly fabrics were traditionally made of silk, but today the luxury and beauty of silk is within every budget. Silk takes dyes with exceptional purity and clarity; it is soft to touch; and it gives the wearer a sense of elegance and luxury. Silk also has insulation properties; it feels cool in summer and warm in winter. Its lightness contributes added comfort, and its absorbency prevents its feeling clammy. It is washable, sheds wrinkles quickly, and is the strongest natural textile fiber known. A filament of silk is stronger than a like filament of steel of the same thickness!

As with other natural fibers, silk is also being used more in combination with other natural and synthetic fibers to achieve new and desirable effects in fabrics—these are usually labeled *silk blend*.

In the United States silk fabrics represent only a fraction of one percent of total textile production, amounting to less than 20 million square yards a year. Only in Japan has silk output remained fairly constant, at a rate of 180 million square yards a year. Of 20 countries producing silk, China, India, Korea, and Italy predominate after Japan.

Silk has embraced ready-to-wear apparel and the decorating field. It is used by designers of lingerie, scarves, knits, millinery, suits, dresses, evening gowns, jackets, slacks, sport shirts, ties, linings, vests, robes, and top hats for men. In the home-furnishing field, it opens unlimited vistas for decorating because of its many textures and its unmatched range of colors in solids, prints, and patterns for every decor—antique to modern.

HIDES AND FURS

We must not forget hides and furs in our discussion of fibers and fabrics. Even though they are technically neither fiber nor fabric, they are important fashion *materials*. They were the first body coverings of our Stone Age ancestors, who killed wild animals for food and used their hides to sleep on and to protect their naked bodies from the cold.

Throughout past centuries furs were used mostly by the aristocracy and the wealthy. The precious ermine trimmed the robes of kings and queens and thereby became a symbol of royalty. Today there may not be many ermine coats or stoles, but many women own mink.

Furs today are used mostly for women's coats—exterior, lining, or trimming. Hides are mostly used for footwear, handbags, luggage, wallets, and outerwear. However, in recent years, fur has also been used by designers for men's coats more elegant than the "raccoon coat," which was often seen in the 1930s at college football games and is now popular again for both men and women.

Among the furs and hides must also be included the camel, alpaca, vicuna, angora, and cashmere goat. As wild animals are rapidly disappearing, however, there will probably be fewer furs available from exotic sources such as leopards or tigers. Furs will not vanish completely from the market, since animals such as mink, sable, goats, sheep, and other similar types will continue to be bred on farms and ranches.

As conservation and ecology become more important, there will be growing pressure to save the remaining wildlife and their natural habitats. Endangered species will be protected. Therefore, the fashion industry will probably confine itself to those animals raised for food or pelts and their synthetic counterparts.

In recent years, synthetic furs have made an appearance on the fashion market and have grown in importance as a substitute for the real thing. They are warm, fine imitations, and the methods of dyeing and finishing pile fabrics have become sophisticated. Synthetic furs are so ingeniously made that sometimes

it is difficult to tell the real skins from the artificially created pelts until you examine them closely.

The leather and allied leather-products industries employ about 350,000 men and women and produce a variety of fashions, and consumer and industrial products, which annually add more than $5 billion to the American economy.

The prime sources of leather are cattle, goats, and sheep. Other sources include: wild and domestic hogs, kangaroos, alligators, deer, water buffalo, seals, elephants, sharks, snakes, and lizards. Alligators, crocodiles, and some species of lizards are now protected as endangered species.

Some 300 tanneries scattered across the United States produce the tens of millions of square feet of leather which provide a livelihood for thousands of American workers in shoe and leather-goods plants. While most of the leather produced in the United States comes from cattle raised here, millions of skins are imported each year from other countries.

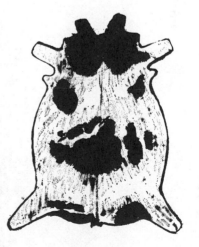

Leather was man's first clothing material. The hunter and his mate soon found that they could cure and use hide for sandals and crude garments. Ages before they domesticated wool-bearing animals or learned to plant cotton and spin cloth, people were skilled in the tanning and use of leather. Archaeologists have found bits and pieces of leather scattered as far and wide as ancient people wandered. Decorated leather thong sandals have been unearthed from the tombs of Egypt; leather garments have been found in the bogs of Scotland; leather containers for water, grain, and other household items have been found in ancient Crete.

Tanning in this country goes back to the days before European settlers landed on these shores. The American Indian made a crude form of leather from deerskins for moccasins, cloaks, and tents. The early settlers soon adapted and refined the deer and buckskin tanning; leather became one of the most common and widely used materials in the new world. Famous frontiersmen like Daniel Boone and Davy Crockett dressed in supple deerskin shoes, pants, and shirts. The first tanner set up business in the colonies in 1623.

Today chemists and tanners are teamed to produce leather with deep, lasting colors, handsome textures, and greater durability. It is a far cry from the hides used as clothing by primitive civilizations to the pressurized leather suits worn by the first astronauts as they rocketed into the skies.

Leather shoes keep more than 200 million Americans walking in fashion, comfort, and health. Leather jackets, coats, dresses, skirts, handbags, belts, and a host of other articles are important fashion items in every wardrobe. Lightweight leather luggage makes travel easier. Elegant leather furniture brings beauty into the home, office, and automobile.

With the emergence of the space age, leather-like materials have been created synthetically with polyurethane, such as Corfam and Naugahyde. More will probably be produced, with even wider uses and applications.

SYNTHETIC FIBERS

Before the advent of synthetic fibers (often called man-made fibers), clothing and other textile goods could only be made from the natural fibers already mentioned.

Production of synthetic fibers on an experimental basis was initiated midway through the 1800s. The first synthetic fiber produced in the United States was rayon in 1910. Rayon is manufactured from cellulose, the fibrous substance of all forms of plant life, which is regenerated into fiber form.

FORMS OF MAN-MADE FIBERS

Monofilament Yarn. A single filament (fine thread) of continuous length.

Multifilament Yarn. Two or more continuous monofilaments assembled or held together by twist or otherwise.

Tow. Large bundles of continuous monofilaments assembled without twist.

Staple. Discontinuous lengths of fibers which have been cut or broken into desired lengths from large bundles of continuous monofilaments (tow).

Source: *Man Made Fiber Fact Book* (1975).
Courtesy of Man-Made Fiber
Producers Association, Inc.

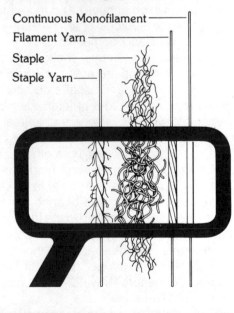

Continuous Monofilament

Filament Yarn

Staple

Staple Yarn

---

man-made fibers

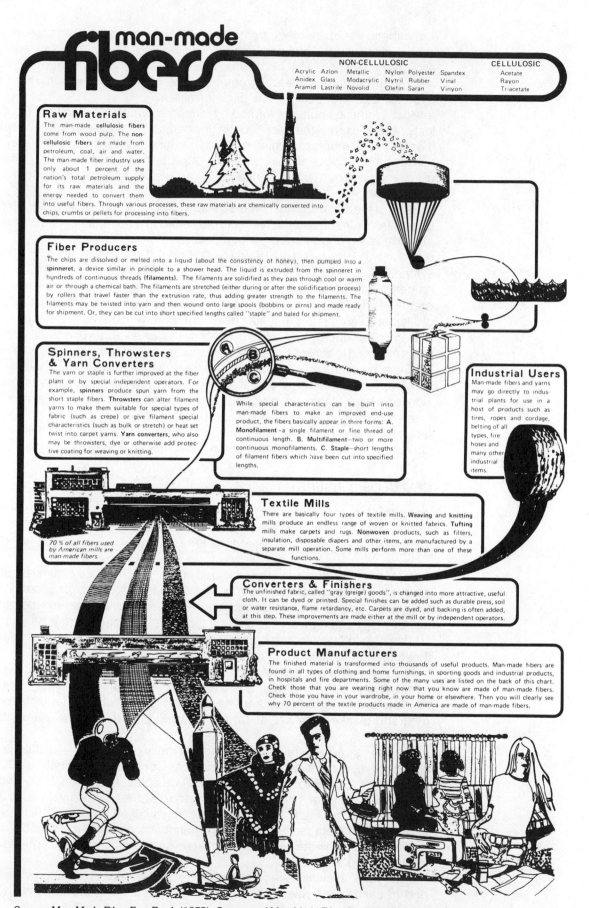

NON-CELLULOSIC						CELLULOSIC
Acrylic	Azlon	Metallic	Nylon	Polyester	Spandex	Acetate
Anidex	Glass	Modacrylic	Nytril	Rubber	Vinal	Rayon
Aramid	Lastrile	Novolid	Olefin	Saran	Vinyon	Triacetate

Raw Materials

The man-made **cellulosic** fibers come from wood pulp. The **non-cellulosic** fibers are made from petroleum, coal, air and water. The man-made fiber industry uses only about 1 percent of the nation's total petroleum supply for its raw materials and the energy needed to convert them into useful fibers. Through various processes, these raw materials are chemically converted into chips, crumbs or pellets for processing into fibers.

Fiber Producers

The chips are dissolved or melted into a liquid (about the consistency of honey), then pumped into a **spinneret**, a device similar in principle to a shower head. The liquid is extruded from the spinneret in hundreds of continuous threads (**filaments**). The filaments are solidified as they pass through cool or warm air or through a chemical bath. The filaments are stretched (either during or after the solidification process) by rollers that travel faster than the extrusion rate, thus adding greater strength to the filaments. The filaments may be twisted into yarn and then wound onto large spools (bobbins or pirns) and made ready for shipment. Or, they can be cut into short specified lengths called "staple" and baled for shipment.

Spinners, Throwsters & Yarn Converters

The yarn or staple is further improved at the fiber plant or by special independent operators. For example, **spinners** produce spun yarn from the short staple fibers. **Throwsters** can alter filament yarns to make them suitable for special types of fabric (such as crepe) or give filament special characteristics (such as bulk or stretch) or heat set twist into carpet yarns. **Yarn converters**, who also may be throwsters, dye or otherwise add protective coating for weaving or knitting.

While special characteristics can be built into man-made fibers to make an improved end-use product, the fibers basically appear in three forms: **A. Monofilament** –a single filament or fine thread of continuous length. **B. Multifilament**–two or more continuous monofilaments. **C. Staple**–short lengths of filament fibers which have been cut into specified lengths.

Industrial Users

Man-made fibers and yarns may go directly to industrial plants for use in a host of products such as tires, ropes and cordage, belting of all types, fire hoses and many other industrial items.

70 % of all fibers used by American mills are man-made fibers.

Textile Mills

There are basically four types of textile mills. **Weaving** and **knitting** mills produce an endless range of woven or knitted fabrics. **Tufting** mills make carpets and rugs. **Nonwoven** products, such as filters, insulation, disposable diapers and other items, are manufactured by a separate mill operation. Some mills perform more than one of these functions.

Converters & Finishers

The unfinished fabric, called "gray (greige) goods", is changed into more attractive, useful cloth. It can be dyed or printed. Special finishes can be added such as durable press, soil or water resistance, flame retardancy, etc. Carpets are dyed, and backing is often added, at this step. These improvements are made either at the mill or by independent operators.

Product Manufacturers

The finished material is transformed into thousands of useful products. Man-made fibers are found in all types of clothing and home furnishings, in sporting goods and industrial products, in hospitals and fire departments. Some of the many uses are listed on the back of this chart. Check those that you are wearing right now that you know are made of man-made fibers. Check those you have in your wardrobe, in your home or elsewhere. Then you will clearly see why 70 percent of the textile products made in America are made of man-made fibers.

Source: *Man-Made Fiber Fact Book* (1975). Courtesy of Man-Made Fiber Producers Association, Inc.

Synthetic fibers are made from plentiful, low-cost, basic raw materials found almost everywhere. The fibers can be "engineered" to exhibit special qualities and characteristics. A fabric may be made from a synthetic fiber or a blend of natural and synthetic fibers. By changing the blends and proportions of each fiber, the end products can be almost limitless.

Most synthetic fibers are formed by forcing a syrupy substance of the chemical or blend used in the fiber through tiny holes. This is called *extruding* the filaments. The filaments emerging are then hardened or solidified. After they have hardened, the fibers are stretched. Through suitable control of the conditions of spinning and hardening, the fiber size and shape can be altered to form useful textile fibers.

Each of the synthetic fibers has special properties and capabilities which set it apart from others, and each fiber is produced in a number of different forms to adapt its special properties for particular end uses.

Nylon was introduced at the New York World's Fair in 1939. It was the first true synthetic fiber because it was made entirely by chemical process and contained no cellulose. Synthetic yarns have a variety of properties. The bulk or stretch properties add an important new dimension to textile fibers. In addition, texturing of filament yarns imparts a soft hand to the yarn. Colored pigments may be added to produce pure-colored fibers with remarkable resistance to fading when exposed to sunlight, salt water, perspiration, soot, washing, and weathering.

Since the chemical composition and treatment in production of the synthetic fibers varies, the fibers are classified and defined by the Federal Trade Commission, and have also been assigned generic names. Synthetic fibers fall into two classifications—cellulosic and noncellulosic. The cellulosic fibers include: acetate, rayon, and triacetate; the major noncellulosic fibers include: acrylic, modacrylic, nylon, olefin, polyester, saran, spandex, and vinyon.

CELLULOSIC FIBERS

Since the first synthetic fibers were produced from cellulose, the fibrous substance of all forms of plant life, it was natural to call them cellulosic fibers. Now the cellulose is almost entirely derived from spruce and other soft woods.

Rayon. Rayon, the first of the cellulosic fibers, is composed of almost pure cellulose. It was discovered in 1910 in the laboratories of the American Viscose Company. Due to its high absorption, this fiber is easily dyed a wide range of fast colors and, because it accepts a high twist, is used a great deal in crepe fabrics. When first produced, rayon was sleazy and gave a bad name to synthetic fabrics for years.

Today it is very popular because it is highly absorbent, soft, easy to dye, economical, and easy to drape. It is used mostly in clothing, millinery, tire cord, medical-surgical products, draperies, slipcovers, upholstery, tablecloths, bedding and blankets, as well as for floor coverings and industrial products.

Acetate and Triacetate. The other two cellulosic fibers—acetate and triacetate—were developed by the Celanese Corporation, acetate in 1924 and triacetate in 1954. Fabrics made from acetate fibers drape beautifully and have a luxurious hand or finish. Acetate is also relatively fast-drying and shrink-resistant, and retains a "crispness." It is mostly used in fabrics such as satin, faille, crepe, taffeta, and brocade. In addition, you will find it in foundation garments, dresses, lingerie, and knitted jerseys, and as fillings in comforters, pillows, and cigarette filters.

Triacetate, a relative of acetate, is shrink- and wrinkle-resistant, resists fading and is easily washable. Fabrics made from triacetate fibers maintain pleat-

METHOD OF SPINNING ACETATE YARNS[a]

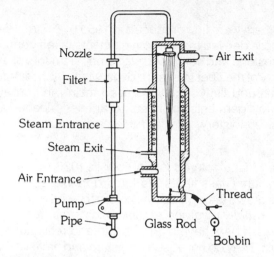

Nozzle —
Filter —
— Air Exit
Steam Entrance —
Steam Exit —
Air Entrance —
Pump —
Pipe —
Glass Rod
Thread
Bobbin

ONE METHOD OF SPINNING RAYON YARNS[b]

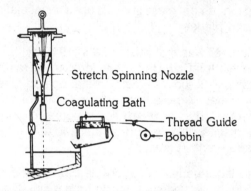

— Stretch Spinning Nozzle
Coagulating Bath
— Thread Guide
— Bobbin

[a]Passage through the heated spinning chamber evaporates the solvent and the pure thread of cellulose acetate emerges at the base to be wound onto bobbins.
[b]There are variations of the method, but the "stretching" principle is common to most nowadays.

Source: *Man-Made Fiber Fact Book* (1975). Courtesy of Man-Made Fiber Producers Association, Inc.

retention and a crisp finish. They are used mostly in garments in which pleat-retention is important, such as skirts, dresses, sportswear, textured knits, tricot fabrics, and other popular fabric constructions including sharkskin, flannel, taffeta, jersey, and faille.

NONCELLULOSIC FIBERS

The introduction of nylon, the first of the fibers produced by chemical synthesis, represented a breakthrough in the application of science to noncellulosic fiber production. Nylon was followed by many other noncellulosic fibers.

These fibers generally soften at high temperatures, and fabrics may therefore be heat-treated to set pleats, develop shape-retention, or receive embossed designs. They are generally abrasion-resistant, which allows them to withstand surface wear and rubbing, and are resilient and spring back when crushed.

They are relatively nonabsorbent and dry quickly. The smooth, nonporous surfaces of most of these fibers do not allow dirt and grime to become embedded. Most noncellulosic fibers are nonallergenic and are not affected by moths or mildew.

Acrylic. Acrylic fibers were first produced in 1950 by E. I. du Pont de Nemours & Company. Acrylic is derived mainly from elements taken from coal, air, water, petroleum, and limestone and combined with small elements of other chemicals to improve the ability of the fiber to absorb dyes. Many fabrics made from acrylic fibers are soft, light, and fluffy. Acrylic is used mainly in carpeting, sweaters, skirts, dresses, baby garments, blankets, draperies, fleece fabrics, ski and snow suits, socks, upholstery, pile fabrics, slacks, and work clothing (trade name "Orlon").

Glass. Glass was manufactured into a fiber in 1936 by the Owens-Corning Fiberglass Corporation. Glass fibers are formed from a special glass formula. The molten glass is drawn through a small hole in the bottom of the melting kettle and collected on a rapidly revolving carrier which stretches the filament to extreme fineness. Glass fibers have high strength and resistance to heat, flame, and most chemicals. They do not absorb moisture and have little stretch but can be made into soft, flexible fabrics. Fabrics made from glass fibers are heavier than most other textiles and are used for draperies in public places requiring fire resistance. Batting made from glass fibers is used for insulation in buildings, railway cars, boats, and planes.

Metallic. Metallic fiber was first produced in 1946 by the Dobeckmun Company, now merged into the Dow-Badische Company. It is a manufactured fiber composed of metal, plastic-coated metal, metal-coated plastic, or a core completely covered by metal. Metallic filaments are used for many decorative purposes in apparel fabrics. They are also used in household draperies, shoelaces, table linens, bathing suits, ribbons and braids, and as packing material for gifts and perfumes (trade name "Lurex").

Modacrylic. The laboratories of Union Carbide Corporation created modacrylic in 1949. Modacrylic fibers are made from resins. This fiber can be softened at low temperatures, retains its shape, is resilient, easy to dye, abrasion and flame-resistant, and quick drying. The low softening temperatures of modacrylics allow them to be stretched, embossed, and molded. Modacrylic is used mainly to simulate furs, and for fleece fabrics, industrial fabrics, nonwoven fabrics, flame-resistant draperies and curtains, deep pile coats, scatter rugs, stuffed toys, paint rollers, knit pile and fabric backings, carpets, hairpieces and wigs, men's lightweight summer hats, and institutional awnings and decorations (trade name "Dynel").

Nylon. Nylon actually refers to a whole family of polymers, called polyamides, perfected by E. I. du Pont de Nemours & Company in 1939. Nylon is made from raw material obtained from petroleum or natural gas (carbon), air (nitrogen and oxygen), and water (hydrogen). These are spun and stretched after cooling to give the desired properties.

Nylon is exceptionally strong, elastic, abrasion-resistant, lustrous, easy to wash, resistant to damage from oil and chemicals, smooth, resilient, low in moisture and absorbency, and can be dyed in a wide range of colors. Its filament yarns provide smooth, soft, long-lasting fabrics, while its spun yarns lend fabrics lightweight warmth.

Aside from its known use in clothing and furnishings, it is also used in tents, hosiery, racket strings, sails, conveyor belts, tire cords, parachute canopies, sleeping bags, tarpaulins, rope, nets, and harnesses, and in the space program.

UNITED STATES MILL CONSUMPTION OF FIBERS (MILLION POUNDS)

	1960	PERCENT	1970	PERCENT	1972	PERCENT	1973	PERCENT
Man-made fibers[a]	1,874.7	28.6	5,501.3	57.6	7,570.2	64.9	8,652	70
Cotton	4,196.1	64.0	3,773.6	39.5	3,849.8	33.0	3,642	29
Wool	480.0	7.3	273.3	2.9	247.5	2.1	182	1
Raw silk	6.9	0.1	1.8	—	2.0	—	3	—
Totals	6,557.7	100.0	9,550.0	100.0	11,669.5	100.0	12,479	100

[a]Including textile glass fiber.

Source: *Man-Made Fiber Fact Book* (1975). Courtesy of Man-Made Fiber Producers Association, Inc.

Olefin. Olefin, first manufactured as monofilaments for various specialized uses in 1949, was changed into multifilament form in 1961 by Hercules Incorporated. Olefin fibers are products of the petroleum industry. The fibers possess a dry hand and a unique wicking characteristic, which means the ability to draw body moisture away from the skin and up through the fabric to the outer surface. This gives olefin a desirable comfort factor in resisting weather, stain, and deterioration from chemicals, mildew, rot, and perspiration. It is strong, sensitive to heat, and easy to dye. Olefin is used in carpeting, both indoor and outdoor; hosiery, sports shirts, sweaters, rope and cordage, sandbags, ties, undergarments, pile fabrics, upholstery, filter fabrics, sewing thread, and knitwear.

Polyester. Polyester was first commercially introduced by E. I. du Pont de Nemours & Company in 1953. It is produced from fiber-forming material derived from coal, air, water, and petroleum. This material is spun. Polyester fibers are strong, resistant to stretching, shrinking, and chemicals, and easy to dye. These fabrics also dry quickly, keep their crisp and resilient hand when wet or dry, resist wrinkling and abrasion, and retain heat-set pleats and creases. Polyester fabrics are very popular in all types of clothing, particularly permanent press. They are also used in furnishings. Polyester fiberfill, because it is resilient, lightweight, nonallergenic, and nonmatting, is used in pillows, comforters, sleeping bags, mattresses, automobile cushions, ski jackets, snow suits, and robes. Textured polyester fibers are used in woven and knit fabrics (trade name "Dacron").

Rubber. Natural rubber fibers are made from the concentrated sap of certain trees. The U.S. Rubber Company, now UniRoyal, Incorporated, first produced synthetic rubber fibers in 1930. The softened rubber is extruded as a monofilament. Rubber fibers are generally used as a core around which the yarns of other fibers are wound to protect the core from abrasion. Rubber core yarns are used in fabrics requiring stretch and elasticity—for instance, in foundation garments, surgical supports, and elastic webbing.

Saran. Saran was first produced by the Firestone Plastics Company, a predecessor of Firestone Synthetic Fibers and Textiles Company, in 1941. Saran fibers wear well and resist common chemicals, sunlight, staining, fading, mildew, and weather. Fabrics made from saran fibers can be easily washed with soap and water and are nonflammable. They are mostly used for upholstery in public conveyances, deck chairs, and garden furniture. The weight of saran fibers is too great for wide use as a general textile material. In thin sheet form it is familiar to us as an airproof wrapping, especially for foods.

UNITED STATES ANNUAL PER CAPITA CONSUMPTION (POUNDS)

	1960	1970	1971	1972	1973	PERCENT INCREASE, 1960 TO 1973
Man-made fibers[a]	10.1	27.8	33.0	37.8	41.8	+314
Cotton	23.3	19.7	20.5	20.0	17.6	− 24
Wool	3.1	1.7	1.3	1.3	0.9	− 71
Totals	36.5	49.2	54.8	59.1	60.3	+ 65
Population	180.7	204.8	207.0	208.8	210.4	+ 16

[a]Including textile glass fiber.

Source: *Man-Made Fiber Fact Book* (1975). Courtesy of Man-Made Fiber Producers Association, Inc.

Spandex. Another product from the laboratories of E. I. du Pont Nemours & Company is Lycra Spandex, which was first produced in 1959. It is light, soft and smooth, and resistant to body oils. Lycra spandex is stronger, more durable, and more powerful than rubber. When stretched repeatedly, it will return to its original shape. Spandex fibers do not suffer deterioration from perspiration, lotions, or detergents, and are supple and abrasion-resistant. Because of these qualities, spandex lends lightweight freedom of movement to apparel such as girdles, foundation garments, bras, support and surgical hose, football pants and other athletic apparel, ski pants, slacks, bathing suits, and golf jackets.

Vinyon. This fiber was first produced by the American Viscose Corporation in 1939. Vinyon fibers also soften at low temperatures but have high resistance to chemicals. They are most commonly used in industrial applications as bonding agents for nonwoven fabrics and products. In some countries other than the United States, vinyon fibers are referred to as polyvinyl chloride fibers.

SOME TRADE NAMES AND EXAMPLES

Pity the poor, confused consumer who is confronted with a barrage of trade names used by every major fiber company for its particular generic brand of synthetic fibers.

It is not surprising that in a recent consumer survey the most common response to the question, "What does du Pont make?" was "nylon stockings." (Du Pont, of course, does not make nylon stockings but manufactures some of the nylon yarn used by hosiery manufacturers to knit nylon stockings.)

FIBERS TODAY AND TOMORROW

During the next 25 years, fiber companies will have to innovate to give consumer satisfaction. Preplanned shapes and constructions must be programmed for wearing and using so that fiber planning will be as important as fabrication. Exact characteristics must be built into garments and home furnishings to meet the specific usage. The fashion concept in fiber engineering will be most important, both in apparel and home furnishings.

FIRM	TRADE NAME	FIBER
Allied Chemical	Caprolan	Nylon
American Cyanamid	Creslan	Acrylic
American Enka	Encron	Polyester
	Enka	Rayon
	Crepeset	Nylon
	Zantrel	Rayon
	Enkalure	Nylon
Beaunit Mills	Vycron	Polyester
	American Bemberg	Rayon
Celanese Fibers	Fortrel	Polyester
	Celanese	Rayon
		Acetate
		Nylon
	Arnel	Triacetate
Courtaulds (North America)	Coloray	Rayon
Dow-Badische	Zefran	Acrylic
	Zefkrome	Acrylic
	Lurex	Metallic
E. I. du Pont de Nemours	Orlon	Acrylic
	Dacron	Polyester
	Accle	Acetate
	Antron	Nylon
	Cantrece	Nylon
	Lycra	Spandex
	Mylar	Metallic
	Qiana	Nylon
Eastman Chemical Products	Kodel	Polyester
	Verel	Modacrylic
	Chromspun	Acetate
	Estron	Acetate
(F.M.C. Corporation) American Viscose Division (AVISCO)	Avlin	Polyester
	Avron	Modified Rayon
	Avisco	Modified Rayon
Hystron Fibers	Trevira	Polyester
Monsanto Textiles Company, an operating unit of Monsanto Company	Acrilan	Acrylic
	Blue "C"	Polyester and Nylon
	Actionwear	Nylon
Phillips Fibers	Quintess	Polyester
	Marvess	Olefin
	Phillips 66	Nylon
Union Carbide	Dynel	Modacrylic
UniRoyal	Vyrene	Spandex

USE OF FIBERS IN 1973 MILL CONSUMPTION[a]

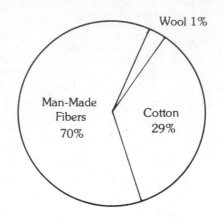

Wool 1%

Man-Made Fibers 70%

Cotton 29%

[a]Silk and linen together account for less than 1%.

Source: *Man-Made Fiber Fact Book* (1975). Courtesy of Man-Made Fiber Producers Association, Inc.

Fiber companies will direct more concentrated efforts at retail personnel, explaining the new fashion looks and their significance. Fibers and fabrics will be discussed at sales promotion meetings covering technical details so that store personnel will become knowledgeable. Major retailers realize the importance of a strongly promoted fiber brand name and will seek to increase their local cooperative advertising with fiber companies.

Statistical data on the synthetic fiber industry in the United States show that it is big business. The synthetic fiber-producing plants in this country represent almost $4 billion of invested capital. In 1974 industry sales of these fibers produced amounted to over $4 billion. Over 100,000 people are employed by the industry, according to a 1974 report. Of these, 82,000 were wage earners on direct production and 30,000 were salaried. The gross annual payroll of these people has more than doubled since 1959. In 1974 the gross payroll for personnel in the entire industry amounted to over $800 million. That same year over 7½ billion pounds of synthetic fibers were produced—almost 30 percent of the total synthetic fiber production in the world.

The largest increase in United States production during the past 18 years has been in the noncellulosic fibers. In one year alone, production of these fibers increased 37 percent. According to 1974 statistics, the annual consumption of synthetic fibers averaged almost 26 pounds for every man, woman, and child in this country.

In 1974 the imports of synthetic fiber textiles into the United States totaled about 3 billion square yards. Foreign countries involved in the manufacture of synthetic fibers include Belgium, Luxembourg, France, Italy, the Netherlands, and West Germany—or the European economic community. Members of the European Free Trade Association include Austria, Denmark, Norway, Portugal, Sweden, Switzerland, and the United Kingdom—all of which manufacture synthetics. Japan is also a ranking producer of synthetic fibers. The foreign competitors of the United States have a well-established trend of an increasingly favorable balance of trade in these fibers, but the volume of U.S. export trade remains relatively stable.

Today all the natural and synthetic fibers can be used by themselves in improved form and, more important, in combination with other fibers to make textiles that combine the advantages of the various fibers. By using synthetic and natural fibers in various combinations, there are now fabrics that are absorbent, comfortable, long-wearing, and which dry quickly when laundered. To be specific, men's shirts or women's blouses were often made of 100 percent cotton up to the early 1930s. Today a good portion of all shirts and blouses are made of cotton and polyester, one of the most important synthetic fibers.

Since many current synthetic fibers include petrochemicals, the cost of synthetic fabrics will increase as oil becomes more scarce and higher priced. Probably in the near future there will be pressure to develop non-oil-based fibers.

60% OF ALL FIBERS USED IN APPAREL ARE MAN-MADE

100% of all women's pantyhose   65% of all night wear and underwear
 82% of all women's dresses   54% of all men's shirts
 69% of all sweaters   52% of all men's suits, slacks, and coats

Source: *Man-Made Fiber Fact Book* (1975). Courtesy of Man-Made Fiber Producers Association, Inc.

FIBERS AND FABRICS

Never before has man had so many fibers or threads from which to choose in making fabric or textiles. Each of these fibers has particular characteristics. Up until the turn of the century, man had only natural fibers to work with. Virtually all fabric was of wool, cotton, flax-linen, or silk. Wool was used for heavier cloth—coats, suits, and sweaters; and cotton was used for lighter-weight garments—shirts and sheet linen, and many articles of wearing apparel.

Fabrics made from all the various fibers or combination of fibers fall into two major textile classifications—woven fabrics, sometimes called "flatgoods," and knitted fabrics. Each of these major categories has hundreds of variations.

In woven goods the major breakdown is into plain or solid fabrics and printed fabrics. In knits a principal breakdown is single knits versus double knits.

The advantage of flat goods is that they hold their original shape well. Knit goods stretch and recover. Hence most hosiery, sweaters, and other garments that require "give" are usually knitted.

If we were to take the various fibers and yarns into the textile mills and follow them through the extensive processes that turn fibers into fabrics, it would require a very enlarged and technical book. The methods differ somewhat in the beginning, depending on the fiber or fibers used. The methods of cloth construction would vary only according to demand and current fashion. Today, through the genius of the dyers and finishers, most fibers can be made to look or feel like each other, and inexpensive synthetic fabrics often look like the more expensive ones. Fabrics may be made firm or soft, bright or dull, warm or cool, colorful or drab. The variety of finished cloth is bounded only by the imagination of the designer and finisher.

Basically all fibers are made into textiles by weaving. This weaving is accomplished in textile mills on machines called looms. In the case of cotton and wool the fibers must be "combed" and/or carded, meaning the process of getting the strands in long, thin threads.

After weaving, the fabric is dyed and/or printed and finished by various other processes as the situation requires. The finished fabric emerges from the mill ready for shipment to garment manufacturers. The exception is greige, or gray goods, which is shipped to a converter who does the finishing to the specific order of an end user.

CONCLUSION

Without fibers there is no fabric; without fabric there is no fashion. A knowledge of fibers and fabrics is essential to those in the business of fashion.

Each season millions of yards of fabric are dyed in the newest colors, which change from season to season. New prints are constantly created, thus assuring new looks, new color combinations, and an endless variety of patterns to suit every taste. New techniques of dyeing and printing are frequently introduced, assuring a constant stream of innovative fashion ideas. It is a long trip from fiber to finished cloth, and thousands of people from all parts of the world have been involved. Each contributes to making it possible for today's men, women, and children to wear the most practical, comfortable fabrics modern technology can produce.

Currently there is experimentation with fused, extruded, and spun fibers. A world of new technology may one day see us mold on, spray on, paint on, or roll on our "look for the day."

It is a long trip from fiber to finished cloth, and thousands of people from all parts of the world have been involved. Each contributes his or her part to help make it possible for today's men, women, and children to wear the most practical, comfortable fabrics modern technology can produce.

REVIEW QUESTIONS AND DISCUSSION

1. What are the natural fibers?
2. What are some of the most important synthetic fibers?
3. Describe a process used in making synthetic fibers.
4. What are generic names?
5. What are some of the copyrights or trademarked names of leading synthetic fibers?
6. Relate the trade names of question 5 to their generic families.
7. Name at least five different types of fabrics.
8. Give examples of what type of fabric might be best suited for particular garments.
9. Discuss the relation of fibers to fabrics.

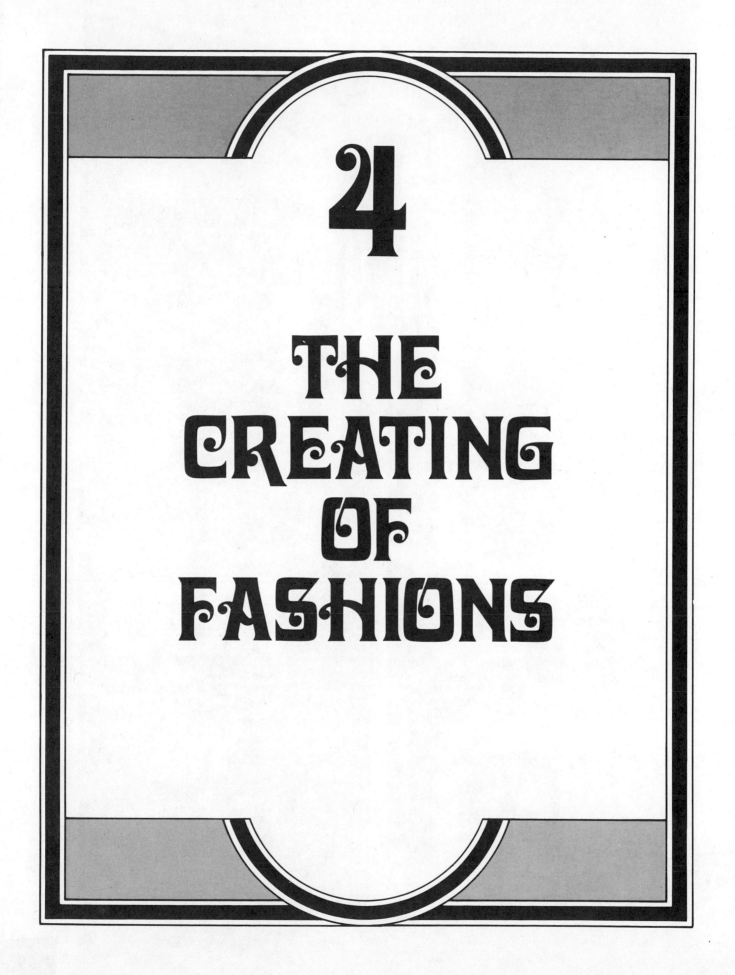

4

THE CREATING OF FASHIONS

After fiber has become fabric, the fabric is ready to be cut and sewn according to demand and style. Nothing has contributed to the speed of this process more than the sewing machine—one of the most important inventions to affect the fashion industry. It made possible the mass production of apparel which was the beginning of ready-to-wear, as opposed to individual, handmade garments. Later, the sewing machine went into the home and into the small shops of dressmakers and tailors. Let's look at the history of the sewing machine, for in part it is also the history of fashion and apparel.

An attempt at mechanical sewing was made in England in 1790 by one Thomas Saint with a machine having a forked, automatic needle which made a single thread chain. Forty years later, in 1830, B. Thimonnier, a French tailor, patented a wooden device with a hooked needle. In 1841 he used 80 of these machines to make uniforms for the French army.

Several men experimented with eye-pointed needles, one for glove making. However, it was Elias Howe who made the first successful machine in 1846, using an eye-pointed needle and an intermittent feed. After perfecting various features and defending his patents, he made a fortune from his machine.

A. B. Wilson invented an automatic feed in 1850 and later perfected the four-motion feed, an essential feature of later machines. Before 1850 all machines were operated by hand, and the cloth was fed by various clumsy devices, such as a separately moving belt with projecting steel spikes. Wilson also invented the rotary bobbin and hook.

Howe's first sewing machine

Isaac Singer is credited with the invention of the foot treadle. He also coordinated previous inventions to make a modern machine, gave it commercial status, and began large-scale manufacture of the machine.

Two types of sewing machines, the chain and the lockstitch, operate on the same principle. An eye-pointed needle, raised and lowered at great speed, pierces the material lying on a steel plate, casting a loop of thread on the under-

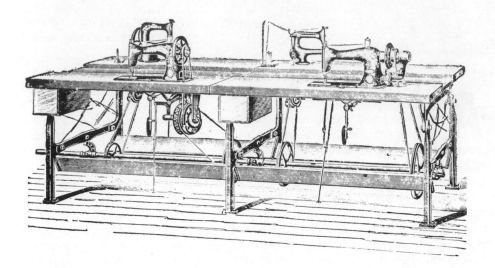

Singer power sewing machines

side of the seam. In the lockstitch machine a second thread, fed from a shuttle (bobbin) under the plate, passes through the loop and is interlocked with the upper thread as it is drawn up tightly by the rising needle. In the chainstitch machine, the loop is held under the seam while the needle rises; the cloth is fed forward, and the needle descends again, engaging the loop and drawing it flat under the cloth. Both types of machines are made for home and industrial use. Most home machines are the lockstitch type.

Electrification and an ever-increasing number of attachments for hemming, gathering, tucking, quilting, and other operations have improved the efficiency of the household machine.

Power-driven, highly specialized machines for industrial use include many used in clothing manufacture, such as those for buttonholing, button sewing, seam finishing, and embroidery. Shoes, gloves, hats, hosiery, girdles, and upholstery are sewn on specially devised machines. The United States leads in the manufacture of sewing machines and ships them all over the world. Recently the Japanese and European machines have been competing for world markets.

Once the sewing machine had been introduced on an industrial basis to make military uniforms, it was only a short step to begin to use it for everyday apparel. As uniforms were men's clothing, it was an easy transition to make everyday jackets and trousers on the same machines. So industrial production of apparel began with men's clothing, though dressmakers and home sewers still made women's garments. This mass production of men's clothing was the beginning of ready-to-wear garments which could be bought in a store instead of being custom made by a tailor or a dressmaker.

The sewing machine, then, made mass production possible. Let's now follow the manufacturing process and see how a garment is created.

DESIGNING FASHIONS

Once a fabric has been made from raw materials, it is either sold for the home sewing market or made available to designers of manufacturing companies. Many designers agree that the selection of fabrics for a garment line is often the key to good fashion.

The designer of fashion begins by looking at and selecting fabrics from the many textile firms. Hundreds and hundreds of fabrics are reviewed and "swatches" obtained. A swatch is a small sample of the fabric. After carefully examining and eliminating many of the fabrics for one reason or another, a number are selected for "yardage."

SPECIAL FABRICS AND COPYRIGHTED TEXTILES

Often large apparel manufacturers are in a position to "steer" or demand special fabrics made to their specifications. Such firms can have the textile mills dye specific colors to meet their requirements for coordinates and go-togethers.

A sidelight on special fabrics is the use of copyrighted textiles or motifs. For example, Mickey Mouse, Superman, 007, Batman, Popeye, and similar characters can be used only when royalties are paid to the copyright owners.

A great print can make an outstanding garment. Occasionally a particular print is so outstanding that it is "knocked off." This means it is copied or imitated by firms other than the original creator. It is difficult and bothersome to copyright every print, as hundreds if not thousands are created each season. By slightly varying the imitation, it is often possible to escape legal action. However, the originator usually has the advantage of lead time. By the time the imitators produce copies of the original, the season is well on its way.

The designer orders approximately three or four yards of the selected fabrics, which is enough to make a sample garment. The designer perhaps has traveled to various fashion centers to get ideas. Now he or she is ready to create garments forming the season's line.

Each designer has an individual way of working. Some are artists who sketch out their ideas and have others execute them. Others cut a muslin prototype of the garment to be made and drape it first on a dummy form and then on a live model. Still others take the fabric itself and begin to drape and "play with it" on a live model or dress form.

In addition to the basic fabric needed for the dress or garment, there are often a number of "findings" necessary to complete the model. Findings may include belts, buttons, trimmings, lace, embroidery, linings, interfacings, or inserts of other fabrics. Occasionally garments require a number of fabrics. An example of this would be a coordinated outfit with a knitted top dyed to match or contrast with a skirt and jacket. The skirt and jacket would be made of a flat cloth. This same outfit might have buttons on the jacket that match a belt on the skirt.

Often the designer has a concept of a color scheme and idea to be carried out, such as a "nautical look." This may require white and navy fabrics, embroidered anchors, a patent leather belt in navy with a gold buckle, and brass buttons on the garment. Some designers go so far as to say it is often these details that make the model a success.

Finally, a garment is created from muslin or the selected fabric in a model size, usually an 8 or 10, or, if a junior house, a 7 or a 9. This garment, when completed, is given a number and tentatively put in a line. When a sufficient number of model garments have thus been created, the entire line is usually reviewed by the key executives of the apparel firm. They may start with as many as 150 garments. Some garments are eliminated, others modified, and then the line is priced and "ready." The showing may now be pared down to 80 or 90 models.

SHOWING THE LINE AND SELLING

Once the line is ready, it is then shown to the retailers who come to the market in New York or other cities during market weeks or "openings." The lines are open for showing in the showrooms of the manufacturers. Here during key periods

BEHIND THE PRICE TAG OF A $110 SUMMER DRESS

Cotton and polyester dress: Wholesale price $ 59.75
Retail price $110.00

<table>
<tr><td colspan="2">MANUFACTURER'S COST</td><td colspan="2">RETAILER'S COST</td></tr>
<tr>
<td>Fabric
2¹¹/₁₆ yards at $1.60</td><td>$ 4.30</td>
<td>$59.75 less discount for
prompt payment</td><td>$ 55.00</td>
</tr>
</table>

MANUFACTURER'S COST		RETAILER'S COST	
Fabric $2^{11}/_{16}$ yards at $1.60	$ 4.30	$59.75 less discount for prompt payment	$ 55.00
Lining 1¾ yards at .75, plus interlining, ¾ yards at .60	1.54	*Markdowns* Averaged over all dresses in stock	11.00
Belt Including covered snaps, elastic	2.28	*Shortages, Pilferage, etc.*	2.00
Labor, Wages Operator, finisher, presser	21.03	*Alterations* Cost of maintaining department, averaged out	2.00
Labor, Fringe Benefits Health and welfare, Social Security, vacation, pension	6.73	*SALARIES* Sales Staff	5.00
Overhead Rent, insurance, utilities, salaries, costs of samples, trade discounts, etc.	19.87	*Merchandising and Buying Staff* Including expenses	3.00
Total Cost	$55.75	*Clerical and Stock Room* Receiving, marking, deliveries, etc.; including expenses	3.00
Taxes	2.00	*Advertising, Display, Sales Promotion*	4.00
Profit	2.00	*Administrative* Executives, credit and accounting offices; including expenses	8.00
		Employee Fringe Benefits	2.00
Wholesale Cost of Dress	$59.75	*Overhead* Rent, insurance, utilities, cleaning, security	9.00
		Miscellaneous	2.00
		Total	$106.00
		Taxes	2.00
		Profit	2.00
		Selling Price	$110.00 (plus tax)

Source: *New York Times*, April 23, 1974.
©1974 by The New York Times Company.

they are modeled by live models before an audience of buyers and merchandise executives from various stores. These showings are generally held twice a year, in May or June for the fall market and January for the spring market.

All manufacturers have one or more designers or creators. This, of course, is a key role in the making of apparel. In Paris, the name of the designer, or couturier, is the name of the firm. For example, the House of Dior was made famous by the designer Christian Dior. Dior died some years ago, but the firm still bears his name. Currently, the head designer is Marc Bohan. Whoever the designer may be, however, the firm continues as Dior.

In America, the name of the firm is usually that of the owner or an adopted name the owner has chosen, such as Russ Togs, named for its owners, the Russos; Kayser-Roth, a merged firm, named after its two founders; or Jonathan Logan, an adopted name chosen by its founder, David Schwartz.

There is more to selling a ready-to-wear line than just showing it during the opening weeks. There is often a great deal of preliminary work, such as mailing

announcements of the opening of the line to all store buyers who-have bought the line before, as well as to prospective buyers and to the press.

Some firms have "road salespersons" who make appointments and visit the buyer in the store or show the line in a hotel in town. Still other manufacturers have regional showings in Chicago, Denver, Dallas, or Los Angeles.

Stories about apparel salespersons are legion. Some are said to succeed by wining and dining their customers. It is true that apparel salespersons in the top brackets make as much as $150,000 to $200,000 a year! These salespersons usually have territories which include top stores that do hundreds of thousands of dollars in business with the salesperson's firm. Such salespersons may book several million dollars' worth of business each year and receive 10 or 15 percent commission.

However, typical apparel salespersons make normal salaries or commissions comparable to those of moderately successful executives. Often big stores that are customers of apparel firms are considered "house accounts," which means no commissions are paid on the business done with them.

Occasionally salespersons are able to represent several noncompetitive firms in their region at the same time. This is becoming an increasing pattern as the cost of selling continues to rise. The cost of selling has risen sharply as the cost of transportation has increased as well as the cost of hotel rooms and food. Not so many years ago the plane fare from New York to Chicago was $55, and the cost of a good hotel room $12 a day. Today the plane fare is over $70, and the same room $19 a day. Three good meals used to cost $15 a day; today the same menus cost $24. The markup of apparel has not kept pace with many other rising costs. Regional fashion presentations are often held in centrally located cities, which makes it unnecessary for buyers from the stores to come all the way to New York to see the line.

Part of promoting the line also includes entertaining store buyers, especially those from the large stores that do as much as several hundred thousand dollars a year in volume. Buyers from these stores may be given the "red carpet" treatment.

The resident buying offices are important to the manufacturer. These organizations, which we will discuss in more detail later (see Chapter 15), also place orders. They represent many stores, and their buyers are often powerful and influential with their member store buyers.

Some manufacturers sell through jobbers, firms set up specifically to sell for manufacturing firms, often with regional offices throughout the country. Jobbers usually have a number of noncompetitive lines and show them all to various store buyers in their regions. They act as "branch offices" for a manufacturer: taking orders, forwarding them to the main office or factory, handling complaints, and visiting the customers. The manufacturer is sometimes called the wholesaler.

In addition to this personal selling, many leading apparel firms do trade advertising. Some also promote their lines through national advertising to make the consumer aware of their brand names. These aspects will be discussed in detail in Chapter 12.

After the store buyers have reviewed the lines, they place their orders for the specific garments they have selected. Later the manufacturer checks over all the orders and, if there is a sufficient number of orders for a specific garment, orders a "cutting." At this point models that have too few orders are eliminated, and the line that began with 150 garments may now be as few as 40 to 50.

MANUFACTURING FASHIONS

After the fashions have been designed and promoted and the line has been fixed at a certain number of garments, the firm enters the manufacturing phase. This phase begins when a cutting is ordered.

CUTTING

A cutting is made from hundreds of yards of the same fabric as the sample garment shown. The fabric is ordered in the colors that the store buyers were offered in the list provided by the garment manufacturer.

Making thousands of garments in various sizes and colors is obviously much more complicated than creating one sample garment the way a dressmaker or a home-sewer makes a dress. Manufacturing is accomplished in two major ways.

The first is in the plants owned and operated by the manufacturing firm itself. The second is by apparel contractors. Contract manufacturers, as they are called, are firms whose sole business is to manufacture apparel under contract from ready-to-wear firms. Most of these plants are located in areas where real estate is not so expensive, such as the outlying New Jersey or Pennsylvania areas, or in the South.

In either case, whether in the ready-to-wear firm's own plants or in contract plants, the method of mass producing garments are the same. In both cases it is up to the executives of the ready-to-wear house to exercise quality control, insuring that the garments are produced according to the design specifications and meet quality standards.

SIZING

The process of sizing begins by taking the original model or sample that the designer has created and making a working sample. This sample is broken down into pieces: the body, the sleeves, the skirt, and so forth. It is then "graded."

Grading is the method of taking the original sample, which was made in a size 8, and making models in sizes 10, 12, 14, and 16. Each size is made according to averages sizes of the American woman worked out by the Department of Commerce from statistics obtained from women entering the Armed Services. The government has set standards for uniforms for nurses, the Women's Army Corps, the Women's Naval Auxiliary, and women Marines. Those measurements are generally used by cutters as a basis for sizing.

In the United States four major size ranges have been worked out. The first, known as "misses sizes," usually run in even numbers from 6 to 16. Junior sizes are odd numbers, from 5 to 17. The third classification, called "half-sizes," is for larger, slightly heavier women, and runs from 12½ to 24½. Finally there are large sizes or extralarge sizes running from 32 to 46.

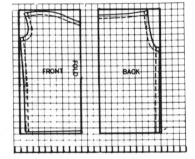

Junior sizes 5 to 17 are generally thought of as younger styles because they are designed with higher busts and slightly slimmer waists. However, junior or misses sizes 6 to 16 are not designed for age groups but relate to the individual figures of the customer. Many older women wear junior sizes, while many young women wear misses sizes.

Patterns are made from the specifications in each size range and for each piece of the garment. These patterns, usually cut out of thin, strong cardboard, are placed on top of layers of fabric laid out on long cutting tables. These layers are usually different colors, so that when patterns are cut there is an assortment of colors for each size and style. An automatic cutter with a rotating blade cuts through the entire stack of fabric, which may have as many as 20 or 30 layers.

ASSEMBLING

The next step is to take the separate pieces of each garment to the sewing department. Here, at long rows of sewing machines, employees sew the sleeve to the body, the body to the skirt, and all other pieces which must be sewn together to complete the garment. Generally one sewer does a single operation and passes the sewn section on to the next sewer, who completes the next operation. Depending on the complexity of the garment, there can be from five or six separate sewing operations to 20 or 30 in the case of gored skirts or inserts of contrasting fabrics.

When the dress is assembled, it is given to trimmers who trim off threads and clip surplus hems and seams. Then inspectors check to see that the garment is correctly made and that a size 10 torso does not have a size 16 bottom or sleeve. Now the garment is ready for pressing; then on to tagging and finally packing and shipping.

PACKING AND SHIPPING

The last step—packing and shipping—is important, for if garments are not packed right, they will require further pressing, which is costly and unnecessary. Often they are shipped on racks on hangars, rather than folded in boxes. The trucks then deliver the garments to warehouses, shipping centers, or the Seventh Avenue lofts of the ready-to-wear concerns.

VERTICAL MILLS

There are a number of "vertical" textile mills, but there are very few vertical apparel firms. Vertical is the industry word which means a corporation contains within its own operations all phases of the manufacturing process. With textile mills it would mean they take the raw fibers in at one end of the mill and the finished goods come out at the other end.

In the case of apparel firms this means they have to manufacture the fabric and then turn the fabric into garments. There are several firms that have experimented with this concept. Generally they are apparel firms that require limited types of fabric. For example, an apparel firm that uses mostly solid color knits can operate a knitting mill in addition to its apparel operation. A ready-to-wear firm that uses mostly denim might operate a textile mill producing denim.

A vertical apparel firm owns and sets up a textile mill to produce the fabric it requires, buying the fibers from the fiber producer. The fabric made to specifications is brought to the adjacent garment-manufacturing plant. Here the fabrics are made into garments, sorted, packed, and shipped directly to retail stores whose orders have been processed by computer. In this manner the fiber goes in at one end; the finished garment emerges from the other end and goes directly to the retailer.

RESIDENT BUYING OFFICES

We have discussed how apparel manufacturers produce and sell their products. The *resident buying offices* are often of major importance in the buying and selling process. These firms are set up to buy for stores all over the country in the New York market and other key markets, hence the name "resident," meaning permanently situated. Resident buying offices give independent stores leverage in the market that they could not have individually. Most major offices have large staffs to fully cover each market. For example, there are a number of dress buyers, for budget juniors, moderate-price juniors, better juniors, misses, half-sizes, maternity, and bridal, to name a few. Multiply this a number of times for sportswear and lingerie, and you can understand why resident buying offices have large staffs.

Resident offices may play a very important role in the retail store's operation. Depending on the relationship established between buying offices and their client, the office's services will vary.

Some client stores send direct orders to their buying office for goods from particular manufacturers, stating merchandise and prices. The resident office will then execute these orders and perhaps adjust for substitutions if necessary.

When a client store needs certain types of merchandise, it will instruct its office to buy to fill these specific needs. These orders are called "open-to-buy orders." For example, a client needs 200 dresses to retail for about $29. The office buyer will use his or her judgment in providing an assortment to fill this request. He or she may buy from as many as five or six different apparel firms to complete this order. In another case a client store may request the resident buying office to "fill in" certain sizes, styles, and colors to replenish depleted stocks in the store. These orders are called "fill in" orders.

Some stores do not have their own buyer in a particular dress department. They have a department manager who each day sends the stubs from the tickets of the dresses sold, or a record of them, to the central buying department of the resident office. The resident buying office replaces the merchandise sold on a continuing basis with new merchandise of the same prices as the merchandise sold. By using the resident buying office as a central buying service, the retail store has a constant inventory of new merchandise.

Some stores may instruct their buying offices to advise them of any special purchases they find in categories of merchandise. A store merchandise manager may want a large number of coats for a sale. If a resident buyer sees an opportunity to snap up a lot of coats at a good price, the sale is made instantly.

Many of the larger offices send their buyers to Europe or the Orient to buy merchandise that is not available in the United States or that cannot be duplicated at a low price. This gives the stores an opportunity to have imported merchandise to offer along with their domestic stock. Many stores run an "Import Fair" from one or more countries at least once a year featuring goods from many nations.

The large resident buying offices have a wholesale division. If, for example, a manufacturer has a closeout of 10,000 women's sweaters, only a very large store can use such quantity. A resident office buys the entire lot, warehouses it, and offers this merchandise to its member stores at great savings. Ten stores can each order 1,000 sweaters or 20 stores may take 500. In any case, it gives the stores purchasing power as a group that would not be possible for an individual store.

The major resident offices provide services other than buying. They serve as headquarters for the promotional efforts of their member stores. They produce Christmas catalogs for their stores' charge customers, each set of catalogs separately imprinted with each store's name. Statement enclosures and direct-mail pieces are provided as well. In addition, many of the resident offices offer mats for use in local newspapers and TV spots for use on local stations. The large offices offer numerous services, which can include buying store supplies and providing figure exchange so that stores may compare their results with those of similar stores.

There are four major types of resident buying offices. The first, and perhaps the most important, are the independently owned and controlled offices of major retail firms. In this case, the retail store owns both the retail stores and the buying office. Macy's, Gimbels, Woolworth's, Kresge, Associated Dry Goods Stores, Sears, Wards, Allied Stores, May Company, and Penney's all have their own resident buying offices. Because the buying office and the store are under the same ownership, decisions made in these offices are binding on the store for which the office buys.

The second type of resident buying offices is the independent office. This group represents independent stores throughout the country who pay a fee to the office to represent them in New York and perhaps in other major market areas. The fee is usually based on the retail volume of the store, on the theory that the greater the volume, the more work the buying office will be expected to do.

The third type of resident office is the cooperative office. This office is financed

SOME LEADING RESIDENT BUYING OFFICES

Allied Stores
Associated Merchandising
   Corp.
Atlas Buying Corp.
Frederick Atkins
Belk Stores
Carr Buying
Certified Buying
City Stores
Federated Stores
Gimbel Corporate Buying
Independent Retailers
   Syndicate
Kirby Block
Felix Lilienthal
Macy's Corporate Buying
McGreevey, Werring & Howell
May Company
Murry Martin Foremost
Mutual Buying Syndicate
National Buying Service
Retailers Representives Inc.
Specialty Stores Association
Steinberg Kass
Van Buren—Neiman
Youth Fashion Guild

by its members on a cooperative basis. The member stores share in the cost of maintaining the office.

The last type of buying office is the commission house, which charges a commission on what it buys for its client stores. This type of office is becoming less important, as there is little or no incentive for the office to make good buys. The fee is actually higher if the cost of the goods bought is higher.

Within this framework are a number of variations. There are resident offices, such as the Youth Fashion Guild, which buy only children's apparel. There are others who service smaller women's specialty shops and those who cater to men's stores exclusively, among others.

FASHION CONSULTANTS

Because fashion is such a differentiated business, there are experts who specialize in advising manufacturers, retailers, and others on various phases of the fashion business.

Some are freelance fashion designers and stylists who help accounts during occasional fashion shows or for seasonal lines. Other fashion consultants act as publicists for special shows or events. For example, the launching of a new product may take a special effort, requiring a fashion publicist or a public relations firm specializing in fashion products.

Some fashion specialists are color experts, while others are fabrics and textiles experts. There is a Color Association that, for a fee, helps fashion firms by indicating color trends. There are, of course, home furnishing stylists, decorators, and designers who specialize in this phase of the fashion business. Most of the successful fashion consultants have at one time or another been with a firm involved in the fashion business and have learned how to acquire and use fashion information.

MERCHANDISE CLASSIFICATIONS

We have discussed how a typical apparel manufacturer prepares, shows, and sells a line each season. However, the apparel market has been traditionally divided up into what are called merchandise classifications. These are discussed below.

Dresses. The most common category of apparel is, of course, divided up into many price ranges beginning with casual, brunch styles that retail for as little as $5.00, to formals by leading couture houses that retail for over $500. It is obvious that there are thousands of manufacturers in the dress category alone. Then, if we add the specialization, such as the manufacturer of knit dresses, it is easy to see that between size ranges—junior, misses, women's, and half-sizes in numerous price ranges and some specialization—there are unlimited possibilities for product diversification.

Sportswear and Separates. This classification is growing as more women put together their own costumes. It includes blouses, sweaters, skirts, pants of all kinds, and coordinated outfits. Here, too, you find the various sizes and specializations. For example, there are some sportswear or separates manufacturers who make only leather, suede, or vinyl products; some that make only knits; or still others that specialize in one category, such as blouses and skirts.

Coats and Suits. This is a different market, in the sense that coats and suits need more construction than the more casual clothes. Such construction is called "tailoring." Tailoring usually means putting into a garment's construction labor that is not obvious on the surface, such as "facing" inside the lapels of a coat or jacket or buckram lining in a coat. Suits and coats often need padding in the shoulders to give a better look. Hence, manufacturers of these categories have somewhat different plant operations than dress manufacturers.

Formal, Cocktail, and Bridal Dresses. Again we have an entirely different market, with the end product for specialized use. Formal dresses and bridal gowns are generally characterized by much detail work. Some are elaborately decorated with beads, lace, and embroidery. Usually these classifications are priced considerably higher than the ordinary street dress or costume because of the workmanship and amount of fabric that goes into each garment. The bridal business operates somewhat differently from other ready-to-wear categories. Usually a single garment of a style is shipped to a store to serve as an example of that type. When a woman comes to the bridal department and makes her selection, that garment is often special-ordered in her size, unless the model in the store happens to be in her size. Because of the cost, it is difficult for most stores to maintain a large stock of bridal gowns in a wide assortment of styles and sizes.

Body Fashions. These are also called intimate apparel for daywear (slips, bras, girdles), nightwear (gowns, pajamas, robes), and loungewear. This category, like the others, is a business unto itself. In recent years, the "underworld of fashion" has undergone a number of changes. The most important is that the dividing line between what is worn at home and outside the home has become blurred. Garments once called lounging pajamas now go everywhere. A number of intimate-apparel manufacturers now make items that are interchangeable with sportswear. The old corset is almost gone, and the girdle has been deboned and is made of lighter but stronger fabric with spandex, which stretches and controls at the same time. There is a constant movement to simplify undergarments, eliminate hooks, straps, garters, and metal findings. There is a trend for the body to come into its own with more natural lines and looks—with the body stocking, for instance. Panty hose have become a way of life, in many instances eliminating the girdle.

Specialized Clothing. As the interest in sports and outdoor activities has increased, there has been a growing market for active-sports clothes. Skiing has been growing by leaps and bounds. As recently as twenty years ago there were thousands of active skiers. Today there are hundreds of thousands. This, of course, has created a large new market for ski clothes and what are called après-ski, meaning clothes worn after skiing. Often après-ski clothes have been so attractively designed that nonskiers have often bought and worn them in colder climates. Increased travel has made swimming and bathing a year-round sport. Thousands upon thousands head for sunny islands and other mild climates to escape the icy winds of northern winters. This, of course, has made bathing suits and beach clothes a big segment of the apparel market. And, of course, few people have just one swimsuit—most have several, plus a number of beach costumes or cover-ups. Boating, too, has become a big leisure occupation. It requires a particular type of wardrobe. A growing number of houseboats are being bought as people spend more time on and near the water. Other sports, such as tennis, golf, riding, and bowling, require special clothes or clothes that make participation more comfortable. This entire field offers opportunities for manufacturers, designers, and all the other related talents to cater to these categories of apparel. Tennis apparel has boomed in the 1970s. What will boom in the 1980s?

The Blurring of Classifications. Today the question of apparel classification has become difficult. What is sportswear? At one time it was simple to classify merchandise. The answer to the above question would have been: Casual apparel to be worn for informal occasions. Sportswear consisted of casual dresses and separates—tops, skirts, pants and shorts as well as related items. With the growing trend toward casual dress for all occasions, what was once considered sportswear could easily fall into other categories. Today sportswear may include leather and imitation leather items including coats, vests, and jackets. It may include sparkle dresses and blouses and jeans from blue denims to sequined metallic fabric pants.

The blurring of apparel classifications has not been confined to sportswear—all categories have begun to overlap. Intimate apparel has become leisure wear and often sportswear. Pantsuits are sold in the dress department, knit dresses are sold in the sportswear section, and long "knit shirts" are sold in the dress department. Recently, long nightgowns with underslips have been worn as formals. The lines of classification have broken down—the new rule seems to be sell the customer and don't worry about the category or classification. This poses problems for both manufacturer and retailer who are accustomed to classifying and displaying garments by type.

Dress manufacturers make garments that pass for sportswear. Suit manufacturers make merchandise that looks like dresses and/or sportswear. Sportswear makers in turn make suits and dresses as well as sportswear. When women shop in department stores today they never can be certain what they may find in various departments or boutiques. The lines and categories are no longer clear-cut. This trend will probably continue as more and more women outfit themselves with a total concept in mind.

CONCLUSION

In today's complicated fashion scene, the manufacturing of fashions has become increasingly difficult. As the lines between sportswear, loungewear, dresses and casual wear, formal wear and informal wear become blurred, those in the manufacturing of fashions will have to be alert. As we have said, fashion is change and perhaps one of the biggest changes is the crossing of lines at the manufacturing level. The customer wants to buy and wear attractive apparel —nomenclature and retail-store departmental breakdowns don't interest the consumer. In years to come there will be many changes in manufacturing and at the retail level to satisfy the fashion demands of the customer.

REVIEW QUESTIONS AND DISCUSSION

1. How is apparel designed?
2. Name at least five different categories of women's apparel.
3. Name three size categories of women's apparel.
4. Outline the major steps in the manufacturing and selling of apparel.
5. Do most manufacturers make all kinds and types of apparel? Explain.
6. Discuss the problems of successfully manufacturing and selling apparel.

5

ACCESSORIES IN FASHION

"Great fashion is an individual and timely getting-it-all-together perfectly."

Fashion accessories play an important role in dress. Occasionally an accessory will dominate a costume. No discussion of fashion would be complete without a brief account of the part accessories play in the total fashion picture. Accessories contribute approximately 15 percent of a typical department store's volume.

BREAKDOWN OF ACCESSORIES BUSINESS, EXCLUDING FOOTWEAR AND HOSIERY[a]

CATEGORY	PERCENT
Jewelry	25
Handbags	25
Neckwear	13
Small leather goods	10
Millinery	7
Wigs	6
Gloves	8
Belts	4
Miscellany	2
Total	100

[a]There are slight changes from year to year as one category or another becomes stronger. But the table gives some idea of the relative importance of the categories by breaking into approximate percents of the total.

Sources: *United States Statistical Abstract* and *National Retail Merchants Association.*

HEAD COVERINGS AND WIGS

At one time millinery and head coverings were an important part of the apparel industry. Now hats are no longer a fashion "must." The casual, less formal approach to dressing has meant that many men and women have gone bareheaded all summer and in mild climates all year.

Headgear for colder climates and the winter season is changing, for both men and women, to be more functional and to protect the wearer from the elements. The total headcovering business in the United States in 1974 was estimated at just under $90 million at retail.

A fast-burgeoning field is wigs for both men and women. The development of synthetic hair that looks real and is easy to take care of has brought down the price of wigs and improved their quality at the same time. Until recently, of course, wigs were worn mostly by bald men and women. (We are referring to the twentieth century because powdered wigs and perukes were worn by men and women during the eighteenth and nineteenth centuries. English judges and barristers still wear these old type perukes.)

Now men and women are wearing wigs as fashion accessories. A woman may have a wig for evening or for daytime, and a fall to modify her regular hairdo. Women have found wigs a boon after swimming; they can appear later at a party without a visit to the beauty shop by slipping on a wig. Many wigs or falls are so

cleverly made that if they are matched to the wearer's own hair, few are aware that a wig is being worn.

The growth of the use of wigs has put many millinery departments in this business. After all, a wig is a head covering as much as is a hat. Beauty shops also carry wigs and, of course, wash and set them. Because of the handwork, most wigs are imported.

The "western look" is making its appearance for both men and women in headwear. Also knit headwear is growing in popularity because it is practical, functional, and inexpensive.

Hats can also lend a dramatic or whimsical effect to an outfit, and they can become "trademarks." From time to time famous women have made their hats part of their "personality." Empress Eugenie, wife of Louis Napoleon, made a particular feathered type hat famous. Hedda Hopper, a Hollywood reporter of the 1940s and 1950s, was known for big flower-trimmed hats. The trademark of Bella Abzug, United States Congresswoman from New York, is a big hat.

FOOTWEAR

Probably the most important accessory category is footwear. Imagination and good design have moved footwear from something essentially functional to an exciting accessory. American men, women, and children spend about $10 billion each year on footwear. Though the United States annually produces some 510 million pairs of shoes, imports are increasing.

Through the years footwear has been a key item in a person's total appearance. We have become more aware of this as boots not only cover the foot but rise high on the leg.

Through a combination of fashion and function, there is more variety of foot covering than ever before. Ideas have been taken from the Russian steppes, from French Cavaliers, and from equestrians. Shoes have been created to ventilate and circulate air. Others have been designed to complete ensembles and match handbags or to be a sparkling addition to an evening gown. Some shoes are designed to improve posture.

Most men and women today probably have a greater variety of footwear in their wardrobes than ever before. There are shoes for daytime, evening, sports, beach, skiing, bowling, at-home wear, as well as shoes for different seasons. As the height, width, and design of the heels change, there are new looks. The new looks should correspond to the changes in apparel to make a pleasant total look.

IMPORTANT TYPES OF SHOES

Baby doll Wide, round-toed, sometimes with strap.
Ballerina Following style of ballet or dancing shoe.
Barefoot sandal Backless, low-cut with open shank.
Brogue Low-heeled oxford, usually with perforations and stitching.
Clog Wood- or cork-soled sandal, for beach or poolside.
Crepe-soled Shoe with crepe rubber sole.
Espadrille Rope-soled with rope or canvas upper, ankle tie.
"Earth" shoe Copyrighted rubber-soled with heel lower than toe.
Evening Fancy shoe for evening and formal wear.
Gold Oxford usually with cleats or ridges on sole.
Jodhpur Above-ankle boot with side buckle from India.
Leisure or Casual Almost any type of informal shoe.
Loafer Moccasin-type casual shoe with sole.
Moccasin Soft leather, heelless shoe from American Indian.
Mukluk Eskimo-type low boot of animal hide.
Open back Bare-heel type of shoe.
Open-toed Front portion of upper is cut out, showing toes.
Overshoe Winter-type boot to go over regular shoes.
Oxford Generally, any low-heeled shoe with lacing.
Platform Shoe with thick sole of cork, leather, wood, or other material.
Play shoe Any shoe for beach, play, resort, or cruise.
Sabot Wooden shoe (French).
Saddle Usually, laced oxford with contrasting color across shank.
Sandal Generally, all open-type shoes—"Greek," "Roman," "peasant"; can be made of leather, fabric, plastic, rope, or other material; one of oldest types of foot-covering.
Sneaker Low canvas, rubber-soled, laced; sometimes called gym or basketball shoe when above ankle.
Space shoe Special patented shoe molded to foot.
Sports Any shoe for casual or spectator sports.
Step-in Shoe with no fastening or closing.
Street Generally, low-cut for everyday wear.
Tie shoe Shoe with lacings.
Walking Comfortable for hiking, walking; sturdy, heavy-soled.
Wedge Shoe with large, solid, wedge-shaped heel.
Work Shoe of sturdy construction, heavy uppers and sole, for laborers.

BELTS

Many articles of apparel come with their own belts. Others call for belts that the wearer must add to the outfit. Most men and women have acquired a wardrobe of belts in different styles and colors. This accessory can be made of leather, metal, fur, plastic, or other materials. Belts can range in width from under an inch to as much as 10 or 12 inches, forming a girdle or cinch-type belt. The fastening or buckles have an enormous range of possibilities. As style and fashions change, the belt or sash must adapt itself to each new look. Wide belts with beautiful buckles have become a focal point of many costumes for both sexes. The smaller volume accessories—belts, scarves, handkerchiefs and neckwear—do only about $610 million in retail sales.

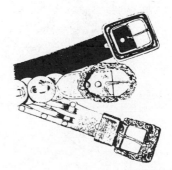

HOSIERY

Covering for the leg has had a most interesting history. In the Western world the leg was the last part of the anatomy that was freed for exposure. Until relatively recently, the leg was always covered. Bathing suits as late as 1910 were extremely modest. Today we laugh at the amount of clothing women formerly wore at the beach, including covering for the legs. Long skirts were worn exclusively by most women all over the world until modern times. In modern times there are cycles of varying skirt lengths. In the Orient most women still wear long skirts.

What women wore on their legs under such long skirts was of little interest for years. Since it could not be seen, what difference did it make? The big revolution in hosiery came in two stages. In the late 1920s and 1930s short skirts came to the United States and Britain. World War I had just ended, and everyone let go in joyous abandon. It was the age of the Charleston and speakeasies. F. Scott Fitzgerald and John Held, Jr., epitomized this time, the former with his writing, the latter with his drawings of the flapper with her short skirts and stockings rolled just above the hemline.

The second part of the hosiery revolution came with the invention of nylon by the du Pont Company in 1938. Women had worn silk stockings prior to this, but nylon offered a longer lasting product at prices every woman could afford. As the invention of nylon coincided with World War II, and nylon was needed for other purposes, nylon hose were rationed during this period.

Now hosiery has become an important fashion item, coming in an enormous assortment of patterns, styles, and colors. Annual retail sales of women's hosiery total nearly $2 billion. Total hosiery sales at retail, including men's and children's, is approximately $4 billion annually.

More important, hosiery has become a major article of apparel. Panty hose have largely replaced the combination of underpants and separate hose and girdle. This has revolutionized the intimate apparel business because hosiery plays a more important role in the total apparel picture, serving as a combination of both undergarment and leg covering.

There is now a tremendous variety in leg coverings. Hosiery has "gone wild" or "crazy." Knee-high socks are worn in all shades of bright mixed colors and patterns. The "crazy toe" has been created with each toe a different color and fitted like a glove fits the hand.

LEG FIGHT!

Until the mid-1970s just about all women's hosiery was sold in department stores and women's specialty shops.

Now the fight for covering legs is on full blast. Supermarkets are vying with the usual hosiery outlets to capture a large share of the $2-billion market. Hosiery as an item combines impulse and need. Women shopping for food are reminded they need hosiery as they pass the display on their way to the checkout counter.

Supermarket brands such as L'eggs, packaged in egg-shaped plastic containers, have in a short time captured a sizable chunk of the hosiery business.

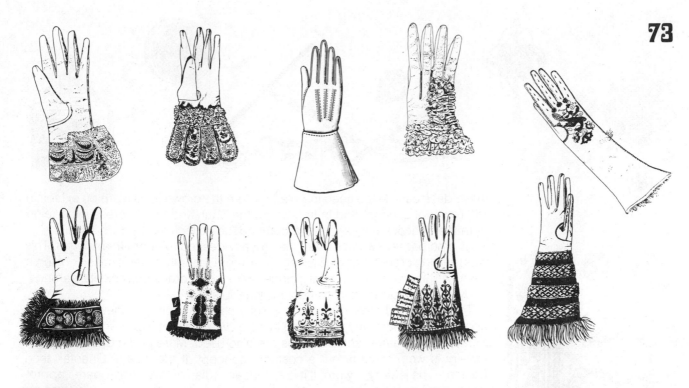

GLOVES

Throughout the ages gloves have been worn both as a fashion accessory and to keep the hands warm. At times they have been tiny and unobtrusive. At other times they have been huge and even dominating. The glove has been the symbol of a challenge—"throwing down the gauntlet" meant that the person who threw it in front of another was challenging that person to a duel. When a woman dropped her glove near a man, it was an indication that she wished to know him better.

Colors and styles run the gamut of small black or white gloves to long styles in every color of the rainbow. Glove lengths are designated by "buttons": a two-button glove is a short one; an eight-button glove reaches the elbow. This description was arrived at when gloves were actually closed with buttons and the number used indicated the length of the glove.

The glove industry has shrunk to about $500 million at retail, with imports getting a larger and larger share of the market.

Prior to World War II, no proper lady who considered herself well dressed, would be seen without gloves—winter or summer. Today, with more casual life styles, the white summer glove is so optional that it has almost disappeared.

JEWELRY

Adornment for women and men is probably as old as history. From archaeological findings it seems certain that the great hunter in the cave-man days often strung the teeth of his more formidable wild animal victories around his neck and later gave them to his mate so she could exhibit the fact that she was the mate of a formidable hunter. From that time to the present, women have adorned their arms, legs, necks, and bodies with jewelry.

Great princes and kings wore jewelry and gave jewelry to their wives and mistresses to prove their power and authority. Jewelry symbolized success and power because only a great prince could afford such luxuries. Carry-overs from

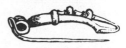

these days can still be seen in Britain, where the crown jewels are on exhibit in the Tower of London, and in Iran where the Shah and his Empress, who reign from the Peacock throne, have a tremendous collection of crown jewels.

As time passed, women other than royalty desired to adorn themsleves. This was the birth of semiprecious jewelry and, more recently, what is called costume jewelry. This type of adornment includes necklaces, bracelets, anklets, earrings, body jewelry, and certain combs and headpieces.

The tastes and fads in costume jewelry change rapidly as new looks come and go. Where formerly most such bangles were of metal and artificial stones, today wood, leather, and ceramics are alsc used. More and more this type of jewelry is worn to carry out a costume concept. If the look is Oriental, then Eastern-type jewelry is worn. If it is American Indian or Western apparel, appropriate adornment of leather, wOod, or Indian-type beading is worn.

Through the years diamonds have been popular jewels. In the Western world an engaged woman usually is given a diamond ring as a symbol of her betrothal. Rubies and pearls (genuine, cultured, and simulated) have always been popular precious stones. However, imaginative combinations of all types of stones, metals, natural materials, and animal teeth and hides are used today in an astounding assortment of body adornments. Many women have drawers full of this type of jewelry and its popularity will probably continue. Costume jewelry retail sales annually come to about $1 billion. There are hundreds of small firms in this business, mostly centered in New England. In addition, handcrafted jewelry, such as the turquoise and silver of the American Indian, is growing in popularity. Both men and women have caught on to the increasing use of silver, turquoise, and beaded necklaces and bracelets.

HANDBAGS

Purses, pocketbooks, tote bags, and carryalls are other names for this accessory. Unlike men, women generally do not have commodious pockets. When women found they needed to carry money, handkerchiefs, and other personal items, they needed an article of apparel to hold them.

The answer is the handbag. As long as a woman needs such an article it might as well be attractive and decorative. So through the years the handbag or pocketbook has developed countless variations, from tiny jeweled and beaded bags for evening to huge pouch or shoulder bags. Every material has been used: metal, chains or links, tapestry, petit-point, precious stones, hides, all types of fabrics, straw, wood, patent leather, and plastics.

Handbags have been made in every conceivable size and of every material, shape, and color. All types of closings have also been used, from a simple drawstring to complicated clasps and buckles. All types, from one large pouch to bags with as many as eight or ten compartments, have been constructed. As long as the bag serves a utilitarian purpose, its popularity will probably continue.

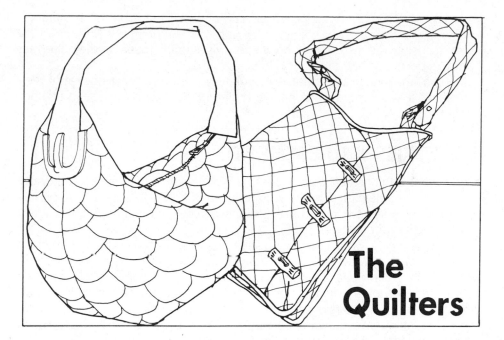

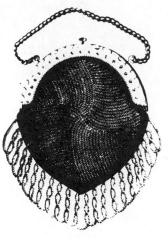

The handbag volume at retail is over half a billion dollars annually, with imports playing an increasingly important role. Some men have begun to carry handbags, particularly those who have a camera and its accessories.

NECKWEAR AND HANDKERCHIEFS

This article of apparel—kerchiefs, neckwear, shawls, ties, and mufflers—has a history of both functional and decorative use. It was only natural that its functional use grew in northern climates where the winters were severe. When outer garments closed, there was often still a small space at the neck that was exposed. Fabrics that could keep the wearer warm were used to wrap this exposed and sensitive part of the body.

Also, in the days of fireplaces, while the front portion of the body was roasting, the back, away from the fire, could be freezing. Hence, the use of a shawl. This item could also be useful for mild early evenings that later grew chilly.

In the case of men whose coats were open at the necks, cravats and ties became natural fill-ins. However, women have often borrowed this idea, and their skirts or blouses have had self-ties, jabots, or scarves, or they have added separate kerchiefs or scarves.

Scarves are easy, colorful accessories to wear. They can be worn loosely around the neck or shoulder, draped over one shoulder, tied on a handbag, worn on the head, and even tied around the body. Scarves can be made in all shapes: small and large squares, triangles, long strips, thin strips, wide strips, and strips as long as nine feet. Scarves can be made of many kinds of fabrics from heavy wooly types for warmth, to light chiffon fabric for summer accents. Scarves are generally colorful, as their principal use is to accent a costume. Recently "signature scarves" have been popular. Famous designers or names in the fashion world have designed scarves and affixed their signatures to the print, thus identifying them.

A small scarf or kerchief became a handkerchief. While this is an accessory because it is carried by men in their pockets and women in their handbags, it

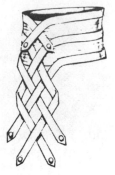

is not given too much importance visually, but a great deal of importance functionally.

Not too long ago men and some women wiped their noses on their sleeves! Today in polite society, this is not done.

Men still may wear a decorative handkerchief in the breast pocket of their jackets while retaining a white handkerchief for sanitary purposes in another pocket.

TOILETRIES AND COSMETICS

Are toiletries and cosmetics an accessory? Some certainly are, if an accessory is defined as something worn to accompany and enhance a person's appearance and other items of apparel. Artificial eyelashes, for example, are actually worn like other accessories.

When perfume is worn it cannot be seen, but it has quite an effect. Many men claim they can find a woman in the dark by identifying her particular brand of perfume. We need not argue the point; there is no question that toiletries and cosmetics enhance a woman's appearance and affect the very air around her. Men have also been users of colognes for a long time, and in recent years men's toiletry counters have grown considerably. Colognes and scented aftershave lotions are widely used and advertised.

The use of cosmetics goes back to ancient societies. Vials of cosmetics and various cosmetic accessories have been found in the tombs of Egyptian and Sumerian women living thousands of years ago. Even the Bible talks of incense, myrrh, and scents.

The idea of women beautifying themselves has had a long history. There were times when it seemed they carried things too far in terms of artificiality and superficiality. Huge, white powdered wigs plus skin whitened by cosmetics made women look almost like porcelain dolls. At other times excessive perfume was used to cover odors caused by lack of personal cleanliness.

More recently the natural look has become popular. Some women jokingly refer to this trend by commenting, "It takes me much longer to make up to look natural than it used to when I didn't look so natural!" Color plays an important fashion role as lipstick, nail polish, and rouge must coordinate with apparel.

With reference to cosmetics, it is certain that fads will come and go as tastes change and differ. As we have mentioned earlier, prominent women, important movies or TV shows, or hit shows in the theater can all affect the concepts of beauty and style.

UMBRELLAS AND PARASOLS

Parasols were once very much a fashion accessory for women, particularly in the seventeenth and eighteenth centuries. This was a time when women prided themselves on their white skin and used a parasol to protect themselves from the sun when they went out for even a short walk. Parasols were also often a flirtatious accessory as women could play "peekaboo" with men of their choice.

Today the umbrella is an occasional accessory in rainy weather. Umbrellas come in many colors and styles, and some are made to fold conveniently into a small space. Men mostly use the ordinary black umbrella, both regular and folding. In climates such as England's, the umbrella is almost a standard item of daily apparel, as it often rains there without advance warning.

Umbrellas for women are occasionally made as part of rain ensembles, and the colors coordinated with or matched to an all-weather coat or a folding raincoat. Today the "golf umbrella," with its multicolor segments, is popular.

WHY DIDN'T RAIN FALL ON THE FIRST UMBRELLA?

The umbrella's first purpose was to provide shade from the sun. *Umbra* is Latin for "shade."

In early times, only a privileged few could afford the protection of umbrellas. It was, in fact, a status symbol. An Oriental king would describe himself as the "King of the White Palace, and the Lord of the 32 Umbrellas."

The British became umbrella-conscious in the eighteenth century. Brian MacDonald, a dandy of the day, is credited with introducing it there.

EYEGLASSES AND SUNGLASSES

Sunglasses have become an important fashion accessory in recent years. They are worn all year in all seasons. They are made in a wide assortment of shapes, sizes, and colors.

Some who normally wear glasses have prescription sunglasses made so they can not only be in fashion but see as well with their sunglasses as with their normal spectacles.

In the beginning eyeglasses were primarily functional, correcting the wearer's vision. Today many men and women wear them as a fashion accessory. Some have a "wardrobe of glasses" for daytime, evening, beach, and sportswear. Recently, singer Elton John has made glasses famous and faddish.

A leading manufacturer of eyeglass frames estimates that there are over a thousand varieties of frames currently on the market.

 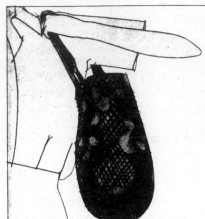 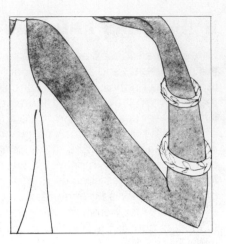

CONCLUSION

Accessories play an important role in fashion. To many fashion experts, accessories can "make or break" a costume. The right accessories can make a simple or ordinary outfit outstanding. A current fashion expression is "get it all together." This is another way of saying that a careful selection of headwear, handbag, belt, jewelry, shoes, cosmetics, and glasses can pay off by creating a great total fashion look. As fashion becomes more individualized, men and women will continue to choose accessories that will both complete an outfit and make a personal statement.

REVIEW QUESTIONS AND DISCUSSION

1. What is meant by *accessory*?
2. What are some of the major accessory categories?
3. What is meant by coordinating a costume with accessories?
4. How do apparel fashions influence assessories? Explain.
5. How important are accessories to fashion? Explain.
6. What are some of the current trends in fashion accessories?
7. Discuss the relation of color to accessories and apparel.

6

FASHIONS FOR CHILDREN

Children's clothes in their own right did not arrive on the scene until the mid-1770s. Until that time a child was dressed in smaller versions of adult clothes. There was, of course, wide variance between the apparel of well-to-do children and that of the poor. Sketches of children in the fifteenth, sixteenth, and seventeenth centuries show that the small world had to endure clothes that were obviously uncomfortable, impractical, and perhaps even cruel.

Children's fashions and apparel have always interested artists and photographers. This is probably because children themselves are delightful subjects and whatever apparel they have worn through the years has been depicted along with them. The simple straightforwardness and disarming frankness of children are shown in sketches and pictures throughout history.

Two young heroes of American literature are Tom Sawyer and Huckleberry Finn. Theirs were images of real American boys with no frills or "sissy stuff," which mothers often insisted that their little boys wear.

However, while boys might be allowed to wear clothes suitable for climbing trees and similar occupations, little girls, like Becky Thatcher, were to be "sweet and nice, like sugar and spice."

When sis and junior had their pictures taken from time to time, they were usually shown in their Sunday best. This means that we have little visual evidence of what many children may have worn on less formal occasions. No mother wanted her children painted, drawn, or shown in ordinary play clothes or torn, dirty apparel. It is indeed unfortunate that we do not have pictures of average children of antiquity. Few people except royalty could afford to have children painted by artists, so it is the children of royalty and great lords and ladies we see recorded throughout early history. These same children are shown in court dress or dressed up, so we aren't sure how they may have looked at everyday play.

One pattern of children's dress emerges clearly. That is that the young people, except infants, wore junior versions of their parents' apparel. Pictures from earlier eras demonstrate that down through the years the little man and the young lady were just that, imitations of adults on a smaller scale.

1840

Infants' and babies' clothes have probably changed the least. Centuries ago infants wore long, white dresses, and they are often still dressed that way today. Their undergarments have improved, and today disposable diapers and rubber or plastic pants have made this portion of dressing easier and more sanitary.

MANUFACTURING AND MARKETING CHILDREN'S WEAR

The apparel market became more and more segmented and specialized after World War I. All apparel manufacturers based their operations on garment patterns and appropriate fabrics for the merchandise they produced. It was obvious that because children were smaller than adults and were growing, there must be separate patterns for them and for each age group. This made it necessary to break down the various segments by ages and sex. The exception was infants' apparel, which could be pretty much the same for both sexes. Fabrics used for most children's clothing were often different from adult apparel.

Little boys' clothing could be made very easily by the same operations that made little girls' apparel. However, when it came to larger boys' clothing—8 to 20 and up—these manufacturing operations were the same as those of the men's industry. It was in this manner that the market divided the manufacturing of children's clothing. Today the children's market is broken up according to manufacturing convenience—infants; toddlers—both sexes 2-3 years; children—little boys and girls 4 to 6; girls 7 to 14; subteen girls; and teens. Boys' sizes 8 to 12 and sizes 14 to 20 are separated from the other children's manufacturers and structured along the lines of the men's apparel industry, which was organized by the Amalgamated Clothing Workers' Union. All the rest of the above categories belong to the International Ladies' Garment Workers' Union.

These classic breakdowns and divisions were carried out at the retail level in stores throughout the country and labeled accordingly—infants, toddlers, children (little boys and girls), boys, girls, subteen, young men, and finally in the adult categories, juniors for girls and college shops for boys. Once such markets were set, they became traditional with their own resources, buyers, and methods of sizing.

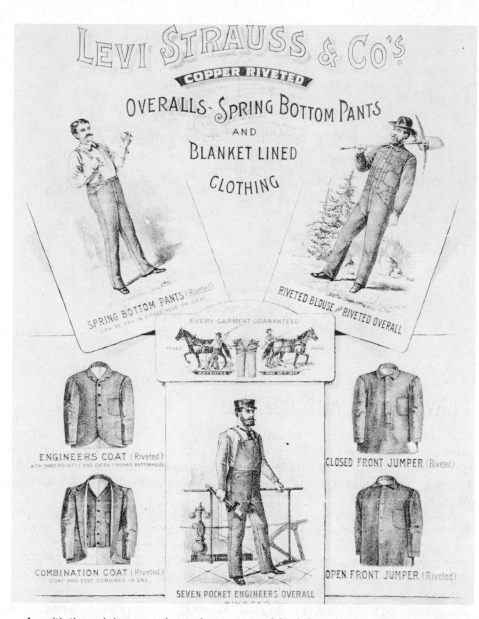

As with the adult women's markets, most of the infants' and children's markets are located in New York. The same type of workers and union scales cover both areas. However, the boys' market is spread around the country, although almost all boys' manufacturers have showrooms in New York. Many denim resources which are particularly important in the boys' market are located in the west. It is easy to understand why the older boys' clothing was grouped with the men's manfacturers. This apparel could be made on the same machines using the same technique required for the men's apparel. Girls soon found out that jeans and pants made by the women's manufacturers did not compare favorably with those manufactured by the men's manufacturers, and so the men's jean manufacturers gained a big new market and still have it.

Advertising for children's and young people's apparel is almost exclusively the province of the retail stores. There are very few nationally advertised brand names recognized in these categories. The few that do exist are usually young versions made by manufacturers of adult clothing—Levi Strauss, Jantzen, Arrow, and Manhattan, among others.

PLAY, GAMES, AND SCHOOL

Many toys and games of today are identical with or takeoffs on what children have been playing with for centuries. We see pictures of hoops, balls, and dolls going back to antiquity. Illustrations show children teasing cats and dogs and riding ponies, mules, or small horses. We also see them in small carts or wagons.

A major change from early days is the educational pattern. Up until the seventeenth and eighteenth centuries many children from lower income families received no formal education. What little education they received they got from their parents, who were usually not well educated themselves. These children wore "hand-me-downs," clothes worn by older brothers or sisters, patched and adjusted for the younger children. Often they began working young, first helping around the home or on the farm and later, when industrialization took hold in the late 1700s, in the mines and factories. Child labor laws did not come until the late nineteenth and early twentieth centuries.

What these children wore was of little concern to anyone. They were usually poorly dressed. As it became apparent that children must be educated if society were to make progress, the habits of dress changed considerably.

It was one thing to allow a child to go ragged around the home or poorly clothed to a factory or mine. It was quite another thing to have children compare what they wore with others in their classrooms.

School attendance brought a number of changes to children's apparel. It brought the concept of uniforms—all children would dress alike so there would be no comparisons, no discrimination. This rule is still followed today by Catholic schools and many other schools in England, Japan, the United States, and other countries. Some of the uniforms for schools such as Eaton and Harrow have been the target of humor for years.

Another interesting aspect of children's clothes was the influence of trendsetters. The well-to-do parents would dress their children in a certain manner, and then those who wished to "keep up with the Joneses" would imitate these so-called upper classes, and a whole fashion trend would spread.

SELLING CHILDREN'S APPAREL

The selling of children's apparel is geared to selling the mother. Seldom do young children have much to say about what they wear except in a general way. It is mother who makes the selection, with some assistance from the child. Thus manufacturers and advertisers for children's clothes aim at what is believed to be mother's concepts and ideas of what her children should wear. Mother usually does the laundering or sees that it is done, so easy care appeals to her. Mother is interested in good hems that can be let out as sister grows, or reinforced wear in junior's pants or sweaters to make them last longer.

Retailers, well aware of these factors, try to stress practicality in selling to the mothers. Every fall there is a big push on children's apparel known as "back-to-school." Most stores run large ads in newspapers featuring apparel appropriate for school. It is at this time that junior and sis tell mother "what all the girls or fellows are wearing." It is then that Susie gets her plaid skirt and Johnny his

new slacks like the other girls and boys. A larger percentage of children's clothes are sold in the fall than in any other season.

There is a strong tendency toward conformity in most children, so it is no wonder that even when some schools had no official uniforms, the children often dressed alike. When Johnny or Susie came home and insisted that all the other children wore certain clothes, their parents usually gave in and bought similar apparel for them.

MANUFACTURERS OF CHILDREN'S APPAREL

Until the turn of the century, mother made her own clothes for the most part or, if more well-to-do, had dressmakers make her clothes. This, of course, meant that daughters' and sons' clothes were also made by mother.

As the population swelled, the market for clothing for all age groups grew, and it attracted firms that specialized in particular apparel for these age groups. As mother began to sew less and buy her own ready-to-wear clothes, she also began to buy more for her son and daughter. The Sears Roebuck catalog of 1897 had a few styles for boys and girls featured on its pages. In that same catalog there are still many pages of fabrics and trimmings and very few of ready-to-wear.

It has been difficult to estimate the amount of business done in each of the children's categories, as there is a good deal of overlapping and duplication of figures. For example, many children's manufacturers make sizes 3 to 6x and 7 to 14 and don't break down their figures. Then there is the difficulty of estimating the accessories sold in the children's market. Most of these items are manufactured by the same firms that make the items for the adult market. However, educated guesses estimate the total volume of this fragmented market including all categories as about $10 to $10.5 billion annually.

Until about 1950 children's clothing pretty much followed the fashions and styles in the adult market. Then gradually and in recent years with a quickening pace the young people's markets became more individualized. Of course, the girls' market was and still is more concerned with fashion than the boys' market. It has been said of boys' fashions, "How different can you make a shirt and a pair of jeans?" In the girls' market for many years plaids of various types and colors have been popular in the fall for back to school. Red is almost always a good color in the children's market.

It has been obvious to children's dress manufacturers that both parents and grandparents like little girls to look "cute." So there has been, and probably always will be, a market for "cute" dresses for little girls. In recent years, however, many manufacturing decisions are based on easy care more than style.

The girls' market does to some extent follow the adult market, imitating one-piece, two-piece, and three-piece styles as they come and go in the adult market. This market also styles clothes at the subteen level to imitate the "older" girls, because the wearers of these clothes are particularly conscious of their age and want to look "grownup."

Proportionally, children's apparel is expensive. Often just about as much labor goes into children's clothing as adult clothing. In some cases the more "fussy details" required for this market make the cost of labor even higher than for an adult garment. The amount of fabric saved because of the smaller sizes does not offset the additional labor costs. Adults are often surprised to find that girls' dresses for the 7 to 14 group and the subteen group cost about the same as adult garments of a similar make. Many parents are shocked to discover that in children's shoes and accessories the same principle holds true, and the amount of workmanship and cost do not differ greatly from the adult market. Some manufacturers claim that it is more difficult to make small versions of apparel than

large items because of the cramped allowances for maneuvering the machines that make them.

Children's ready-to-wear has grown into a multimillion-dollar industry with hundreds of manufacturers specializing in clothes for boys and girls. These clothes are broken down by age groups and sizes. Each size range and merchandise category has a different manufacturer. For example, one ready-to-wear maker will make only girls' knits, perhaps in two size ranges, 3 to 6X and 7 to 14. Another will make only dresses, and still another only sportswear or coats.

BREAKDOWN OF CHILDREN'S CLOTHES BY AGE GROUPS AND SIZES

GIRLS		BOYS	
Infants	0 to 18 months	Infants	0 to 18 months
Toddlers	2 to 3X	Toddlers	2 to 4
Little girls	3 to 6X	Little boys	3 to 7
Girls	7 to 14	Boys	8 to 12
Subteens	6 to 14	Bigger boys	14 to 20
		Some clothes in small, medium, and large	

Other groups of apparel manufacturers will cater to the boys' markets, one making only dress pants and slacks, another sweaters, still another shirts or pajamas. As boys wear fewer suits, there are more manufacturers of sweaters, shirts, slacks, and jackets in the boys' market.

One manufacturer of the famous blue denim jeans, the Levi Strauss Company, has given the name "Levis" to the jeans they make. In the beginning they only made blue dungarees for men, then, later, smaller sizes for boys. Still later they began to manufacture khaki pants for the military that became a popular civilian item called "chinos."

Today this firm, along with many other men's pants manufacturers, is making pants for women to meet the growing demand for "boys' clothing" for women. In addition, Levi Strauss now manufactures jeans for younger children as well. As men and boys borrow from women's fashions, girls increasingly borrow apparel ideas and clothing from the boys' market. The up-to-date "uniform" for both boys and girls has been blue denim slacks in various versions—stove pipe, flared, ragged, tie-dyed, faded, and regular—often decorated to individual taste with patches, embroidery, nailheads or whatever.

FADS IN CHILDREN'S APPAREL

Fads have not played a large role in children's clothes. They have been a fringe business. The biggest fad in recent years has been the T-shirt fad. These shirts are manufactured with the latest topical news or hero or comic character. Each season as the news changes there is a proliferation of T-shirts, which can be printed quickly and easily with the latest slogan or phrase. Some have endured for years—Superman, Mickey Mouse, Peanuts, Stolen from the Athletic Department of (various schools), and prisons such as Sing-Sing or Alcatraz. Many fads are local and just about "everybody" at a particular school will wear a certain type of shirt during a season or year.

As with the adult market, the long-range trends in the children's markets seem to be in the direction of practicality. The clothes that wear best and are easiest to keep clean are winning out. Easy care has become a by-word in almost all categories of children's apparel. Today most children's clothes are easy to wash, hygienic, and practical. There is new emphasis on flame- or fire-retardant fabrics, especially for sleepwear.

DESIGNERS OF CHILDREN'S APPAREL

While there are a number of famous designers in the children's field, they are known mostly in the market and not by the consumer. In children's apparel the name of the manufacturer is publicized rather than the name of the designer. In this way when a designer leaves or a company changes designers, which happens often in this merchandising area, the company has continuity. There are quite a few firms that have been in business a number of years, and stores recognize their names and hope to build a following for these names. Among those recognized by a number of consumers are Girltown, Kate Greenaway, Cinderella Frocks, White Stag, Joseph Love, Justin Charles, and Danskins; and in boys' wear McGregor, Donmoor, Chips & Twigs, and Wrangler.

CONCLUSION

It has often been said that parents are willing to spend more on their children than on themselves. At any rate the children's market is a big and good one, and by all indications it will remain so. The children's fashion industry is not "kid stuff"; it's big business.

REVIEW QUESTIONS AND DISCUSSION

1. Does children's apparel follow adult fashions? In what way?
2. What are the major children's size ranges?
3. Do the same companies make both adult and children's apparel?
4. What is the usual approach to marketing children's merchandise?
5. Discuss how you would promote children's apparel for a retail store; for a manufacturer.

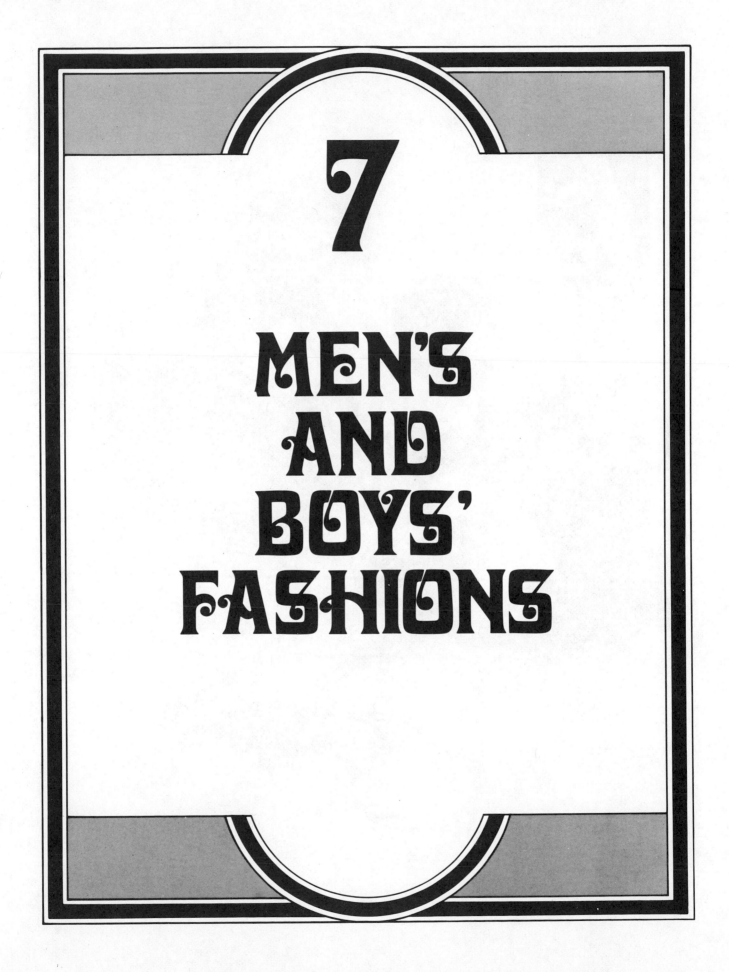

7

MEN'S AND BOYS' FASHIONS

Like the history of fashion in general, the evolution of men's fashions is closely related to expanding means of travel and communication. We are apt to forget that, until relatively recently, it was difficult to travel from one place to another. A man might spend his whole life in a village and assume the rest of the world consisted entirely of villages like his, with men dressed exactly like himself. Clothes changed so slowly that for centuries the average man was not conscious of any development. His father and grandfather had worn clothes similar to his, so he saw no reason for himself or his sons to wear anything different.

A HISTORY OF MEN'S CLOTHING

Wars and increased travel brought knowledge to other peoples. Wall paintings show that Egyptians were aware that captured peoples did not wear the same apparel as themselves. The ancient Greeks knew that the "barbarians" on their borders wore trousers, unfamiliar to themselves. However, the ancient world as a whole showed very little interest in such matters as what people wore.

One type of apparel in which men were extremely interested was battle clothes. This could mean the difference between life and death. After animal skins and simple cloth, the first other article of apparel was foot covering that would allow a man to walk or march over rough ground. Then came head protection and crude shields that could protect him from leaping animals or other men's spears.

As military weapons improved, men's fighting apparel changed. Helmets and breast plates later became entire suits of chain mail and full metal armor. Bullets and gunpowder made such outfits obsolete. It might be noted in passing that "uniforms," similar clothing for all men from a particular country, helped to distinguish friend from foe in battle.

Fashion in the modern sense emerged in the last half of the fourteenth century. Beginning in the luxurious courts of France, it soon spread to other countries. One of the earliest attempts to picture fashion was that of Ferdinando Bertelli, who published a costume book in Venice in 1592. German and French books illustrating apparel soon followed. Shakespeare was probably aware of Cesare Vecellio's *The Clothing and Apparel of Diverse Parts of the World,* published in 1590, which included costumes of Asia and Africa.

It seems certain that women made the early clothing for men as well as for themselves. This work included spinning yarn and making fabric. Later, probably beginning in France and England, men's clothing was made outside the home by tailors, who constructed men's clothing on a somewhat different scheme from women's apparel. All early work on both was done by hand, as the sewing machine was not invented until about 1830.

We have also seen that the first mass-produced garments were soldiers' uniforms in France and later for the Civil War in the United States. It was only a small transition from making uniforms to making civilian apparel. So it was in men's wear, *not women's wear,* that the ready-to-wear concept got its start.

In 1880 a book appeared that changed the course of apparel making. It was *Human Proportions in Growth, Being the Complete Measurements of the Human Body for Every Age and Size During the Years of Juvenile Growth* by Daniel E. Ryan. This scientific, statistical summary virtually gave blueprints for the men's and boys' manufacturers for proportioning their ready-made garments.

As mentioned in previous chapters, men's clothing in the beginning was functional. In warm climates a loin cloth sufficed, and in cooler climates, a tunic was

worn over the loin cloth. In cold climates fur wrappings or layers of heavy fabrics served as protection. The addition of sleeves made garments fit better. This type of clothing or apparel was not fashion as we know it today. This was body protection.

It was most natural in the beginning that kings, lords, and royalty sought to distinguish themselves by dress, so it was generally in the court of the ruler that styles were set. It took some time before such styles came into wide use because travel was slow and difficult, and few visited the court and saw the apparel worn there.

When royalty began to exchange ambassadors for the first time and trade developed between nations, the apparel of one country could be influenced by that of another. It is not difficult to imagine how a lord of one court might admire the garments of a visiting dignitary. The visitor in turn might carry home some of his host's ideas and on his next trip present gifts from his own country.

FASHION AND FUNCTION

If you analyze contemporary men's apparel you will find a number of details that are carry-overs from early functional clothing. For example, because most men rode horses, many types of boots were developed to protect legs from chafing and becoming sore from saddles and stirrups. Coats were split up the back to divide over the horse's back; buttons were sewn at the top of the slit to reinforce the seam. Collars were put on coats to turn up against harsh weather.

A vest filled in the space left by an open coat and protected the wearer from the cold. Vest pockets were used to carry pocket watches; breast pockets carried handkerchiefs. Scarves kept the neck warm.

Other pockets were used for keys, flint boxes, and later matches, money, papers, and an assortment of such things as pocket knives, magnifying glasses, spectacles, and work tools—compass, ruler, needles, pins, hammer, or blood-letting paraphernalia. There were, of course, differences between the apparel of courtiers, gentlemen, tradesmen, and peasants. The latter's clothes were determined by his trade or function.

During most of this period, women's clothing was designed to please the eye and add to the appearance of the wearer. Much of women's apparel was not only not functional but actually created difficulties for the wearer. For example, hoop or full skirts constantly got in the way and had no useful purpose.

OCCUPATIONAL DRESS

As men did many different kinds of work, there was often a costume or special apparel for each occupation. This special apparel developed over a period of years and was based on trial-and-error experience. Let us examine a few of these occupational uniforms.

The earliest specialized costume was probably that of the hunter. When man had to cover his body to protect it from the cold, he first used skins, then heavy fabrics. However, when he needed hunting implements he needed a place to put them while keeping his hands free. It is thought that the belt or girdle was one of the first accessories. A hunter could put an ax or hunting knife in a belt and carry his spear in his hand. Belts were easy to make; strong vines, leather strips, heavy fabric, or combinations of materials were available.

A number of other occupations all needed variations of the same garment—the apron. A blacksmith who needed protection against flying sparks and dirty horses' hooves developed a heavy, leather-type apron that would prevent his getting burned or the horses' hooves tearing his regular clothes. Others that needed aprons included bakers, carpenters, stonemasons, and barbers, who were also in part physicians. These aprons were often different in material and in placement of special pockets adapted for tools of the trade.

1300

1400

1500

1800

1850

1890

1935

1940

1945

1600

1700

1890

1900

1920

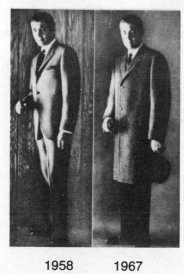

1958   1967

1970s

Women borrowed the idea of the apron. It has come down through the years in various forms and is still in use in the home when a woman wants to protect clothing while in the kitchen. Aprons from time to time are used in various costumes as a fashion look.

Let us return to men and their occupations. Trousers or pants were probably developed by societies in which the horse was used extensively. Egyptians, Greeks, and Romans were not normally horsemen, so we see them dressed mainly in loin clothes, tunics, and togas. However, we see that the so-called barbarian who was a horseman often wore trousers or pants, making it easy to sit astride a horse. This is an important fashion concept because it ultimately becomes the major differentiation between men's and women's dress. If we look at the Greek, Roman, and other early civilizations, men's and women's dress was almost identical.

It is interesting to note how fashions are being more and more influenced by what the other sex wears. Men's clothing is becoming more colorful and borrows ideas from the women's field, just as women's apparel is taking ideas from the men's clothing market. For example, women for years have worn lightweight fabrics such as batiste and chiffon. Now men have discovered that such lightweight fabrics make excellent summer shirtings, and even lace is comfortable, letting in air and permitting perspiration to evaporate. Men's shirts have also become brighter and more colorful. In the past the white shirt was standard. Today there is almost as much variety of color and design as in women's shirts. Women have discovered that pants are comfortable and practical, and pants are now worn for all occasions. There is even a "borrowing" of designers—Brooks Brothers makes women's shirts and Yves St. Laurent designs men's shirts, to name two examples.

Currently some young men and women wear identical clothes—tunic blouses, jeans, sandals, and beads, and long hair.

The major question about such trends as the "hippies" or the motorcycle or motor-bike set is how much they will influence other fashions or how long these trends will last.

THE MEN'S AND BOYS' FASHION INDUSTRY

The men's and boys' fashion industry is set up in various distinct categories, which are divided by the basic products manufactured. There are the clothing manufacturers, which in the men's field means suits and coats. Shirt manufacturers make both dress and sport shirts. Pants manufacturers make slacks and jeans. Then there are the sportswear manufacturers who produce a mixture of apparel such as bathing suits, shorts, tunics, sweaters, and related items.

In men's apparel the famous names and brands were an early mark of the industry. Such names as Arrow, Van Heusen, and Manhattan go back many years.

In the manufacture of men's suits, such names as Hart, Schaffner and Marx, Kuppenheimer, Society Brand, and GGG Clothes go back to the early 1900s. These firms were the largest of any apparel firms, employing thousands of workers at a time when a very large women's apparel firm might have had 50 employees. So you might say that men's apparel emerged as an industry when women's apparel was still made up of numerous small shops. This came about because millions of women were still making their own clothes, while men were buying ready-made suits and shirts for themselves.

It was not long before these giant men's industries had the matter of sizing down to a science. In the men's shirt business, it soon became apparent that the critical areas of fit were the sleeve and collar. As the early styles of men's shirts called for stiff, starched collars, these were made detachable so they could be laundered separately from the shirt. The collar and sleeve lengths were graduated. The collars were generally 14 to 17 inches long, measured by the length around the neck. These were graduated by half sizes such as 14, 14½, 15, 15½, 16, 16½, 17.

The sleeves were made in lengths measured from the center of the back of the neck to the wrist bone, from 31 inches to 36 inches. When these measurements were set, men could buy shirts by size. It was a short step to conceive of men's clothing sized along similar lines, making certain that alterations could be accomplished at strategic points. Men's suits were manufactured according to graduated sizes, allowing for the sleeves to be shortened or lengthened slightly and the bottom of the trousers adjusted by length and waist to individual needs.

A man could now buy a ready-made suit in a store and have the store's tailor make alterations to insure a better fit. Today this is still the standard practice, but the sizing and fitting have become more sophisticated. Instead of graduated sizes of from, for example, 28 or 30 to 44 or 46, there are now within each range "shorts," "regulars," and "longs," allowing for men of different stature. There are even "short shorts" and "extra talls" to cover variations of variations. This means fewer alterations are necessary. As time goes by, it becomes more difficult for retail stores to get skilled alteration people, so it is preferable that a suit be made to fit each individual better to begin with.

As short a time as one hundred years ago, almost every man had to have his suit made to order; today only wealthy men have custom-made suits. The ready-made suit in all its variations is in many respects a better, more comfortable suit

BILL BLASS LTD.

than many of the individually made, custom-tailored suits of yesteryear. Well-known men's designers include Hardy Amies, Ralph Lauren, Pierre Cardin, and Bill Blass (the latter two also design women's fashions).

There is now much more variation in weights of fabric, colors, and styles. In an age of heated and air-conditioned rooms, it is not necessary to use the heavy fabrics formerly needed for men's clothing. Most men today have a wardrobe of suits including summer weights, year-round weights, and, in cold climates, winter weights. Heavier overcoats are generally in less use for urban living because men go from heated homes to heated transportation to heated offices or work areas.

Today men's clothes are increasingly casual. Only a few years ago a man's sport clothes wardrobe might consist of a few slacks and sport shirts. Now he might have a large selection of casual clothes and fewer business suits. As men engage in more active sports there are costumes for each. The sale of bathing suits for both men and women has increased tremendously. With easy travel, swimming, in fact most sports, are year-round activities.

Winter sports have become more important, too, so ski clothes have become more common. There are now a number of resorts where you can both ski and swim during the same vacation! Boating, fishing, tennis, and golf have also grown more important as more leisure time becomes available. The "slicker" is essential for boating enthusiasts, as well as rubber-soled footwear to protect the boat deck.

Golf shoes often have spikes or cleats to give firmer footing. Smooth, rubber-soled shoes are mandatory on tennis courts, and special ski boots are necessary for skiing. For most sports that are carried on in the sun, sunglasses are usually worn to protect the eyes from glare. These have become fashion accessories for men as well as women, coming in many shapes and colors. For skiing, glasses become goggles which wrap around the face to protect against fine, driven snow and ice.

BOYS' WEAR

The men's clothing industry also includes older boys and youths. Very young boys are served by the children's industry.

Boys' wear has through the years been a junior version of what daddy wore. As with men's clothing, the tendency has been to a more and more casual approach through the years. Mothers have always known that boys can be very destructive to their clothing. At first this was deplored, for boys did not have both play clothes and regular clothes. The Sunday suit was demoted to the everyday suit, and a new suit bought for the Sabbath.

Today mother buys junior blue denim jeans. When the young man comes in from play with a hole at the knee, it is stitched or patched. In fact, old, faded, and worn jeans have become a "status symbol," especially among teenagers.

It is interesting that manufacturers of boys' clothing, noting this trend, began to make jeans with ragged edges and a faded look. Now these jeans are made not only for young men but also for their fathers, sisters, and mothers; they are made with "paint smears" and fading, ragged hems. The fading, splattered look is made by "tie-dying," which has also been used on other items of apparel.

BREAKDOWN OF TEENS' AND BOYS' APPAREL SALES
BY TYPE OF RETAILER

	TEENS—BOYS' WEAR SALES (MILLIONS OF DOLLARS)	1975 SHARE OF NATIONAL TOTAL (PERCENT)	1965 SHARE OF NATIONAL TOTAL (PERCENT)
Major Chain Stores (Retail and Mail Order) Authoritative consensus estimate	$ 790	33	20
Discount Stores About 3% of $20-billion total volume	570	22	12
Department Stores (Upstairs and Basement) About 3% of $18-billion total volume	510	21	30
Men's and Boys' Specialty Stores About 6% of $4.8-billion total volume	271	10	25
Boys'—Young Men's Specialty Stores Entire volume of about 200 stores clustered mainly in N.Y., N.J., Penna., Ill., Calif.	23	2	1
Other Retail Outlets Includes volume from variety stores, children's shops, rural general stores, house-to-house salesmen, etc.	302	12	12
Total	$2,460	100	100

Source: *Teens & Boys* magazine. By permission.

Boys' clothing includes many T-shirts, sweaters, and jackets, which are ideal for active youngsters. As with the adult line, the sizing ranges are well covered. There are even "husky sizes" for the bigger, heavier boys. In boys' footwear the single most popular style is the sneaker or gym shoe. These shoes have now been improved, reinforced, and ventilated, often with built-in arch supports. They are virtually the "must" of every boy's wardrobe.

Like their fathers, the young men often have wardrobes that include active sportswear, swim trunks, ski clothes, baseball outfits, and football uniforms or portions of them.

Fads play a fairly important role in boys' clothes. For instance, with the landing of the astronauts on the moon, astronaut T-shirts, sweatshirts, and caps became popular. Sweatshirts of various types are periodic fads. They include such subjects as Superman, Batman, G-Man-007, Mickey Mouse, the Beatles, football heroes, baseball heroes, war heroes, Buck Rogers, Indian chiefs, the Lone Ranger, Tonto, Super-Spy, Sesame Street, VIP, Gunsmoke, Men from Mars, and spacemen.

Communications Carrier
(Earphones, Microphones)

Emergency
Oxygen Supply

Closed Loop Oxygen
and Water Systems

Backpack Control Box
with Electronic and
Mechanical Linkages

Portable Life Support System
(Backpack)

Extra-Vehicular Communications
System VHF Radios

Neck Ring

Arm

Multiple Water Connector

Electrical
Power Source

Inlet Gas Connector

Suit Electrical Harness

Exhaust Gas Connector

Pressure Gauge

Pressure Relief Valve

Biomedical Data
Transmission Belt

LM Restraint

Glove

Palm Restraint

Urine Transfer Fitting

Self-Sealing
Medical Injection Disk

Boot Bladder

Boot Restraint

CONCLUSION

It is clear that males are becoming more fashion-conscious as the years pass. Not long ago men left fashion to the women. While women might change their wardrobes twice a year—spring and fall—men wore their apparel until it was worn out. Men's suits changed little from one year to the next. All this is changing; men's clothes are becoming brighter and more interesting. Men no longer look like the cartoons that show identical men carrying their briefcases to catch the 8:11 train.

In many cases the younger male generation has gotten away completely from the "Ivy League" look and the businessman's approach to dressing. There is little doubt that men's apparel will in some degree follow the women's pattern of more changes and variety over shorter periods of time. No longer will what was worn last year be the fashion for next year in the men's field of ready-to-wear.

For a number of years the men's apparel industry was not realistic. In spite of the obvious trend toward more casual dress, many segments of the men's apparel market ignored what was taking place. Most men were simply not wearing hats in mild climates. Advertising and promotion could not make them do so. The business suit was becoming less important among large sectors of the men's world, yet many firms were slow in switching to casual and leisure clothing. Only recently has the men's apparel industry responded to meet the needs and demands of men instead of trying to influence trends.

The concept of individualism marks the future of men's apparel. Each man will select the clothes he believes suit him best and fit his personality and occupation. This means that at any given time there will not be a few major styles but a variety of styles, all popular with different groups or segments of the masculine market.

From this may emerge simplification and functionalism. Each man will wear the most comfortable and simplest clothing for his particular needs. This will mean regional differences due to climate and weather as well as occupational differences. An office worker's clothes will be different from an engineer's, and both will be different from a factory worker's clothing. Men's apparel will be a far cry from Adam's animal skins and leaves.

Men's fashions have moved slowly compared to women's. However, now there is every indication that men's fashions will become increasingly varied, colorful, and casual.

REVIEW QUESTIONS AND DISCUSSION

1. How does the men's fashion business differ in major aspects from the women's apparel business?
2. Does men's apparel change as rapidly as women's? Why or why not?
3. What are current major trends in men's apparel?
4. Do men's and women's fashions influence each other? How?
5. What are some men's items that are found in women's apparel?

8

FASHION IN HOME FURNISHINGS

Throughout the ages there has been great concern for the outside appearance of buildings, for many people pass them every day but do not enter them. But buildings are really created to satisfy the needs of people who live, work, pray, or find amusement within them. Buildings, especially homes, should be and can be attractive and comfortable inside.

Early men lived by fishing, hunting, and gathering berries and edible herbs. The only homes they had were caves, tents made from animal skins, or easily constructed huts. There was neither the desire nor the opportunity to have more permanent homes or to make these temporary homes more comfortable or attractive. The caves and tents usually had only a few skins for the occupants to sleep on, a fire, and a few implements. The most that could be said for this type of shelter was that it kept out some of the cold in winter, was perhaps a bit cooler in summer, and served as a protection from wind and rain at other times. At least there was a dry floor of earth or rock.

From about 3000 B.C., according to archaeological discoveries, people of the Middle East began building primitive houses of unbaked bricks. These were permanent homes in which families lived for a lifetime. Such a house had a door with perhaps a mat of reeds or rushes hung over it and an unglazed window for light and ventilation. This early home had seats and possibly a table and later an oil lamp.

We can still see homes such as this in Africa and some of the outer islands in the South Pacific. Naturally, the climate had a great deal to do with architecture and whether heavier or lighter materials were necessary. In certain areas where civilization was advanced, as in India, Egypt, China, Greece, and Rome, rulers and wealthy individuals had homes that contained far more than the bare necessities.

These homes often had handsome, colorful floors, walls, and ceilings decorated with paintings, mosaics, hangings and fine architectural details. While the poor might live in small, cramped quarters with few if any sanitary facilities, the wealthy often lived in splendor. There were chairs, stools, cabinets, and rugs or mats, all of fine workmanship. There were many sizes and types of pottery and earthenware for water and food and sometimes for containing small fires or charcoal to heat rooms in cooler weather.

In Egypt building materials included stone and granite. In Rome different color marble was used, sometimes to form graceful columns or pillars modeled after

Adobe house in American
Southwest

Roman chair.—couch

those of classical Greece. Furniture was carved or decorated with ivory, gold, or tortoise shell, and couches or beds had mattresses, cushions, blankets, linens, and quilts for comfortable sleeping.

From ancient times to the Middle Ages and on to the sixteenth, seventeenth, and eighteenth centuries, housing continued to improve for the wealthy and, more important, for the growing middle class. Compared to modern life, the medieval household was an open unit. It often consisted of not only blood relatives, but also a group of industrial workers as well as domestics whose relation was that of secondary members of the family. Young men and women of the upper classes got their knowledge of the world by serving and waiting upon noble families.

In earlier eras, homes only two or three stories high were built in continuous rows around the perimeter of their rear gardens. Freestanding houses exposed to the elements, wasteful of land on each side and harder to heat, were relatively scarce. Even farm houses were often part of a solid block that included stables, barns, and storage bins. We can still see a carry-over of this idea today in the row houses of older American cities such as New York, Baltimore, Philadelphia, Boston, and Washington, D.C.

Even into the nineteenth century, very few builders bothered to consult architects about designs for working class housing. Working people as a rule could not pay much rent, so nobody saw any reason why they should expect good housing. As for the middle class, things continued to improve but could have been better. Their houses were larger and built of better materials, often with elaborate fronts. However, the inside was often dismal, with numerous open fireplaces to be tended. Coal might have to be carried up several flights of stairs, and taking a bath meant carrying hot water from the boiler or stove to the bathroom. Cooking was done on coal-fire ranges with no temperature control possible. Cheap domestic help made life somewhat more tolerable for the middle class.

In our own century, advances in technology and improvements in social conditions have caused drastic changes. Homes have become more livable and comfortable, and a large percentage of the population in the Western world enjoys these comforts.

The modern home meets the requirements for these comforts. Electricity, oil, and gas give hot water at the turn of a tap. Electrical gadgets remove much of the drudgery of housework. Furniture can easily be kept clean. There are fewer dust-catching crevices and ornaments. Comfortable chairs and beds allow relaxation, and upholstered furniture contributes to genuine comfort. Refrigerators and freezers keep precooked or prepared foods edible almost indefinitely.

Buildings and homes are constantly improving. Larger windows are used for more light; central air-conditioning and heating provide year-round controlled temperature. Interior spaces and surfaces are more flexible and utilitarian. As homes have improved so have interiors. The choice of furnishings has expanded to suit every taste and creative concept. A home of today can be created in the image of its occupant.

THE MANUFACTURE OF HOME FURNISHINGS

At first everything in the home, including the home itself, was made by the people who lived in it, perhaps with the help of their immediate family or tribesmen. Simple tools and furnishings were made by hand. The mats or rugs, as well as any fabrics, were woven by the women; the tools and implements were made by the men. Stools and tables were crudely carved and chopped from nearby trees, and pottery was created from clay found close at hand. That completed furnishings.

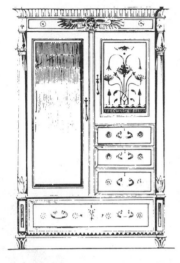

Chest ca. 1850

EARLY FURNITURE CRAFTSMANSHIP

At first chiefs and leaders, who were usually warriors as well, began bringing home articles captured in conquests. Also, captured prisoners or slaves were set to making things for leaders' homes. Craftsmen became skilled in making furniture and household implements, and in weaving, building, carving, and decorating. Not only prisoners but the kings' or lords' helpers or servants aided in making the household and its furnishings comfortable.

Once the basic necessities were taken care of, craftsmen and artisans began to decorate and make beautiful all articles for the nobleman's home. Wood was carved elaborately for furniture, cabinets, and benches. Banners, tapestries, and wall and floor coverings were made by groups of artisans working together. This was the beginning of crafts and guilds, the forerunners of our modern labor unions. Soon, in addition to furnishing for the noblemen, craftsmen and artisans began to produce their goods for the wealthy tradesmen as well.

Instead of working within the walls of a castle, the artisan now worked at the craft in the town or village, supplying others with furniture, glass, pottery, fabrics, and household goods that formerly were only available to the nobleman. Manufacturing had begun in a small way.

From these early beginnings grew the crafts and trades that became guilds and finally developed into industries. Today each category of home furnishings is made by large manufacturers who specialize in one type of product only. There are floor-covering manufacturers with large weaving, tufting, and related facilities; and furniture factories that specialize in one category of furniture, such as beds, chairs, tables, upholstered furniture, chests, or cabinets.

In addition, there are now thousands of items for the home in every category. For example, there are hundreds of lamp manufacturers. China manufacturers all over the world create an infinite variety of patterns, colors, and styles. Thousands of buyers annually visit centers which carry particular categories of home furnishings.

MODERN FURNITURE CENTERS

Furniture manufacturing areas or centers have been developed in certain parts of the country where lumber and labor are easily attainable. Two such areas are Grand Rapids, Michigan, and High Point, North Carolina.

Each January there is a showing of new furniture in High Point. Gathered there are exhibits of furniture to be placed on the market in the coming year. The Grand Rapids furniture is sometimes sent to High Point or to Chicago, where there is another showing. At High Point each category of furnishings is grouped for display as bedroom, living room, or dining room furniture. Retail store buyers can choose from vast assortments.

Chicago has become the marketing center for housewares as well as furniture and floor covering. One of the largest buildings in the United States is the Merchandise Mart. In this building almost every important home-furnishings manufacturer in every category of merchandise has a showroom. Because Chicago is centrally located, buyers can easily come from any part of the country to see this merchandise. In addition to the Merchandise Mart, there is another large building, called the Furniture Mart, which houses additional resources. Between these two buildings, one can see virtually every home-furnishings line manufactured domestically or imported.

Each year there is a housewares and home-furnishings market in Chicago. At the markets in High Point and Chicago buyers place their orders for the merchandise they want for the coming season. Just as New York is the fashion center, High Point and Chicago are the home-furnishings centers. Many of the smaller decorative items and giftwares are now imported, as they often involve hand labor which make manufacture in the United States prohibitively expensive.

New York has become the center of much of the import market in giftware, lamps, china, and objets d'art, though most of these lines can also be seen in Chicago and some in High Point. As transportation and communication improve, it becomes easier to find and ship items from remote parts of the world, so you see more and more imported merchandise in the homes of today.

"UNDER ONE ROOF".
THE WORLD'S BIGGEST BUYING CENTER

The Merchandise Mart showrooms are open MONDAY through FRIDAY, fifty two weeks a year, with personnel in attendance. Here buyers select merchandise gathered from all corners of the earth, and are able to shop leisurely with never a thought of outside weather conditions.

FLOOR	
18	FLOOR COVERINGS · BEDDING · FURNITURE
17	FURNITURE · BEDDING · CONTRACT FURNITURE
16	FURNITURE · CONTRACT FURNITURE
15	GIFTWARES · GLASSWARE · CHINA · SILVER · WALL DECOR · LAMPS · ACCESSORIES · ANTIQUES
14	GIFTWARES · GLASSWARE · CHINA · SILVER · WALL DECOR · LAMPS · ACCESSORIES · HOUSEWARES
13	CURTAINS · DRAPERIES · FLOOR COVERINGS · FABRICS—CONTRACT FURNISHINGS
12	LAMPS · FURNITURE · ACCESSORIES CONTRACT FURNITURE · FURNISHINGS
11	CONTRACT FURNITURE-FURNISHINGS—FURNISHERS · FABRICS · WALL COVERINGS
10	FLOOR COVERINGS · TEXTILES—CONTRACT FURNITURE
9	WOMEN'S AND CHILDREN'S APPAREL
8	MEN'S AND BOYS' APPAREL · OFFICE OF THE MERCHANDISE MART · BUYER SERVICE DEPT
7	CONTRACT FURNITURE-FURNISHERS—OFFICES
6	RESIDENTIAL AND CONTRACT FURNITURE · FABRICS · LAMPS · WALL AND FLOOR COVERINGS
4	CONTRACT · APPAREL · TOYS · HOUSEWARES · OFFICES
2	RETAIL STORES · RESTAURANTS · M & M CLUB · CONTRACT FURNISHERS · ELEVATED STATION
LOBBY 1	RETIAL STORES · BANK · POST OFFICE · RESTAURANTS · DRUG STORE
LOBBY EAST	CONTRACT · GIFTWARES

a sectional view of the World's Biggest Buying Center with general headings of the various lines of merchandise available on each floor

THE CHICAGO MERCHANDISE MART

The Mart covers an area of two entire city blocks, has 18 floors, and a tower which rises to 25 stories. The gross area of a single floor is 217,000 square feet. The total floor area is approximately 4,229,000 square feet, or the equivalent of 97 acres. There are approximately 7½ miles of corridors. There are 1,000 showrooms displaying about 2,600 home-furnishings lines. The Mart is larger than many U.S. cities.

On a daily basis, 20,000 persons either work in the showrooms and offices or transact business in the Mart. During major markets, the number swells to 60,000. The Mart has its own post office, zip code, security force, electrical shop, carpentry shop, and paint shop. The housekeeping department employs about 150 persons to maintain the building. There is a heliport on the roof, a boat landing below the plaza, railroad tracks beneath the building, and car-parking facilities for about 12,000 cars.

Source: Based on information provided by the Merchandise Mart. By permission.

HOME FURNISHINGS AND FASHION FURNITURE

Cabinet ca. 1750

Chair ca. 1570

When furnishings for the home were difficult to obtain, no one worried much about their looks or appearance. As the years went by and the noblemen accumulated beautiful home furnishings by conquest and booty or through the work of artisans, appearance as well as function became important.

We saw in our brief history how at first even the grandest castles and homes were sparsely furnished. What little furniture they did have was usually massive and heavy, and most of the furniture was made by carpenters who were mainly concerned with constructing the buildings themselves. These men thought of a bench as built-in and fixed to a wall. A table consisted of planks set side by side resting on crossbar legs and joined by dowels (wooden pegs). None of this work was light or graceful, but it served its purpose.

Toward the close of the Middle Ages, craftsmen who specialized in making furniture began to supply furniture to those who could afford it. They believed that benches, chairs, and tables should exist in their own right as things of beauty and not as part of a building. They thought that furniture should also be lighter in weight so that it could be moved around and arranged to suit the occupants' needs.

In joining pieces of wood together, they used ingenious joints that did not look as crude as nails or dowels. Still later, in the seventeenth century, another class of craftsmen came into being. These were cabinetmakers who specialized in making fine cabinets, tables, and related items. Now furniture could be obtained in different woods with different motifs, influences and looks.

Fashion in home furnishings was born. Since the Renaissance, the appearance of furniture has undergone numerous and radical changes. Many experts can tell by looking at a piece of furniture when it was conceived and in what period it was made.

There is Tudor furniture of oak, which is much like earlier English furniture. In France lighter and more elaborate styles developed. These styles or periods are named after French monarchs reigning at the time—Louis XIV, Louis XV, or Louis XVI. This furniture has fine carving and is often covered with tapestry or other rich fabric.

A musical corner ca. 1910
contrasted with a modern music
room

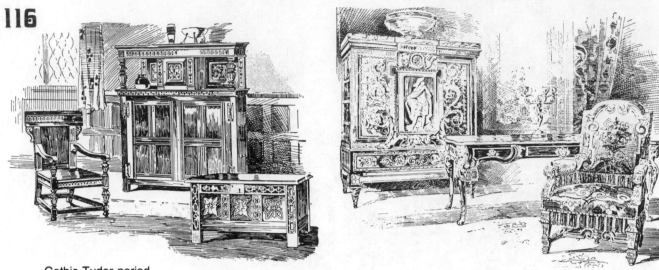

Gothic Tudor period

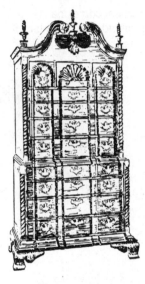

After the French kings came Napoleon; his period was called Empire, as befitted France, a nation with an emperor.

These periods or styles are to furniture what the same periods are to apparel.

Furniture that was made for country homes or outlying estates had a different flavor than that made by urban artisans and craftsmen. This type of furniture is called provincial—from the provinces. In individual countries of Europe, different types of this furniture were created. Thus we have French, Italian, or Spanish provincial.

Meanwhile, in England certain cabinetmakers and furniture craftsmen were creating their own designs. The best of these became famous and gave their names to styles such as Duncan Phyfe, Hepplewhite, and Sheraton. In America we had Colonial, a style developed in early settlement days, often of maple wood and simply made. Later came the Federal period with eagles as a motif. After that, distinctive furniture was created in New York, Maryland, Philadelphia, and New England.

RETAIL SALES VOLUMES, 1974 (BILLIONS OF DOLLARS)

	SUBTOTALS		TOTALS	
	NATIONAL	MIDWEST	NATIONAL	MIDWEST
Furniture and Home Furnishings				
Household furniture, floor covering, china, and glassware			$19.0	$4.6 (25% U.S.)
Household Furniture	$9.8	$2.6 (28% U.S.)		
Upholstered	$3.8	$1.2 (30% U.S.)		
Case Goods	$3.2	$0.8 (25% U.S.)		

Source: U.S. Department of Commerce, *1972 Census of Retail Trade,* updated with monthly government report.

Now there are thousands who can afford to decorate their homes in French provincial, Louis XV, Early American, modern, or various combinations. The aim is to have pieces that are related by period, taste, or design. Just as a woman may put a costume together, a room is put together using furniture that complements the scheme and with appropriate accessories.

Once the type of furniture is decided upon, the furnishings and accessories are planned to go with the concept and enhance its appearance. An entire home need not necessarily be done in the same decor. Different rooms can be in different periods or related periods. For example, a living room might be Early American, and a bedroom French provincial of about the same period with an English period dining room. Let us turn to several other important home-furnishing categories.

Just as furniture developed through the years, floor covering took its own route. From the earliest floor coverings of grass, straw, and animal hides, there evolved more durable fibers woven in the same manner as straw. This soon led to blankets and rugs of various types made of available fibers—flax, wool, and cotton. It was soon discovered that while such items were being woven, they could be given color and design at the same time. Probably the first design was to have all the threads going in one direction in one color, and all the threads going in another direction a contrasting color.

From this simple beginning and with the development of looms and shuttles, rugs became heavier, more colorful, and more beautiful. Because weaving was essentially a hand operation, only people with time or those whose labor was not too costly could engage in making elaborate rugs. Primitive women spent days making blankets and rugs, some of which we can see today in museums. We have reconstructed many of these designs and have modern copies of these lovely creations.

Early traders and conquerors bought or brought back as booty beautiful rugs from the Middle and Far East, particularly colorful and well made. This was the beginning of the Westerner's desire for Oriental rugs, with their intricate designs and multicolor patterns. Today many oriental rugs are used in homes, as they can fit into almost any decor and come in thousands of patterns, colors, and sizes.

In recent times huge weaving and tufting machines have been built that can make broad widths of floor covering. This type of floor covering is called carpeting; because it is woven on wide looms, it is called "broadloom" carpeting. It is generally made in a wide assortment of solid colors and can be cut to any desired width or length or pieced in large sections to go wall to wall, covering the floor completely.

Another category of floor covering is called "hard surface." It consists of linoleum, fabricated tiles, and plastics. This type of floor surfacing imitates the original marble, stone, mosaic, or concrete floors of famous palaces, churches, or buildings. Because of its durability it is generally used in kitchens, dens, and play areas and is now made in a huge variety of colors, patterns, and designs. Ceramic tile and slate are also used.

ACCESSORIES FOR THE HOME

In addition to furniture and floor coverings, there are necessary and decorative items for the home called accessories, or decorative accessories. They include such items as clocks, lamps, pictures, bric-a-brac (sometimes called *objets d'art*), china, glassware, silver, hangings, and decorative pillows.

There are literally thousands of these decorative accessories. For example, lamps come in every shape and variety—floor, table, hanging, wall, and desk, to name a few. Each of these comes in a variety of styles using fabric, china, metal, glass, porcelain, plastic, straw, and combinations of these materials to achieve all period and decor effects.

Pictures or wall hangings can be anything from genuine paintings of old masters to inexpensive posters, fine etchings, or prints of originals. They can

vary in size and can be framed and mounted in hundreds of ways, to go with each category of interior design.

CURTAINS AND DRAPERIES

These are not included in decorative accessories because they form a separate category of home furnishings. As windows have become larger and more important, so have window treatments. Just as there are hundreds of possibilities for furniture and accessory combinations, there are hundreds of decor possibilities for window treatment. The fashion part of home furnishings plays a role in arranging drapes and curtains to go appropriately with the particular period planned for the furniture and floor coverings. Modern technology has added Venetian blinds and shades to window decor. In tropical climates, screens, jalousies, or mosquito netting can be used. Window coverings play an important role, along with floor coverings, in the home-furnishings fashion picture. Interior decorators have illustrated this point by completely furnishing a room, with the exception of window and floor coverings. Such rooms usually look barren and unfinished.

BEDDING

Bedding has become an important fashion category of home furnishing. It includes mattresses, pillows, comforters, blankets, sheets and pillow cases, also called "white goods" or "linens"—both are misnomers as today they are probably neither white nor linen. Mattresses and box springs add a great deal to our sleeping comfort, and these items now come in a number of sizes and in various degrees of firmness. They can be constructed of springs and bindings, foam rubber, shredded synthetic batting, or horsehair. Pillows can also use these types of filling, substituting feathers, down, and foam rubber for the springs and binding category. In Europe there are still down and feather mattresses as well. Beds, sheets, and mattresses, now come in king, queen, regular, and single sizes. Fashion plays a much more important role than ever before in this area.

Where once almost 100 percent of all sheets and cases sold were white, it is now estimated that more than 50 percent are solid colors or prints. Printed sheets include all colors and patterns and can be coordinated with towels and bathroom accessories if desired. These categories, formerly known as white goods, are now a riot of color.

The most important home-furnishing fashion bedding item is the bed cover. This is visible at all times, and its color and design make an important contribution to the look of the entire bedroom. Often the bedspreads and bedroom window coverings are carefully coordinated.

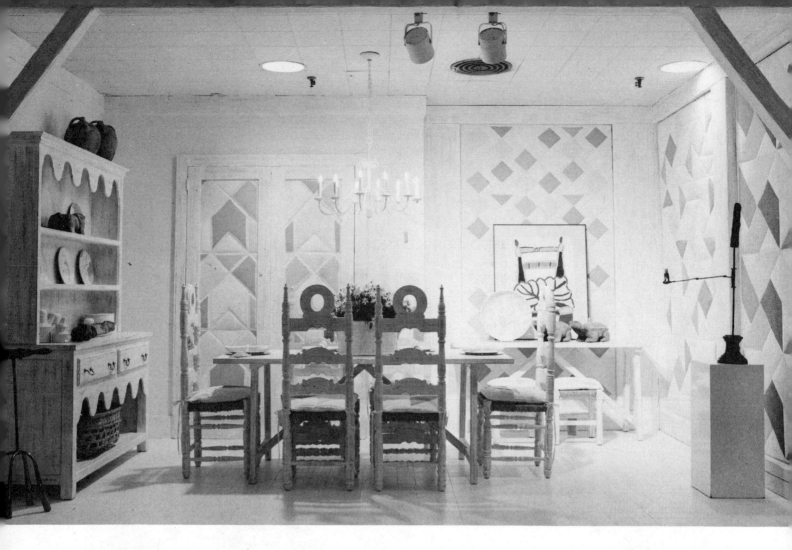

MISCELLANEOUS HOME FURNISHINGS

In this category we will place all the items we passed over in the main classifications of furniture, floor coverings, decorative accessories, and bedding.

These miscellaneous home furnishings include such items as housewares (pots, pans, and kitchen accessories) and related items. Then there are bathroom accessories—hampers, soap dishes, tissue holders, towels, towel racks, toothbrush holders, mirrors, and cabinets.

There are all types of electrical appliances—steam irons, toasters, waffle irons, electric coffee makers, blenders, mixers, ice crushers, electric carving knives, dishwashers, vacuum cleaners, and more. Some of these items such as toasters and coffee makers are highly visible at all times.

Then there are china, glassware, and tableware—also called "silverware" and "flatware," a huge category of its own. Many homes have china cabinets with open shelves or glass doors where the fine china is exhibited for all to see. Many dining room sideboards exhibit pieces of silver, antique coffee urns, and similar items. There are also kitchen towels and linens to be considered in coordinating the kitchen decor. And now that pots and pans come in various colors and patterns, even they have fashion appeal. Also, kitchens are now sometimes carpeted, as are bathrooms, which is still another item to consider in planning the decor for these two rooms. Finally you might add fireplace accessories—screens, andirons, ash shovels, tongs, rakes, and pokers.

A category, not strictly home furnishing, that can add much to the appearance of almost any room is plants. As we have become increasingly city or urban people, we tend more and more to bring the outside inside. Today millions of homes have real and artificial flowers and plants in all types of containers —from red clay pots to elaborate vases, from brass urns to hanging gardens. This trend promises to continue, as it gives most of us a sense of well-being to surround ourselves with living, growing greens and flowers that bring us closer to nature right in our own homes.

BATHROOM FURNISHINGS

In recent years, the bathroom has come into its own as a room with many possibilities for fashion decor.

Towels, rugs, and toilet bowl covers are coordinated with shower curtains and window curtains. This room often has colorful tiles on the walls and floor, with the fixtures themselves in pastel colors. Some bathrooms are elaborately decorated with waterproof wallpaper, mirrors, and pictures.

Where space allows, large sunken tubs are installed—sometimes these tubs and sinks are made of marble. The faucets and tap handles are made of gold colored metal, fancy porcelain, or marble. The bathroom of today may turn into a glamour room of tomorrow, with small swimming pools replacing tubs!

CONCLUSION

It is easy to see the important and growing role of fashion in home furnishings. Where once the bedroom linens were white, now they are colored and patterned. Where once pots and pans were silver color or copper, now they, too, may be colorful and hung in the kitchen in plain sight for all to see.

Everywhere you turn in the home you see color and decor ideas. Home furnishing is as much fashion as apparel. Putting together period ideas and various items is as skilled a task as creating an apparel concept. Persons who do this type of work are sometimes called interior decorators or interior designers. They might also be called home-furnishings coordinators.

In order to sell home furnishings, stores and manufacturers need home-furnishings fashion coordinators. These persons must give direction to the store or manufacturer and explain how his or her products fit into the larger picture of trends for the home. A fashion person must be able to help make the home beautiful and exciting by suggesting carpeting, furniture, decorative accessories, curtains, bedding, and other items to fit into a comprehensive, pleasing scheme. If this is done well, a home can be a delight to the eye as well as a comfortable place in which to live.

Home furnishings in recent years have become more and more "fashion-conscious." The American family has become aware that a lamp can add much

to a room besides giving light, carpeting and rugs can create an ambiance as well as covering floors, chairs and sofas can be beautiful as well as comfortable. Today home furnishings are *fashion* furnishings.

REVIEW QUESTIONS AND DISCUSSION

1. Why should home furnishings be considered in a fashion context?
2. What are five major categories of home furnishings?
3. Name the major American furniture centers.
4. Name at least five period or furniture styles.
5. What are the three major categories of furniture?
6. If you were creating an ad for furniture, what would you emphasize?
7. What does the word *decor* mean?
8. Discuss what is meant by a decorator or interior decorator.

9

FASHION CENTERS AND THEIR INFLUENCE

Centuries ago courts of kings and rulers were the fashion centers. What was worn at court became the style for those who could afford to dress well. All others had to do the best they could to imitate the affluent. The greater portion of the population wore more functional apparel, but it often reflected the overall tone set by the lords or by royalty. As the middle class grew, more and more people could consider clothing in terms of fashion and style instead of function alone.

It must be remembered that most people wore clothes made at home, and only the well-to-do could afford tailors and seamstresses. As time passed, men's clothes were made by tailors, while women made their own or had personal dressmakers. This pattern continued almost to the present day. Ready-to-wear as we know it really began toward the end of the nineteenth century. At that time apparel manufacturers began turning out single categories of apparel in various sizes to be sold in retail stores.

As the ready-to-wear business expanded, larger cities with their groups of dressmakers and tailors became centers for its production. People came to the cities to have their dresses or suits made. Sewers and tailors began to anticipate business by making garments in advance. This became the ready-to-wear business and gradually was organized by major categories and subdivisions. A manufacturer would buy fabric and hire sewers and tailors to make up garments for sale through stores which catered to apparel customers.

Posh shoe store ca. 1845

W.S.&C.H.THOMSON'S SKIRT MANUFACTORY.

Such cities as Paris, London, New York, Chicago, Rome, and others became centers for the ready-to-wear business. Soon the products that went into local stores were also being shipped elsewhere, and the mail-order firms began to expand their offerings of ready-made apparel. The United States, the most highly industrialized country, became the leader in this ready-to-wear business.

AMERICAN FASHION CENTERS

Today there are many diverse fashion looks in a country as large as ours, and different American cities have evolved as centers for different fashions. Let's examine some of these fashion centers.

NEW YORK CITY

New York City, a major port and the focal point of the United States eastern seaboard, has always attracted thousands of transients each year. About the turn of this century, New York City stores became centers for shopping. As the demand for ready-made apparel grew, New York began to cater first to local women, then to the entire East, and finally to the whole nation. The breakthrough for ready-made apparel began when blouses became fashionable. A woman would still make her own dresses, but feminine, frilly blouses could be made better and cheaper in factories. As a result, thousands of blouses were factory-made. Dresses and children's clothes followed, and by World War I almost all articles of apparel were being manufactured in large quantities in various major cities.

As specialization took hold, New York City became a center for all women's apparel, accounting for about 65 percent of women's and children's apparel produced in the United States. Los Angeles, Boston, Philadelphia, and other cities produced a limited amount of women's apparel, but New York produced more categories of clothing. Soon store buyers from all over the United States

·35· **1913 – 1919**

1913
The Semi-tailored effect.
High Waist line, and narrow draped skirt.

1914 →
The Climax of the Draped Skirt. extremely full at top and skimpy below. The "Sheath" skirt.

1915
Radical change from the narrow to the full skirt. Many of us said we would never wear them, but we did.
The change was almost too sudden to grasp at first but ever so much more sensible than the dangerous narrow skirt.

1916
Full Skirt continues.

1917
Novelty Effects with modified fulness, tho distinctly a drop-off from the full Skirt.

1918
Back to the simple and the slim, which was gratefully received for the next few years, tho Evening dresses often showed fulness.

1919
Novelties and

began coming to New York; the great market in women's ready-to-wear was established, and it became known throughout the world as "the garment center."

As time passed this center became in reality a series of garment centers. The lingerie and intimate apparel manufacturers congregated on Madison Avenue; the sportswear and separates manufacturers flocked to 1407 Broadway and adjacent buildings; and the children's manufacturers moved to 34th Street and Sixth Avenue. Certain buildings became centers for particular apparel classifications; certain blocks in the garment district became known for particular categories and price ranges. In this way an out-of-town buyer could visit more manufacturers with less footwork. Many smaller, lesser-known apparel makers in particular categories moved near the larger manufacturers so that it would be little extra effort for buyers to visit them.

It must be understood that in the early 1900s this concept of apparel was unique. The rest of the world was still making clothes at home, while the well-to-do were having private tailors and dressmakers make their clothes. New York was a pioneer in the mass manufacture of women's apparel.

As the demand grew, the ready-made market became larger and larger, covering more categories, more size ranges, and more specializations within each category. A manufacturer might become famous for cotton blouses and so expand cotton lines and styles and perhaps drop the other fabrics. Soon he or she might become a specialist in tailored, cotton blouses. Multiply the concept hundreds and thousands of times, and you have an entire market of specialists with each manufacturer making a particular type of garment in a particular price range.

Every store in the United States began buying and stocking goods from manufacturers in New York, and in the 1920s and 1930s stores featured "the latest fashions from New York." As the reputation of the New York garment center grew and visitors from all over the world viewed its operation, the ready-to-wear concept began to spread worldwide. Paris, the leader in couture fashions, has recently begun to pay attention to this idea.

di SANT'ANGELO INC.

ANNE KLEIN and company

bill blass

SOME OF AMERICA'S LEADING DESIGNERS, PAST AND PRESENT

Adolpho	Halston	Lew Prince
John Anthony	Stan Herman	Lilly Pulitzer
Scott Barrie	Chuck Howard	Roxanne (Samuel Winston)
Geoffrey Beene	Charles James	Clovis Ruffin
Bill Blass	Victor Joris	Gloria Sachs
Ellen Brooke	Kasper	Pat Sandler
Stephen Burrows	Gayle Kirkpatrick	Sarmi
Patti Cappelli	Anne Klein	Scaasi
Albert Capraro	Calvin Klein	Don Simonelli
Hattie Carnegie	John Kloss	Adele Simpson
Bonnie Cashin	Ronald Kolodzie	Willi Smith
Justin Charles	Hubert Latimer	Karen Stark
Betsy Daniels	Ralph Lauren	Stavropoulos
Jane Derby	Tina Lesser	Gustave Tassell
Oscar de la Renta	Claire McCardell	Jacques Tiffeau
Georgio di Sant'Angelo	Mary McFadden	Teal Traina
D D Dominick	Hanae Mori	Pauline Trigère
Luis Estevez	Jean Muir	Sally Victor
Anne Fogerty	Anthony Muto	Diane von Furstenberg
Jack Fuller	Leo Narducci	Ilie Wacs
James Galanos	Albert Nippon	Chester Weinberg
Rudi Gernreich	Norman Norell	John Weitz
Bill Haire	Mollie Parnis	Ben Zuckerman
	Sylvia Pedlar	

CHICAGO

We have talked about women's fashion and its history. Let us turn to the men's fashion business and see what has been happening in this industry. Until the nineteenth century, every family made its own clothes. However, while a dress could be made at home without too much difficulty, a man's suit was much more complicated. It had interlinings, difficult seaming, and perhaps shoulder pads and buckram shaping. Many men went to local tailors who showed them fabrics, from which they selected a particular one for a suit. After a few fittings, the individual, custom-made suit would be finished. For the less affluent there were garments made by lower-priced tailors, and there was a big market for second-hand clothing. When an affluent customer grew tired of a suit, he might sell it to a dealer in old clothes.

In Chicago a number of famous men's tailors catered to large numbers of private customers. They began hiring hands to take the various parts of a man's suit and sew them together. Each suit was still custom-made and fitted, but a particular hand became adept at sewing pockets, sleeves, or buttons. Soon the large tailors had enough business to keep a man busy just making pockets. It is said that men's "store clothes" first made their appearance in the Andrew Jackson era, which began in the later 1820s, and as we mentioned, that mass manufacturing of men's clothes got its real impetus during the Civil War with the making of soldiers' uniforms. This was the era of rising capitalism, but while other industries grew from small firms to great corporations, the clothing industry at first remained small. Though machinery was introduced, clothing makers, in

Packing Away the Season's Profits

Down they go—into the basement instead of the bank—those profits tied up in your unsold high priced stock suits.

You can change all this for Fall. Put in the Ed. V. Price & Co. line. Insure the success of the season ahead of you by getting this Quality Tailoring Service in back of you.

Sell Before You Buy!

Largest tailors in the world of
GOOD made-to-order clothes
Chicago

CHICAGO APPAREL CENTER

The new Chicago Apparel Center was dramatically "sewn up" (topped out) when the last steel beam was put in place in September 1975. The sewing-up ceremony marked the completion of the steel construction of what will be the country's largest wholesale buying center of women's and children's apparel under one roof.

The grand opening of the 1.7 million square foot Apparel Center (also called Style Exhibitor's Center) is scheduled for mid-1976. The building is adjacent to the Merchandise Mart and, like the Mart, is privately owned by the Joseph P. Kennedy family.

The new Center will be a major fashion resource for 31,000 Midwest apparel buyers and a hub of business activity for the city of Chicago. When completed, the Apparel Center will house over 1 million square feet of permanent, year-round apparel showrooms, containing more than 3,500 brands of clothing. The new Center will contain five times the number of apparel showrooms now lo-cated in the Merchandise Mart. The center will enable buyers to shop hundreds of brands never before available to them in the Midwest. Apparel will span the price and fashion spectrum, from moderately priced to couture ready-to-wear.

The new building will host a minimum of five major fashion markets annually in Chicago, each attracting as many as 15,000 buyers from Mid-America. It is estimated that the Apparel Center will produce $3 billion in sales annually.

In addition to fashion showrooms, the Apparel Center complex will contain Expocenter/Chicago, the second-largest privately owned exhibition hall in the nation; the 527-room Mart Plaza hotel, managed by Holiday Inn Corporation, with swimming pool, meeting facilities, and restaurants; and a full-scale model retail store.

The 6 million square foot Mart Center complex—including the Merchandise Mart, the Apparel Center, and Expocenter/Chicago—is the largest wholesale buying center in the world.

Source: Based on information provided by the Merchandise Mart. By permission.

essence, remained peddlers in what had become an industrial society. As late as 1860 there were under 200 firms in the men's apparel business in the United States, and most were small.

By the early 1900s there were a few really large men's clothing firms. Several were located in Chicago (Society Brand, Kuppenheimer), including one of the oldest: Hart, Schaffner, and Marx. Chicago, Rochester (New York), and Philadelphia became important men's clothing centers and remain so today. Chicago became the home of a number of the largest men's manufacturers. Perhaps as a result of this, both of the leading men's magazines, *Esquire* and *Playboy,* were founded in Chicago.

Until recently, men's fashions changed little from one year to the next. Stores throughout the country had racks of men's suits made by the leading firms; these became national brands as they advertised their products year after year. A well-dressed man in the 1940s and 1950s was said to look as if he were "a page from *Esquire*." The Chicago influence was a national institution in the men's clothing business.

LOS ANGELES

The newest and still growing apparel market is California. This market's special contribution is casual sportswear for both men and women with a particular look and colorings. Because of the California climate and casual approach to dressing, California manufacturers design apparel appropriate for California and other parts of the United States with mild climates. The Los Angeles Apparel Mart has become the west coast center for fashions. A number of retail stores have successfully promoted "California Fashions." Another factor contributing to the success of California apparel is that many western cities are closer to California than to New York and buyers shop there for sportswear.

INTERNATIONAL FASHION CENTERS

Fashions in this country and all over the world are continuously influenced by trends developing in Europe, the Orient, and other areas of the world. Our discussion of fashion would be incomplete if we failed to mention the role of these international fashion centers.

PARIS

While the ready-to-wear apparel concept was flourishing in the United States, the couture concept was thriving in Paris. As we have mentioned before, many women had their dresses made by dressmakers. Paris became a geat center for dressmaking. Prosperous women from Europe, and later from all over the world, found that Paris dressmakers were leaders in ideas and creativity. The French styling was exciting. The fabrics were unusual, and the clothes, when finished, fit and looked better than any apparel made anywhere else in the world. They were expensive, but each garment was uniquely made and fitted for each person.

When these prosperous women met at affairs, they would ask, "Who made the charming frock you are wearing?" Soon certain names began to be recognized as superior dressmakers. These particular makes were sought after, and because they were in such demand, they raised the price of their garments and hired seamstresses to help sew the garments that were ordered. This group of leading coutures soon began to be known as the "haute couture," the creators of high fashion.

PARIS

ROME

LONDON

These leading designers began to have small showings for their good customers prior to each season. They would invite these customers to the openings and have models show the new creations.

As certain names began to come to the fore, it became a status symbol to be a customer of such haute couture designers as Dior, Chanel, Lanvin, Balenciaga, Patou, and others. Their "openings" became important beyond their immediate range of private customers. The world of fashion wanted to know what Dior, Chanel, and the others were doing. What fabrics were they using? What colors did they emphasize? At first no press or reporters were admitted to these private sanctuaries. The press had to interview the customers—"Mrs. Astor, what did Chanel show?" Mrs. Astor might answer briefly what impressed her, and so it went until the openings became a world event and each season the fashion world flocked to Paris to find out what was new in the fashion picture for the coming season. This system still operates today. In July and late January or early February all fashion eyes are on Paris. New names have appeared through the years on the list of Paris greats: Marc Bohan for Dior, Balenciaga, Yves St. Laurent, Ungaro, André Courrèges, Grès, Cardin, Givenchy, and more.

The Paris influence is still strong, but it has lessened since the United States created the casual and sportswear look, which has not done well in Paris. Paris was at its greatest with royal weddings, great balls and affairs, and parties of the famous. As life styles have grown more casual, the need for great gowns and dramatic costumes has lessened. The world has been turning to the American look: jeans, slacks, the Western influence, the more casual approach to dressing. Paris is still important and will probably continue as a fashion center, but as couture becomes less important and ready-to-wear more important, Paris' role will diminish. Already *prêt-à-porter,* French for "ready-to-wear," is becoming more important. Several leading French houses have set up shop on Madison Avenue and in other cities, and more will come. St. Laurent's "Rive Gauche" in New York has been operating successfully for more than six years.

These leading Paris designers often branch out into perfumes and toiletries. Chanel No. 5 is still one of the most famous of all scents, and there are Dior, St. Laurent, Lanvin, and other fragrances sold all over the world. While its influence may diminish in the fashion world, most people in the fashion business simply say "there will always be a Paris."

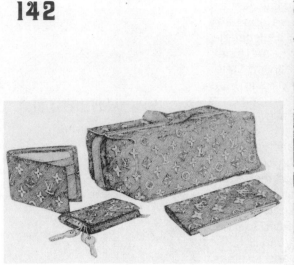

HAUTE COUTURE

To present a united front to the press and the public, the Haute Couture group formed an association called the *Chambre Syndicale de la Couture Parisienne.* This powerful group in recent years has made *haute couture* seem much more important than it is. By skillfully handling publicity and somewhat exaggerating the influence of its members, it has kept Paris at the top of the fashion world.

ROME

Italy has always had a great many skilled craftsmen, so why not skilled dressmakers? Italian silks are famous as well as other fine fabrics, so why not apparel made from these fine fabrics?

In recent years a number of dressmakers in Rome have achieved worldwide reputation. In addition to the famous French names, Italian names appear on the roster of great couturiers. Valentino, Emilio Pucci of Capri, and Gucci for accessories make Rome an important place for fashion buyers to visit. Other Italian designers known in the United States are Fabiani, Fontana, Galitzine, Schoen, Simonetta, and Veniziana.

Emilio Pucci developed an unusual type of colorful prints that make striking dresses. His prints are so individualized that fabric designs resembling these prints are called "Pucci-type prints." His concepts for casual clothes have subsequently become widely copied.

While the showing of Italian fashions may actually be held in other Italian cities, such as Florence, the Italian influence and school of fashion is said to be in Rome. However, the Eternal City will probably continue to play a subordinate role to Paris as long as couture fashion is important in the fashion world.

LONDON

England's capital has had its ups and downs as a fashion center. Everyone in the fashion world is always interested in what England's royalty wears. The ladies of the royal family try to be loyal to their own country in fashions as well as other products, but London designers have often been uninspiring. A few British designers have stood out as leaders: Captain Molyneaux, Hartnell, Cecil Beaton, and Hardy Amies.

London has been a men's fashion center, and many of England's men's styles have been copied through the years by United States manufacturers. The London tailors of Saville Row have been considered pacesetters for men's apparel for years.

Since the early 1960s, when the Beatles, the Rolling Stones, and other groups began influencing American youth culture, young people have looked to London for ideas. The Soho, Carnaby, and "hippie" looks have made their mark on the younger set everywhere. Young British designers such as Mary Quant have influenced fashion trends for American youth. London will probably continue to influence the various facets of the fashion business.

Mary Quant

SPAIN, SCANDINAVIA, AND ISRAEL

As travel has become easier and faster, fashion in a sense has become worldwide. In addition to Paris, New York, and Rome, great new fashion ideas have come from such widely separated places as Spain, Scandinavia, and Israel. Each has developed unique concepts. There is a growing sale of fashions from these countries. For example, certain unique, intricately colored sweaters are called Scandinavian.

Israeli fashions have often combined the looks of the Middle East with Western moods. They are generally aimed for export to the American market and seem to be meeting with growing acceptance. Their knit suits and dresses in unusual colors and classic designs have been particularly popular.

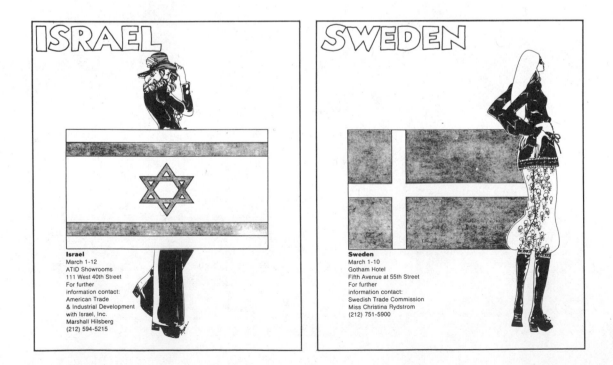

ISRAEL

Israel
March 1-12
ATID Showrooms
111 West 40th Street
For further
information contact:
American Trade
& Industrial Development
with Israel, Inc.
Marshall Hilsberg
(212) 594-5215

SWEDEN

Sweden
March 1-10
Gotham Hotel
Fifth Avenue at 55th Street
For further
information contact:
Swedish Trade Commission
Miss Christina Rydstrom
(212) 751-5900

Spain, like Paris and Rome, has always had its great dressmakers. More recently Spain has produced beautiful handmade fabrics and detailed workmanship which have attracted the fashion world.

THE ORIENT

The huge Western markets have inspired apparel makers from the Orient to make merchandise for the United States and Europe. Fashions from the Orient fall into two main categories: those with great price appeal and higher-priced apparel with exceptional value.

Apparel manufacturers in Hong Kong, Taiwan, and the Philippines have been able to make inexpensive copies of current fashions, which are now widely sold in the United States. Such items as blouses and sweaters have been very popular because they are excellent values.

Labor costs in the Orient are still far below Western standards, and it is possible to buy finely made garments at much lower prices than those for comparable apparel made in the West. When it comes to beading, the application of embroidery, faggoting, and hand operations, the Orient can deliver apparel at prices that can no longer be met in Europe and the United States. Many large retail firms and organizations have set up plants in the Orient to supply their needs. They either own, lease, or supervise production in such plants to insure timely delivery and merchandise that meets the standards and demands of the American consumer.

Once labels such as "Made in Japan," "Made in Korea," "Made in Taiwan," "Made in Hong Kong," or "Made in the Philippines" invoked negative reactions, but today they are often sought after as being excellent values.

IMPORTS

Fashion imports have been steadily increasing through the years. For many years—from the 1860s to about 1920—the most important fashion imports were fabrics. Silks from China and Japan, linen from Ireland, woolens from Scotland and England, colorful prints from Italy and France, lace and embroidered fabrics from Spain and Portugal and other countries were all imported in large quantities.

With the growth of ready-to-wear, the imports of fabrics dwindled, and imported finished fashion products began to increase. From the 1930s to the present, there has been a continuing flood of apparel from foreign countries. Early popular imports were fine sweaters from England and Scotland. Along with these came lavishly embroidered children's clothes and handkerchiefs from Switzerland, Spain, Portugal, the Philippines, and the Madeira Islands. Today thousands of fashion items come from all over the world. The Orient has become particularly important as a source of apparel and accessories because of the price differentials due to the lower cost of labor. Efforts of American manufacturers and labor to get tariffs on such goods have only partially stemmed the tide of these goods.

Marketing experts believe that in the long run, it is good to have world trade based on specialization, in which each nation contributes to the world what it does best at the most reasonable cost. In this way the consumer gets the most value for his or her money spent on merchandise.

IMPORTS OF SELECTED WOMEN'S AND CHILDREN'S GARMENTS (THOUSANDS OF UNITS)

TYPE OF GARMENT	1961	1971	1974
Coats and jackets	558	16,626	14,431
Suits	75	879	1,474
Dresses	3,323	30,324	18,932
Blouses	29,426	129,293	101,010
Skirts	504	9,517	3,012
Sweaters[a]	7,201	116,645	123,648
Slacks and shorts	31,146	138,337	107,078
Playsuits	10,988	20,215	11,957
Raincoats[a]	1,337	6,578	7,026
Dressing gowns and robes	476	3,214	1,797
Nightwear	4,492	18,245	6,873
Underwear	1,650	22,941	17,092
Brassieres	31,523	59,938	74,246

[a]Women's, men's, and children's garments.

Source: United States Bureau of the Census and ILGWU Research Department.

CONCLUSION

Although the centers mentioned in this chapter continue to play a dominant role in the fashion trends of the Western world, fashion is becoming much more diffuse and eclectic. New centers have sprung up to challenge the more established ones. For example, each season at Dusseldorf, Germany, hundreds of firms from as many as fifteen nations show their apparel lines. Estimated attendance at this exposition is from 25,000 to 30,000.

Fashion that not long ago was local is today international. Fashion concepts and apparel come from everywhere. An American designer may use Italian fabric and sell his or her product in Australia. A Scandinavian sweater of British wool will be sold in New York. United States blue jeans are seen on the French Riviera and in Africa. Fashion is truly international and will be even more so as ideas and people travel easily and rapidly everywhere.

REVIEW QUESTIONS AND DISCUSSION

1. Name six fashion centers.
2. What is Paris' main contribution to fashion?
3. Does New York compete with Paris? Why or why not?
4. Give examples of how different fashion centers influence the apparel trends.
5. What is haute couture?
6. Name five famous apparel designers. Discuss their particular appeal.

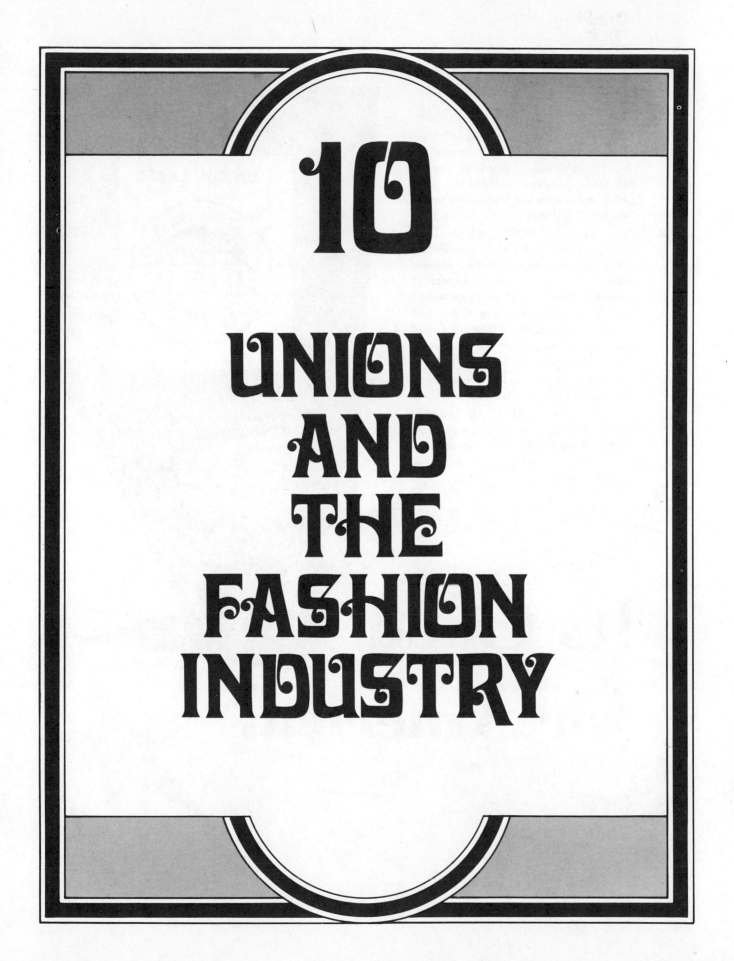

10
UNIONS AND THE FASHION INDUSTRY

D o you know that women's and children's clothing made in decent American factories under fair labor standards, carries the label of the International Ladies' Garment Workers' Union?

The I.L.G.W.U. is the Union of the garment industry representing 450,000 workers, mostly women, many of them the sole support of their families. Through their union, they eliminated the long hours and very bad conditions of the past, and continue to negotiate for improving the standards of today.

We know we have your sympathy. May we ask for your support?

You can help us by insisting on our label on every garment you buy. That is good for the garment workers, good for the communities in which they live, and

UNION LABEL

INT. LADIES GARMENT WORKERS UNION
UNION MADE
ILGWU
AFL-CIO

Symbol of decency, fair labor standards, the American way of life.

It's Good for America!

The labor unions of the United States have played a vital role in apparel. Theirs is an inspiring story of how our nation's working people have been able to achieve one of the highest standards of living in the world. It is an economically important story of how the labor movement has helped to provide a market for the goods our country makes, thus insuring our prosperity.

Where the unions are the strongest, the standards of living are the highest, prosperity the most secure, education the most highly developed, and the culture flourishing. When you find a city with a telephone directory full of labor union names, you will find a city with symphony orchestras, good restaurants, boutiques, antique shops, museums, theaters, and cultural activities.

Whenever you have strong, honest labor unions, the middle class and small businesses prosper. Labor is almost the only group that negotiates its prices. It reaches its pay rates by the bargaining process.

The history of unions in the clothing industry has its roots in the evolution of sewing from a crude home process to today's highly mechanized operations.

EARLY SEWING IMPLEMENTS

Fashion may begin with a needle or an implement of metal to carry the thread in sewing and in various forms of needlework and manufacturing. The earliest needles were merely awls or punches. Stone, bone, ivory, and thorns, with or

without an eye, were used by primitive peoples. Much of the embroidery of antiquity must have required fine needles. China supposedly was first to use steel needles and the Moors are credited with bringing them to the West. The needlemaking trade was established in Nuremberg (Germany) in the fourteenth century and in England in about 1580 to 1600. In 1656 the first needlemakers' guild was chartered. Manufacturing needles by machinery developed slowly. By 1870 most needles were made mechanically. There are now over 250 different kinds of needles: bead needles; carpet needles; and those for shoes, upholstery, and knitting, to mention only a few.

The pin is one of the earliest human artifacts. It was at first made of thorns, bone, or wood, and was used as a clothing fastener and for the hair. The long single-shaft pins appeared early and were often tipped with ornamental knobs. The bent pin was probably one of the earliest uses of the spring coil. Today we call this type of pin a safety pin. Economist Adam Smith, in his *Wealth of Nations,* cites pinmaking as an early example of division of labor. The process was divided up into specific operations: creating the metal, extruding the wire, pointing one end, flattening the head, and so on.

When pins were scarce in the fourteenth and fifteenth centuries, England's parliament limited the sale of pins to the first two days of the year. As they were expensive, women saved their money all year to buy them; hence the term "pin money."

With these two early implements of garment making, pins and needles, we are ready to follow sewing from an individual, personal occupation done in the house and later in small dressmaking and tailoring shops into an enormous industry.

From prehistoric times until the first decade of the nineteenth century when the Industrial Revolution changed the operations of the apparel business, tailoring was predominately a household craft. Alexander Hamilton, our first Secretary of the Treasury, in his "Report on Manufacturers" estimated that as much as four-fifths of all United States clothing was made at home by the inhabitants.

Gradually, between 1860 and 1890, small women's apparel firms sprang up mainly in the hands of immigrant German Jews. Later, during the first phase of the women's garment industry, toward the turn of the century the tendency was toward large shops employing more than a hundred workers. These plants were known as "inside" shops because they did not farm out work to home workers who worked on a piece basis. All the work was done at the factory.

These early apparel shops made the entire garment. They marketed their garments through wholesalers or jobbers. About 90 percent of the workers were female. The majority were English-speaking, native or Americanized. As machinery was introduced, men gradually edged out the women. New immigrants, mostly men from Eastern Europe, many of them Jews, took over. These new immigrants were more politically conscious and began to agitate against the sweatshop conditions.

Between 1880 and 1890 the women's garment industry grew in all directions. The value of the total volume grew from $32 million in 1880 to $68 million in 1890. The number of workers increased from 25,200 in 562 apparel firms to 39,150 in 1,224 shops. Almost all the new workers were men, and three-quarters of them were in New York, even then the center of the trade. Most were employed as sewing machine operators.

As competition became fierce, the conditions of the sweatshops grew worse. Most shops were in slum area lofts where the workers were crowded into hot, dirty rooms, often poorly ventilated. Health conditions were scandalous. Skin diseases were caused by poisonous dyes, and respiratory diseases and rheumatism by overcrowding in rooms either stifling hot or freezing cold. Conditions were ripe for mass action by the workers.

THE INTERNATIONAL LADIES' GARMENT WORKERS' UNION

Almost three-quarters of a century has passed since the women's garment workers of the 1880s and 1890s made attempts fumblingly, painfully, and later furiously, to organize. Today the International Ladies' Garment Workers' Union (ILGWU) is one of the richest and most powerful unions in the United States. There are cloakmakers, dressmakers, pattern makers, cutters, pressers, and finishers who work in underwear, loungewear, intimate apparel, dresses, suits, knit goods, embroidery, laces, plastics, and more.

The philosopher–cloakmakers, immigrants from Europe, stirred up the workers and began organizing them. In the early 1900s these workers were politically on the left. Today they and their successors are mellowed middle-of-the roaders. It was a tough fight to unionize; the employers fought every inch of the way. Finally, in 1900, after confused and desperate struggles which had extended over twenty years, the International Ladies' Garment Workers' Union was founded. It was known as an immigrant union; about 70 percent of the members were Jews from Eastern Europe or Italians. Now, of course, most of the workers are first- or even second-generation Americans with Puerto Ricans and blacks gradually entering into the garment industry.

The pattern changed from hiring mostly men. The dress, shirtwaist, and housedress branches of the industry began hiring women. The apparel business grew to one of the major consumer goods industries in the country. In 1900 there were over 80,000 workers. At a meeting of representatives of cloak makers, shirt makers, and cloak pressers from New York, Baltimore, and Newark, it was decided to form an industrial union of all crafts, to be called the International Ladies' Garment Workers' Union. Each worker was to be assessed one cent a week and each local union was assessed ten dollars a week for an operating fund.

In June of 1900 the AFL (American Federation of Labor) issued a charter to the new union. The International started its career with a capital of thirty dollars and unpaid officers who contributed their time after attending to the regular local union duties. By 1903 there were 51 local unions with almost 10,000 members, of whom 3,500 were women.

Strikes were carefully prepared, and only as a last resort. The ILGWU was interested in the success of the fashion industry and in building its financial strength through workers' benefits. There were hard times for the nation and the unions in the depression of 1904–1908. In 1909 and 1910 in New York City there were two strikes that brought national attention to the women's garment workers. The first involved the shirtwaist makers, of whom 80 percent were women between the ages of 16 and 25. The second was the cloakmakers strike in 1910.

Working hours were often 70 hours a week with pay averaging from seven to twelve dollars per week for regulars, with learners getting about half. The public and a large section of the press were shocked and outraged when these conditions were brought to light. The great devotion of the women in 1909 kept up the spirit of the strikers in spite of arrests for picketing. Wellesley College girls donated $1,000 to the strike fund, and prominent society women organized groups to support the strikers.

When the 1910 strike came to an end, a number of concessions were made by the manufacturers. Hours were reduced, pay increased, working conditions improved, and all strikers taken back without question. More important, it was the first successful mass strike in the needle trades and it formed an alliance between socially minded people of the middle and upper classes and organized labor.

Those were the days when many working mothers always knew where their children were.

In the factory. Working ten or twelve hours a day, seven days a week.

Little time was "wasted" on play or school.

Even when Mother's Day was established— back in 1914—many women and children couldn't celebrate it. They had to work.

Gradually organized labor whittled away at the long work week: 55, 50, 45 hours. Today, throughout most of the ladies' garment industry, the 35-hour work week prevails.

Through our union, 450,000 members of the International Ladies' Garment Workers (80% of us women) have won many benefits: fair wages, decent working conditions, security on the job.

The ILGWU label, sewn into ladies' and children's garments, is our signature. It is a symbol of progress made; and more progress to come.

Look for it when you shop.

A handsome 64-page publication with historic photographs of labor's progress—is available. Send $1.00 to: ILGWU, Union Label Dept., 275 Seventh Ave., New York 10001, Dept. NL-4.

114

PHOTOWORLD, INC.

Woman's right to vote {1920} was union made.
We fought for it.
Use that right this year. Vote.
Vote your conscience.
And buy with a conscience.
Look for the union label when you buy.

International Ladies' Garment Workers' Union, Union Label Department, 275 Seventh Avenue, New York, N.Y. 10001

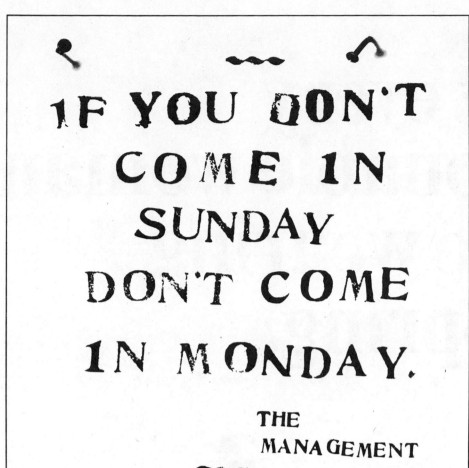

IF YOU DON'T
COME IN
SUNDAY
DON'T COME
IN MONDAY.

THE
MANAGEMENT

AVERAGE HOURLY EARNINGS

INDUSTRY	1961	1971	1973
Women's Garments			
Coat, suit, skirt	$2.26	$3.08	$3.32
Dress	1.85	2.78	2.99
Blouse	1.52	2.37	2.67
Knitted outerwear	1.66	2.55	2.93
Children's outerwear	1.49	2.30	2.57
Other outerwear	1.54	2.30	2.62
Corset and brassiere	1.61	2.43	2.68
Underwear and nightwear	1.42	2.21	2.46
Knitted underwear	1.48	2.31	2.61
All Manufacturing	2.32	3.56	4.07
Nondurable goods	2.11	3.26	3.69
Durable goods	2.49	3.79	4.32

Source: United States Bureau of Labor Statistics.

What every fashionable woman will be wearing this Spring.

Fashions change.
Hemlines go up, go down.
Necklines go up, go down.
Waistlines go up, go down. Go in, go out.
The only fashion prediction anyone can make is that fashions will be unpredictable.
Except for one little thing.
The ILGWU union label. It's sewn into the garments of American women's and children's wear. And it never changes.
It's always in fashion.
The label is the signature of 450,000 members of the International Ladies' Garment Workers' Union, 80% of them women.
It's the symbol of decent working conditions and fair wages. Of progress made. And more to come. Look for it when you shop.
Then, if you'd like, snip out the label and send it to us. We'll send you an illustrated guide to the art of being well-dressed, called "Looking Your Fashionable Age."
It's what every fashionable woman will be reading this spring. ILGWU, Union Label Dept., 275 7th Ave., N.Y. 10001, Dept. T-10.

Dear Mr. Editer

i Went down town with my daddy yesterday to see that terrible fire where all the littel girls jumped out of high windows My littel cousin Beatrice and i are sending you five dollars a piece from our savings bank to help them out of trubble please give it to

the right one to use it for ~~ for them~~ sombody whose littel ginl jumped out of a window i wouldont like to jump out of a high window myself.

Yours Truly
Morris Butler

On March 25, 1911, a tragedy occurred that affected not only the future of the garment industry, but also building codes, fire prevention methods, and factory working conditions throughout the country. It was the Triangle fire in which 146 shirtwaist workers lost their lives. As late as twenty-five years later, the fire was still mentioned. Frances Perkins, Franklin Roosevelt's Secretary of Labor and the first woman cabinet member, commented: "They did not die in vain and we will never forget them." The details of the tragedy are vividly described in Leon Stein's book *Triangle Fire.*

From that time on, the story of the ILGWU is one of continual progress and expansion. In recent years the union has become part of American life and an even larger part of the story of the fashion business. The ILGWU has been a responsible union in the sense of working out with the industry wages and hours that are fair to both sides.

The longtime leader of the ILGWU, David Dubinsky, is himself an example of the strains, conflicts, political trends, and social upheaval of early unionism and his times. The tug-of-war between socialism, communism, Knights of Labor, International Workers of the World, American Federation of Labor, Congress of Industrial Organization, the Republican Party, the Democratic Party, and the

Union vacation spot.

New Deal were all part of his background. For those interested, the early history of the labor movement in the United States, the history of the ILGWU, makes fascinating reading.

The ILGWU has become more than a union. It has planned and built large housing projects which offer to union members low-cost cooperative apartments or low rentals. It has a health, hospital, and medical program for its members, giving them inexpensive complete coverage. It has a summer resort camp for members—Unity House at Forest Park, Pennsylvania. The union founded a college (the Brookwood Labor College, the Workers University at Washington Irving High School in Manhattan, and in 1949 an ILGWU Training Institute). Today the ILGWU has approximately 450,000 members.

THE AMALGAMATED CLOTHING WORKERS' UNION

What the ILGWU has been to the women's apparel business, the Amalgamated Clothing Workers' of America (ACWA) has been to the men's clothing industry. The history of Amalgamated starts with the great Chicago strike in 1910 against Hart, Schaffner, and Marx. First all 7,000 workers of this great men's wear firm struck; then 35,000 clothing workers from other firms joined the HSM strikers. While the unions did not win their demands, the foundations had been laid for building a strong union. Strikes followed in other cities, including New York, Boston, Baltimore, and Cincinnati.

The union began its official life in 1914 by breaking away from the United Garment Workers, a part of the American Federation of Labor. By 1916 most of the men's industry had recognized the strength of the new union and had tried various means to weaken or destroy it. However, the union proved strong enough to weather the storms, and by 1929 the only holdouts were the Philadelphia manufacturers, who signed a collective bargaining agreement. The men's clothing industry was fully organized. During the Great Depression that followed, the union proved its strength by helping the unemployed and preventing unrestricted cutting of wages.

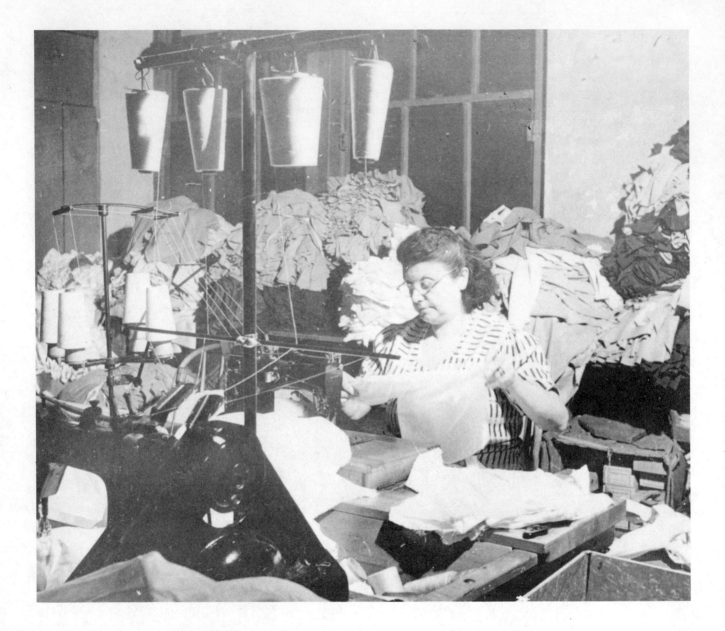

SIDNEY HILLMAN

"We want a better America, an America that will give its citizens, first of all, a higher and higher standard of living so that no child will cry for food in the midst of plenty.

"We want to have an America where the inventions of science will be at the disposal of every American family, not merely for the few who can afford them. An America that will have no sense of insecurity and which will make it possible for all groups, regardless of race, creed or color to live in friendship, to be real neighbors; an America that will carry its great mission of helping other countries to help themselves."

Low-rent apartments built by unions for their members.

With the coming of the New Deal the Amalgamated, along with all other unions, made great progress. Sidney Hillman, president of the ACWA, was an important advisor to President Roosevelt, and urged the support of the Wagner Labor Relations Act, a landmark piece of legislation for unions. In essence, it guaranteed the rights of workers and unions to organize and bargain collectively.

In addition, the Social Security Act was passed which included unemployment compensation and payments to the elderly. A Fair Labor Standards Act was also passed, assuring yardsticks for a labor-wage scale and qualities of workmanship and products.

In addition to the men's suit firms, the men's shirt firms were brought into the union, as well as work clothing, nightwear, sportswear, and miscellaneous related garment industries. Today the ACWA has just under 400,000 members.

Like the ILGWU, Amalgamated has health insurance, real estate, low-cost apartments for workers in some major cities, an insurance company, a bank, scholarships for workers' children, and old-age pensions to supplement public benefits.

CONCLUSION

All manufactured products are the result of teamwork. The team includes management and labor. Without the contribution of the labor unions, the men's, women's, and children's fashion business would not be in the advanced stage it is today.

The almost 900,000 members of the ILGWU and ACWA are the backbone of the apparel industries. These two unions have not only contributed to their

JOBLESS MEN
KEEP GOING
CAN'T TAKE CARE OF OUR OWN
CHAMBER OF COMMERCE

respective industries but to the entire union movement. In addition, they have pushed for much of the social legislation in effect today.

Labor faces both a serious challenge and a greater opportunity in this age of automation and technology. There are many new, advanced techniques being developed for industries using skilled workers. Never in history has so much been spent on research and development to make better products with less labor and effort. In some cases either labor or management has held back from technological progress, fearing what might happen.

Many of the strikes and labor unrest have been caused by the failure to keep pace with technological developments which are coming at an ever-increasing pace. There have been fewer strikes in the garment industry than in most American industries. The unions have become an integral part of the fashion business. They have been among the most cooperative of all unions, often helping manufacturers to solve production problems.

Progress cannot be held back long. We are arriving at an era of end-product engineering, and more durable clothing will be made by new methods. The apparel industry, the unions, and the manufacturers will team up to make this new apparel the best value so far produced. The saying "They don't make things like they used to" will be absolutely true!

REVIEW QUESTIONS AND DISCUSSION

1. What is the name of the labor union involved in women's apparel?
2. What is the name of the labor union involved in men's apparel?
3. What caused the unions to be formed?
4. Why did the unions grow?
5. How important are the apparel unions in the various apparel industries?
6. How do the unions deal with management in setting labor wages and conditions?
7. Discuss the role of unions in our society and their contribution to their members.

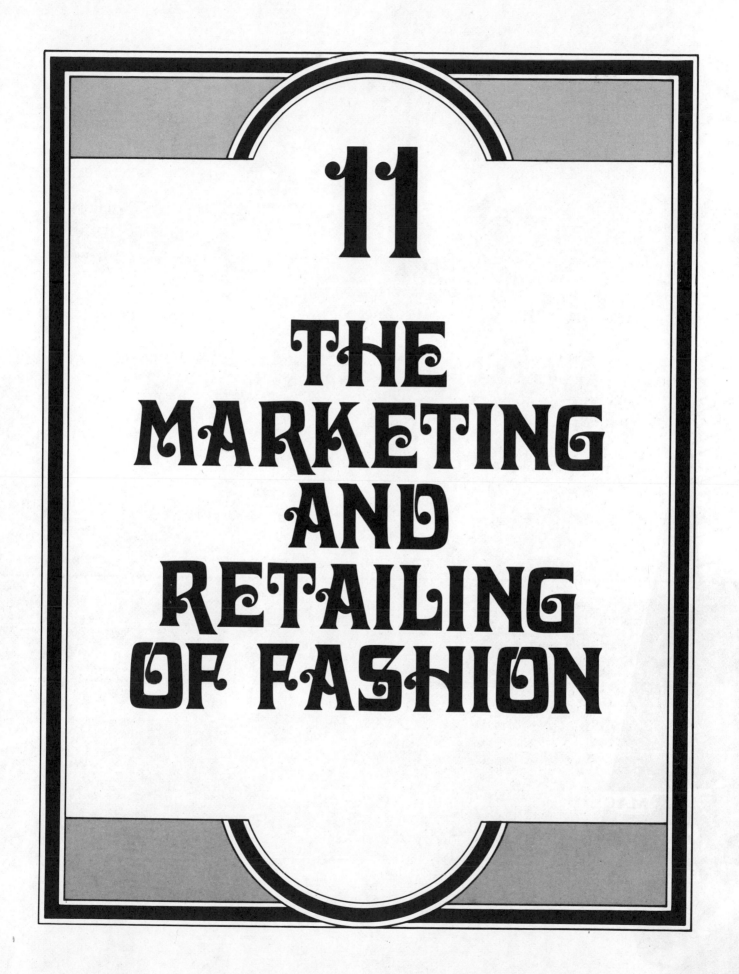

11

THE MARKETING AND RETAILING OF FASHION

Retailing began as peddling. A peddler was an itinerant merchant who, at some wholesale market, would purchase, among other things, bolts of fabric to sell at retail or to small shopkeepers throughout the countryside. Sometimes such peddlers would sell one commodity; sometimes they would have a miscellaneous pack.

By 1850 retail stores were fairly common in England and America in the form of country "general" stores carrying a wide assortment of goods. They performed an important merchandising function for sparsely settled regions. In towns and cities, specialty retail stores grew, many of them developing from the handicraft shops of earlier periods.

An important development was the rise of wholesale merchants who purchased goods from manufacturers and offered them to local retail stores.

Sociologist C. Wright Mills, in his book *White Collar* (Oxford University Press, 1951), sums it up this way:

In the older world of the small entrepreneur there were storekeepers but few salesmen. After the Revolutionary War, there began to be traveling peddlers, whose markets were thin but widespread. By the middle of the nineteenth century the wholesaler, then the dominant type of entrepreneur, began to hire drummers or greeters whose job it was to meet retailers and jobbers in hotels or saloons in the market centers of the city. Later these men began to travel to local markets. Then, as manufacturers replaced wholesalers as dominant powers in the world of business, their traveling agents joined the wholesalers.

There are still trading posts and general merchandise stores in outlying areas. Single-line or specialty shops numerically dominate United States retailing. But the department store, the chain store, and the mail order house, all principally types of this century, are most in tune with our society.

READY-TO-WEAR AND RETAILING

Fairs and bazaars were the predecessors of the retail store. Common items were on display to attract the passersby. However, the more expensive merchandise was not offered to the public. Such categories were kept behind closed doors and shown only to select customers and to the noble families whose coats-of-arms were often proudly displayed by the tradesmen who sold them goods. The department store pioneered in displaying masses of goods for the general public to see, touch, and buy.

Prior to the department store, merchandise was not priced and marked. The buyer and seller normally haggled and bargained over the sale of the item, a procedure still followed in the marketplaces of developing countries. With the coming of the department store, the price of all merchandise was clearly marked and it was no longer a question of bargaining for the best price.

Two important inventions that came between 1880 and the turn of the century helped all retail stores operate more efficiently, honestly, and obtain more data on their day-to-day sales. The first was the cash register, which later also produced a tape of sales, categories, and salesperson ringing up sales. The other important invention was the adding machine, which probably originated from the abacus, widely used in the Orient for calculations. This made it possible for stores to quickly compute essential figures for the operation of the business.

As discussed in previous chapters, ready-to-wear apparel is relatively new. It was only in the late 1800s that a woman could buy garments already made up. Prior to that time she bought piece goods and made or sewed her own clothes. Well-to-do women had dressmakers. The major retail stores all had large fabric departments to cater to their women customers.

Today many large department stores still have piece-goods departments for women who sew, but they are small compared to their predecessors, which often took up most of the main floor of the store. The Sears Roebuck catalog of

No. 31R316
$6.75

No. 31R317
$6.75

No. 31R318
$7.95

No.
31R315
$5.75

No.
31R319
$9 98

No. 31R320
$10.50

LADIES' TAILOR MADE SUITS

When ordering be sure to give all the measurements required, and say what color you desire.

WE FURNISH THESE in sizes from 32 to 42 inches around the bust and from 38 to 44 inches skirt length. The average length of waist in back is 16 inches and the length of inside seam 18¼ to 19 inches. These are regular measurements. Sizes different than these must be made to order, in which case we charge 20 per cent above the regular price. If you fail to enclose 20 per cent for extra size we will make same and charge you with the difference. When postage is not given goods cannot be sent by mail.

If for some reason you have to return the suit to us, never return skirt or jacket alone; return both and we will be pleased to exchange the suit. Parts of suits will not be accepted.

No. 31R315 LADIES' SUIT. Made of a good quality wool mixed repellent cloth, consisting of jacket and skirt. The jacket is made with coat shaped collar and lapels, double breasted front, the back extending to the waist only; dip front, lined throughout with mercerized sateen. The skirt is made with an inverted plait in the back, silk band around the waist, lined throughout with percaline lining, interlined at the bottom and bound with waterproof binding. Colors, black, blue or Oxford gray. Price.............$5.75

If by mail, postage extra, 64 cents.

No. 31R316 LADIES' TAILOR MADE SUIT. Consisting of jacket and skirt, made of all wool cheviot serge. The jacket is made with coat shaped collar and lapels, fly front, cuffs on the sleeves, lined throughout with black mercerized lining. The skirt is made with inverted plait in the back and graduated flounce on the bottom; lined throughout with glazed lining and interlined at the flounce; velvet binding on bottom and silk ribbon band around the waist. Colors, black or blue. Price....(Postage extra, 64 cents) .. $6.75

No. 31R317 LADIES' RAINY DAY OR WALKING SUIT. Made of all wool cloth, consisting of jacket and skirt, coat shaped collar, lapels faced with peau de soie, flaring cuffs. Back of jacket reaches to the waist only, while the front reaches below the waist, three buttons in the front, giving it a very pretty effect; lined throughout with black mercerized sateen lining. The skirt is tailor made with a graduated flounce, stitched all around the bottom, silk ribbon band around the waist and no lining, making it very light and desirable. Color, Oxford gray only. Price..........................$6.75

No. 31R318 LADIES' TAILOR MADE SUIT. Consisting of skirt and jacket, made of all wool Venetian cloth. Eton jacket, new shaped collar and lapels, double breasted front, reaching just a trifle below the waist in front and to the waist in the back of jacket; lined throughout with romain silk lining. Skirt, tailor made, with flounce around the bottom, lined throughout with glazed percaline, and interlined at the bottom, bound with velvet. Colors, black, castor or blush gray. Price..(If by mail, postage extra, 64 cents)....$7.95

No. 31R319 LADIES' TAILOR MADE SUIT. Consisting of jacket and skirt. Made of all wool Venetian cloth. Jacket is made with the new collar and silk faced lapels; double breasted front, made with yoke which is bound with satin straps; wide plait from yoke to bottom of jacket. The back of jacket is made same as the front and it only reaches to the waist; trimmed cuffs. Jacket is lined with romain silk. The skirt is made with a graduated flounce, trimmed with satin straps; is lined with glazed lining and interlined at the bottom and bound with velvet. Colors, black, blue or red. Price.................................$9.98

No. 31R320 LADIES' TAILOR MADE SUIT. Consisting of jacket and skirt only. Made of all wool Venetian cloth, coat shaped collar and lapels, double breasted dip front. The jacket extends in back to the waist only, yoke front, made with yoke which is bound and piped with velvet, fancy cuffs with same trimming. The jacket is lined with romain silk; skirt is tailor made with graduated flounce, piped with velvet where the flounce joins the skirt; lined throughout with percaline lining, interlined at the bottom and bound with velvet. A very desirable garment. Colors, black, gray or castor. Price......................$10.50

1897 had only 15 pages for ready-made women's apparel of all categories: blouses, dresses, suits, coats, and undergarments. Today ready-made apparel dominates the over-1,500-page Sears catalog.

Retailing today is more scientific, aggressive, and competitive than ever before. The major retail volume is done by the giants. It is estimated that Sears, Penney's, Ward's, and Grant's together may do as much as one-third of the total retail volume in the United States! Then, if you add the large store-owned groups such as Federated Department Stores, A.M.C., Allied Stores, The May Company, Macy's, Gimbel-Saks, Dayton Co.-Hudson, and Marshall Field, you have perhaps as much as one-half of all retail volume, apart from food. Apparel accounts for over half of this retail volume.

Such major stores as these and others are proud of their reputation and try hard to maintain standards of service and quality, and to guarantee customer satisfaction. Like all retail stores, they are the last link between the finished product and the customer.

The task of the retail store is considerable. It must stock desirable merchandise in quantities, arranged in an orderly manner so that customers can quickly find what they desire. It must price the merchandise attractively so the consumer gets a fair value. Each category of merchandise must be sorted according to sizes, colors, prices and styles.

JOBS IN RETAILING

A knowledge of merchandise and how to continually evaluate it in terms of materials, workmanship, price, and cost is one of the most important aspects of buying or merchandising for a retail store. To become a good judge of values usually takes years of experience. The best way to begin is to look at and carefully examine merchandise before you look at the price tag and then guess the price. When you find that you are often coming fairly close, this indicates you are developing an awareness of the relationship between price and quality. The more you practice this method, the more it will help you judge this relationship.

Most retail stores expect those who seek jobs as assistant buyers to have selling experience. It is believed that unless you have dealt with customers and heard their comments and complaints you cannot fully understand how the fashion business operates. Listening is a good way to find out what a customer takes into consideration when he or she buys an article of apparel.

Then, too, a buyer or salesperson must understand store policies. Not only must the sales check be written correctly, but the transaction must be completed by seeing that the customer gets the purchase from the wrapping desk or cashier, depending on the store's system.

Most stores carefully wrap or box the goods sold, and if the item is large, deliver it to the customer's home. In many cases the store and the manufacturer guarantee that the customer will be satisfied with his or her purchase. Often the store will extend credit to the customer through charge accounts or time payments.

To accomplish these tasks, stores need many people: buyers who select the merchandise; merchandise managers who supervise the buyers; people who receive the merchandise into the store, mark it with price tags, and distribute it to the various departments; personnel departments who hire and supervise sales people; wrappers and service personnel; bookkeepers; and payroll department, billing department, and store maintenance staffs. Stores must also have display departments to take care of the windows and interior displays. They usually have an advertising department, which we will discuss in detail in Chapter 12. It takes executives to plan and supervise the entire operation and the thousands of employees needed by a large store.

There are hundreds of types and classifications of retail stores: grocery stores, dry-goods stores, shoe stores, hardware stores, bakeries, candy stores, and variety stores, among others. We are going to concern ourselves here with stores that deal in and sell fashion. They fall into seven main categories.

DEPARTMENT STORES

Department stores are familiar to almost every person all over the world. They derive their name from the fact that they are, in a sense, stores within stores. Each category of merchandise is carried in a department in the store, hence the name.

WOMEN'S, MISSES', AND CHILDREN'S APPAREL AND ACCESSORIES

Percents of Year's Total Sales Done Each Month

	JAN	FEB	MAR	APR	MAY	JUNE	JULY	AUG	SEPT	OCT	NOV	DEC
Grand Total—Entire Store	6.5	5.3	7.3	7.9	8.0	7.6	6.1	7.3	8.0	8.6	10.2	17.2
Apparel and Accessories												
Women's and misses' coats and suits	10.0	6.1	10.7	11.3	6.4	2.3	2.6	5.6	8.8	12.7	2.5	11.0
Coats	11.3	6.1	9.2	10.4	6.3	1.9	2.4	5.6	8.1	12.9	13.7	12.1
Suits	5.2	6.4	17.2	15.8	8.0	4.4	3.9	6.2	11.1	11.2	6.1	4.7
Juniors' and girls' wear	—	—	—	—	—	—	—	—	—	—	—	—
Juniors' coats, suits, and dresses	4.6	4.3	9.7	11.2	9.8	6.8	4.6	8.1	9.5	9.3	9.9	12.2
Girls' and teen-age wear	3.9	3.7	8.9	8.4	6.0	5.7	4.9	13.2	8.7	8.3	10.9	17.4
Women's and misses' dresses	5.9	5.1	8.2	10.9	12.0	9.5	6.2	7.1	9.4	8.7	7.7	9.3
Inexpensive	5.6	5.0	7.8	10.6	12.6	10.2	6.2	7.1	9.4	8.2	7.6	9.7
Better	6.4	5.2	8.7	11.2	11.1	8.6	6.2	7.1	9.4	9.3	7.9	8.9
Blouses, skirts and sportswear	5.0	4.2	5.6	7.2	9.4	10.4	7.6	7.4	8.3	8.2	8.7	18.0
Aprons, housedresses and uniforms	6.0	5.0	7.4	9.3	13.2	10.7	7.2	6.4	7.7	7.2	8.0	11.9
Furs	9.7	7.2	7.0	6.9	4.7	1.8	2.9	9.3	8.4	14.8	12.4	14.9
Neckwear and scarves	4.4	4.8	7.0	8.3	8.4	7.3	5.5	5.8	8.0	8.7	10.2	21.6
Handkerchiefs	4.6	5.0	5.0	5.6	5.5	5.6	4.2	4.7	4.7	6.3	12.5	36.3
Millinery	4.9	4.3	12.8	13.6	6.0	4.5	2.8	5.4	11.7	11.7	10.2	12.1
Women's and children's gloves	5.7	3.8	7.2	8.7	5.3	3.6	2.0	2.5	5.7	9.3	14.5	31.7
Corsets and brassieres	8.6	5.9	7.9	9.0	9.0	9.8	7.0	7.4	8.7	8.5	7.4	10.8
Women's and children's hosiery	6.8	6.7	8.0	8.5	8.0	6.1	4.4	5.8	8.3	9.2	9.8	18.4
Underwear, slips, and negligees	5.2	4.7	5.4	6.1	8.3	7.1	6.0	5.6	6.0	6.9	11.1	27.6
Infants' wear (incl. infants' furniture)	5.2	4.5	8.3	7.8	5.7	5.3	5.6	8.6	8.8	9.3	12.3	18.6
Handbags and small leather goods	4.2	3.8	6.9	8.4	8.7	7.4	4.8	5.5	8.5	7.9	9.9	24.0
Women's and children's shoes	5.7	4.5	9.8	9.8	8.5	7.7	4.9	7.8	10.1	9.1	8.8	13.3
Children's	4.6	4.8	11.7	9.8	6.1	5.6	4.3	14.2	10.5	6.9	8.4	13.1
Women's	6.1	4.4	9.3	9.8	9.2	8.3	5.0	6.1	10.1	9.7	8.9	13.1

Source: Promotion calendar of National Retail Merchants Association.

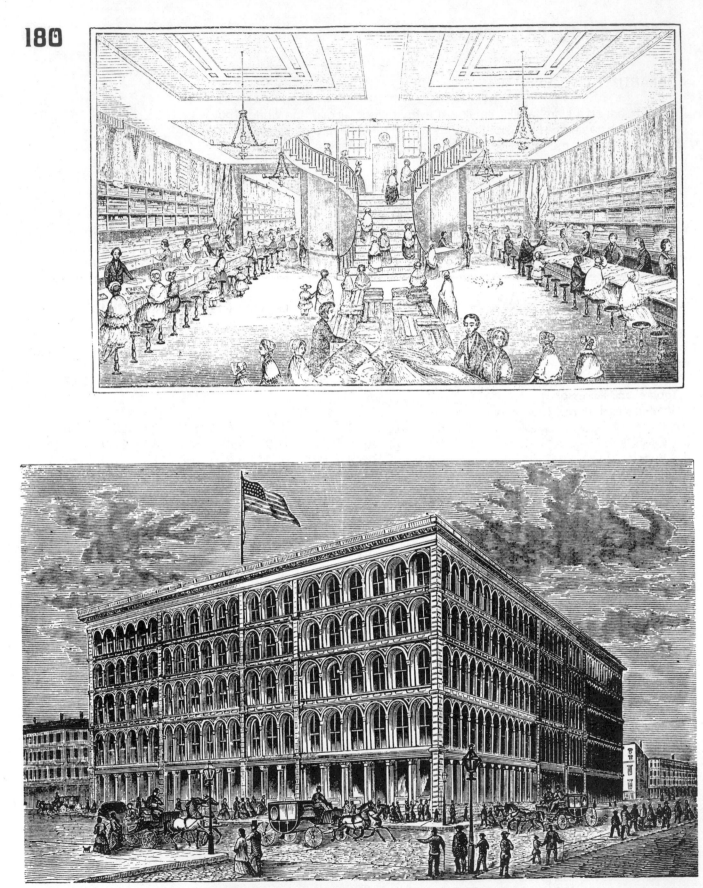

America's first department store, A. T. Stewart's in New York

One of the first department stores was Stewart's Marble Dry Goods Palace in New York City, built in 1846 and later expanded. Now department stores are so familiar that it seems hard to believe that they didn't exist until 150 years ago.

Department stores in large cities throughout the world are usually among the most famous landmarks. Few people visit New York City without seeing Macy's. Such stores as Marshall Field in Chicago, J. L. Hudson in Detroit, Wanamaker's in Philadelphia, Lazarus in Columbus, Rich's in Atlanta, Neiman-Marcus in Dallas, Eaton's in Montreal, Selfridge's in London, Broadway-Hale in Los Angeles, Denver Dry-Goods in Denver, and Galeries Lafayette in Paris, are household words.

The department store leads in terms of overall status and importance in a community. It usually serves a larger segment of the local population than any other type of store except the food supermarket. It generally appeals to a broad range of income groups, as its merchandise covers a wide range of prices.

These stores are usually dominant advertisers in the newspapers and frequently use radio and television. In addition, most large department stores have mailing lists of charge customers and additional names, for direct-mail advertising.

Most of the major department stores have branch stores located throughout their trading area, and some have expanded into adjacent areas and even other cities. This creates a larger market and reduces the cost of advertising, because the branch stores have the same merchandise as the main store and benefit from the same ad. The branch stores and their addresses are usually listed in advertising. Branch stores have created some difficulties in merchandising because they cannot carry the complete stocks that the main store carries. This often annoys the customer who wants the merchandise at once and does not want to wait for it to be ordered from the parent store.

In many cases, however, the branch stores have become so strong that their total volume is more than the volume of the main store. Branches offer parking facilities and easy access for the suburbanites who can drive to a shopping

182

center in a few minutes on a Saturday or an evening when the store is open, instead of going downtown. The branches also afford opportunities for family shopping on Saturdays rather than individual shopping during the week.

The question of night and Sunday openings has been a topic of controversy. It has been obvious for some years that shopping has, in a sense, become a leisure occupation. The trend seems to be toward more Sunday and evening openings as more families shop together.

The retailing picture is constantly changing. Large retail corporations constantly jockey for bigger shares of the consumer's money. They constantly work out new methods of merchandising and selling to capture this huge market. It has been estimated that at least 50 percent of all items sold today were not even conceived of as short a time as ten years ago.

SPECIALTY STORES

From the standpoint of fashion, the women's specialty store, or boutique, has become the next most important store in recent years. The women's specialty retailer generally caters to a particular segment of the women's market—the young girl, the mature woman, the woman who wants sport clothes or separates, or the woman who is after a "look." These stores usually present their merchandise in an exciting, interesting manner, showing different possibilities of mixing, matching, and accessorizing the various costumes. This is somewhat different from the department store where a woman has to visit several departments to "put herself together."

Many department stores, noting the success of these specialty stores, have created boutiques and shops within their stores. In this way they are competing with the women's specialty stores for this category of customer. Of course, there are many types of women's specialty retailers. We have discussed the category that sells outerwear. There are intimate apparel shops, hosiery stores, and women's shoe stores as well. There are also the large specialty stores that sell all categories of women's wear. Some even sell men's apparel. Stores such as these usually have definite ideas about their particular customer—her tastes and ideas about how she wants to outfit herself. These stores succeed because they do not try to please an entire range of consumer but go after a particular segment by having a broader and better selection in their specialties than do the general stores.

Sizzle Shirt

THE DENIM DELUGE

Until a few years ago, blue denim pants were the clothes of laborers—construction workers, cow hands, farmers, and those similarly engaged. Today the denim pants, now called "jeans," are virtually the uniform of the young set. Many stores have "Levi departments," which do a large volume not only in jeans, but also in denim jackets, skirts, shirts, and accessories.

CHAIN STORES

Probably the first chain store in the world was the Great Atlantic & Pacific Tea Company, which from humble beginnings in 1859 grew to mammoth proportions with over 4,000 large stores doing over $5 billion in the 1970s. Their merchandise was food, but it indicated the possibilities of selling other types of merchandise using some of the same techniques, so the idea spread to other categories.

In 1879 F. W. Woolworth opened his first two "Five and Ten Cent Stores" based on the idea of price appeal. If merchandise was inexpensive, customers would buy on "impulse." Advertising was not needed as the merchandise on display "sold itself." This method of merchandising was called "price lining"—creating merchandise to sell at particular prices.

Although the chain store is often similar to a specialty store and a department store, it is a group owned by a single company with stores in various cities in a geographical area or across the nation. Lerner's and Peck and Peck are examples of women's chain specialty shops. Evans is an example of a women's chain shoe store. Included in this group are *variety stores,* such as Woolworth's, Kresge's, and J. C. Penney. Chain stores are operated as a group, with their main headquarters making the important decisions and paralleling the merchandise and promotional operations in each store. For example, during a particular week every store features the same merchandise and has the same displays in their windows and the same ads in the newspapers. These plans are sent in detail to each store manager and not too much latitude is allowed.

However, in a coast-to-coast chain, regional differences are taken into consideration. For example, northern stores are given heavy coats and outerwear, while southern stores have lighter-weight coats and no heavy outerwear. Also, southern stores and California stores are generally given more light colors than northern stores, when color ranges are ordered.

Some major retailers have set up "bargain stores" under different names. These stores operate on the concept that price is the major appeal. For example: Woolworth's has set up the Woolco chain, Kresge has organized the very successful K-Mart chain, and as a regional example, Rich's of Atlanta has organized Richway. This concept follows the old retail adage—"Be your own best competition."

The success of chain stores is based on their ability to buy well, since they place orders for thousands of a single garment. Often garments are tested in pilot southern stores that are "ahead of the season." Most chain operations skillfully appraise fashion trends before they make their decisions.

DISCOUNT AND PROMOTIONAL STORES

The name "discount stores" developed after World War II when certain retail operations gave out cards that permitted the bearer to get a discount off the regular price. These stores at their inception claimed they could sell merchandise at less than the regular stores because they had "low overhead," a trade expression meaning lower operating costs. These discount stores usually had poor locations, few sales people, no advertising, and no charge accounts or credit.

This type of store usually specialized in selling refrigerators, washing machines, dryers, radios, television sets, and electrical appliances, all of which were in short supply after World War II.

It has only been in recent years that the discount stores have branched out to become complete department stores. All discount stores began as local operations; some have opened multiple units in different areas of the country.

Now it is generally conceded that discount stores are really promotional stores because they now have more sales people, and they advertise and extend credit. A promotional store is one that emphasizes price as a major selling feature. Macy's, Gimbel's, and similar stores are considered promotional stores, while B. Altman, Marshall Field, Jordan Marsh, and Broadway-Hale are considered regular department stores. A number of retail experts predict that the category "discount store" will disappear, as there is now little difference between the older promotional store and the newer discount store.

SUPERMARKETS

The fashion industry does not sell much at the present time through the supermarkets, which are primarily purveyors of food. However, as the supermarkets expand the scope of their merchandising concept, they will probably include more staple apparel items in their inventory.

Already some supermarkets are selling such items as women's and men's hosiery, aprons, and men's shirts. In the home-furnishing area they sell bathroom towel sets, scatter rugs, and sheets and pillow cases.

One concept of retailing is that "when you have the traffic you can sell anything." The lines of demarcation that used to clearly mark off what one type of retailer sold are breaking down. Men's stores have put in women's lines; shoe stores sell hosiery; furniture stores sell bedding and domestics. Why shouldn't supermarkets sell some categories of apparel?

Supermarket chains are among the most powerful of all retail organizations. The A & P has one of the greatest volumes in sales of any retailer. Other such giant supermarket chains as Grand Union, Safeway, Kroger, Acme, and First National-Finast do hundreds of millions of dollars in sales annually. As marketing patterns change, they will constantly be on the lookout for opportunities in the apparel field.

In 1900 rural America shopped at the general store—post office at the neighborhood crossroads. This became a meeting place and the source of many jokes and "cracker barrel" humor. A farmer, his wife, or his children picked up the mail, the weekly newspaper, and the staples they needed.

Until about 1898 Rural Free Delivery was carried on in a haphazard manner, but by 1906 Rural Free Delivery was in full force, covering virtually all of rural America. This plus the inauguration in 1913 of parcel post legislation, authorizing the carrying of packages weighing more than four pounds, started a communication revolution in rural America. Now the farmer could read daily papers and receive mail order catalogs and merchandise directly by parcel post.

The original concept of the mail-order house was to build an image of reliability and to offer a wide variety of merchandise through catalogs. At the time these catalog firms got their start in the late 1800s, transportation was slow and difficult. People living in small communities and rural areas had to shop in stores with limited selections. The mail-order houses filled a need by offering rural customers all manner of goods.

Soon women could select from thousands of household and apparel items. The farmer could buy everything from a collar button to a farm machine. In a space of twenty-five years these mail-order houses grew in volume and scope, and soon they were doing hundreds of millions of dollars in business. Names such as Sears Roebuck, Montgomery Ward, Alden's, and Speigel's became household words.

It was originally believed that when transportation and communication improved, the mail-order business might dwindle considerably. This was one

THE NEW TWEEDS
.. born to the purple

Separates of bonded
wool-and-nylon
tweed .. and a
meant-to-mate
knit pullover

(1 thru 4) Donegal-type tweed separates that are perfect for "the new adult" of the '70s. A blend of wool and nylon bonded to acetate tricot. They're in Fall's most important color theme: purple and white, subtly flecked with accent colors. Dry clean.

1 **Princess-line tunic** . . compatible with the pants and skirt but not inseparable. You can opt for wearing it alone at whim. V-neckline; little patch pockets with button trim.
   Misses' sizes 8, 10, 12, 14, 16, 18.
Please state size. Shipping weight 14 ounces.
V7 H 6527F $14.00

2 **Straight-leg pants** . . trim, tailored, terrific. Beautifully made with fly-front zipper and hook closing, bandless waistline.
   Misses' sizes 8, 10, 12, 14, 16, 18.
Please state size. Shipping weight 15 ounces.
V7 H 6528F $12.00

3 **Jacket** . . tailored for flattery. Shaped with princess seaming and fashioned with a natty notched collar and lapels.
   Misses' sizes 8, 10, 12, 14, 16, 18.
Please state size. Shipping weight 1 lb. 2 oz.
V7 H 6525F $15.00

4 **Pleated skirt** . . flattering you by artful design. A trio of inverted pleats at front are stitched down to the hipline. Set-on waistband and a side zipper closing.
   Misses' sizes 8, 10, 12, 14, 16, 18.
Please state size. Shipping weight 10 ounces.
V7 H 6526F $9.00

The Knit Pullover

5 Mock-turtleneck style in purple jersey of Acrilan® acrylic. Soft, supple, clingy. Back neck zipper closing. Machine wash, warm.
   Misses' sizes 8, 10, 12, 14, 16, 18.
Please state size. Shipping weight 9 ounces.
V7 H 6524F $6.00

ORDER YOUR USUAL SIZE
if in doubt, see
pages 770 and 771

THE SHOE

6 Upfront pant shoe with suede leather upper and strap and buckle. Composition sole, 2-in. heel. Coordinates with bag sold on page 294.
Sizes AA(narrow) 7 to 9, B(med.) 5½ to 9, 10.
X54 H 45848F–Purple   X54 H 44848F–Camel tan
X54 H 45448F–Hunter green
X54 H 44248F–Dark brown
State size, then width. Wt. 1 lb. 4 oz $18.00

reason that the mail-order firms built retail stores. However, today mail-order houses still do hundreds of millions of dollars in sales, much of it to city people who find it convenient to order from the huge catalogs, some of which run to well over a thousand pages an issue. There are two major issues a year, with smaller interim catalogs, or "flyers" as they are called.

Today most mail-order firms are also giant retailers with hundreds of stores, mainly in shopping centers in major towns and cities, and some in foreign countries. Sears Roebuck is the largest retail mail-order firm with a volume of over $13 billion. Next comes J. C. Penney, followed by Montgomery Ward. It is interesting to note that Sears started as a mail-order firm and went into retailing, while J. C. Penney started as a retail store and went into the mail-order business by issuing catalogs to supplement its business. Of course, most retail stores do some mail-order business, primarily through monthly statement enclosures and three or four catalogs a year—Christmas, January and/or August White Sales, Home Furnishings, and Fall-Back-to-School.

The large mail-order houses have maintained their image by money-back guarantees for consumer satisfaction.

OTHER TYPES AND VENDING MACHINES

Since World War II the Armed Forces of the United States have maintained a worldwide chain of Post Exchange and Navy stores. These stores cater to servicemen and their wives stationed on every continent and at many military posts in out-of-the-way corners of the world. Merchandise is offered at low prices, and some of the major stores in the PX network are department stores carrying virtually every category of merchandise. A service wife stationed in Germany or Korea can buy most of the goods featured in stores in the United States. The PX is a large operation in terms of scope and total volume, running to hundreds of millions of dollars.

In recent years vending-machine companies have become a factor in retail distribution. Women are able to purchase hosiery, bobby pins, sanitary napkins, facial tissues, and other items by inserting coins in conveniently located machines. There is a possibility that this type of selling can be expanded to cover still larger merchandising areas.

Another growing type of retail operation is the company store. Large firms have stores at their headquarters and major plants. These stores often feature products of the company itself at low prices, plus other merchandise. A variation of this is the factory store or factory outlet, where the public can buy "direct from the factory."

In the future women will probably be able to shop through television, ordering merchandise shown by numbers via electronic phone connections that make the system virtually automatic. Fashions will be modeled and viewed in color, and the woman sitting in her home can dial a number and give her name, address, and the style number selected and receive the merchandise a few days later, with the price deducted automatically from her bank account.

PRESENTING AND MERCHANDISING FASHION

We have discussed how merchandise is manufactured and sold to the retail stores that in turn sell it to the consumer. Now let us look into these retail operations and see how they complete the final step—getting the merchandise into the hands of the customers.

Most stores have what is called a comparison-shopping department. This department has professional shoppers who buy merchandise in stores that are competing with the one at which they are employed. They are particularly concerned with comparable merchandise, that is, merchandise that the customer can compare with what he or she may have purchased at another store.

Comparison-shoppers report to their store that another store has a "better value" in a particular garment or item. The merchandise manager or buyer of the department concerned may decide to reduce the price of that item to make it comparable to that of the competitor. No store wants the reputation of being higher priced for the exact or similar merchandise that its competitors are offering.

MERCHANDISING DUTIES

1. Maintaining stock-control records and inventory, and stock keeping
2. Buying merchandise
3. Handling returned merchandise
4. Handling special orders
5. Analyzing selling trends
6. Marking up and marking down merchandise
7. Reviewing and correcting advertising
8. Working with display department on interior and window displays
9. Protecting merchandise from theft and damage

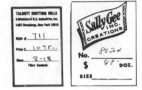

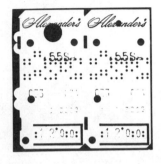

Comparison-shoppers also report on items that their store may have missed. When this is reported, the buyer or merchandise manager attempts to get the items that were somehow overlooked into the store as fast as possible. A good store wants to have the merchandise the customer wants.

Alert buyers or merchandise managers are not caught too often in the position of having missed good items or being overpriced on merchandise. Between the market information they receive when buying and their buying office, they are well aware of the important trends in their particular market areas.

Merchandise is received by the store in the receiving room where it is checked in with a count and examination to see that the merchandise is undamaged and in salable condition. The shipping invoice is marked "received" and the merchandise forwarded to the marking room. In the marking room there is a written form from the buyer whose merchandise has arrived, stating exactly how this lot is to be ticketed. Price tags or tickets indicate in code the vendor, the season, the cost, the department, and, of course, the selling price.

Now the merchandise is ready to go into stock and to the selling floor. This particular lot is misses dresses in six sizes and six assorted colors, a total of 36 garments.

The store buyer has gone into the market with a "buying plan." For example, the store is planning to purchase a total of 500 daytime dresses for the initial spring assortment. It plans to retail them for $10.95, $12.95, $14.95, and $16.95. From past experience the buyer expects 30 percent of the business in misses sizes and the balance in women's and junior sizes. The plan calls for 50 percent of the sales to be in the $12.95 and $14.95 price range, with 25 percent each in the $10.95 and $16.95 categories. With this in mind, the store buyer fills out charts to conform to the plan, putting together the totals from individual charts similar to the one above.

A fashion buyer must understand how to buy against plan and how to mark up and mark down to maintain inventory control. And, of course, he or she must know fashion and choose desirable stock, so that little is left to be marked down at the end of the season. The total assortment must be widely varied in styles, colors, and sizes.

Buyers must plan for advertising and window displays. They must also decide what should be displayed on mannequins on the selling floor in departmental display, which must be changed every week, or two weeks at the most. The ad planned with the help of the advertising department must be used to its best advantage. We will discuss fashion advertising in detail in Chapter 12.

There is to be a fashion show for the spring season. The buyer and the fashion coordinator for the store work together to pick several styles from this group to be featured in the show. Now that all the steps have been taken, we are ready to sell to the customer. It is the duty of the personnel department to train the

TYPICAL ASSORTMENT IN MISSES' DRESSES

SIZE	BLUE	PINK	GREEN	TOTALS
8	1	1	1	3
10	2	2	2	6
12	3	3	3	9
14	3	3	3	9
16	1	2	2	5
18	2	1	1	4

sales people to sell. They must be shown how to fill out sales checks, make out credit slips, and accept returns.

In addition, with the help of sales-training films, demonstration, and role playing on how to handle a customer, it is the duty of the buyer or assistant buyer to explain the merchandise and the selling features. Usually there is a meeting prior to each major selling season, spring and fall, where the fashion sales people are briefed on the major trends and fashion outlook.

BRANDS

What are some of the factors that influence the sale of fashion merchandise other than a customer's confidence in a particular retail store? One, of course, is brand names. A number of major firms have spent a great deal of money to make their brands known. Ads have been run in national magazines so that when a woman goes into a store she doesn't just look for an all-weather coat. She asks for a "London Fog," a "Misty Harbor," or some other leading brand.

The fashion industry as a whole has lagged far behind the food industry, the luggage industry, the drug and pharmaceutical companies, and others in building brand images. Most women would be hard pressed to name *one* famous dress or coat manufacturer.

The apparel industry is beginning to come of age. The smaller apparel firms are merging into larger companies or being put out of business by the larger firms. Retail stores are becoming aware of the value of presold brand names. There will be a growing trend to build brand images for apparel lines so they are recognized at the retail level.

PRIVATE BRANDS

Some major store groups have their "private brands." These are mainly for staple items that the groups buy wholesale and sell at competitive retail prices. For example, A & P in the food field has Ann Page, Jane Parker and Eight O'Clock Coffee. In the department store field, Marshall Field has Fieldcrest, and Macy's has its own Macy brands. Often these private brand items are made by leading manufacturers of that merchandise classification for a specific store or group. Some of the major buying offices have private brands, which they merchandise and handle for their member stores.

One advantage of offering private-brand merchandise is that the store has it exclusively and need not fear competitors with respect to pricing.

CONCLUSION

There is an old quotation: "A chain is no stronger than its weakest link." One of the most important links in the chain of getting products to the consumer is the retail store. There are many types of retail stores, but all have the same objective: *to please the customer.* Only by receiving satisfaction will the customer return to a particular store. That's what the retail business is all about, and the stores that do this best—please the customer again and again—are the ones that are succeeding. Good retail management means timely, fashionable merchandise priced to be fair value. Good fashion is good business.

The twentieth century has seen the development of sophisticated retailing techniques, as well as the growth of giant stores. Although there are seven different categories of retail stores, today the distinction between several of the categories has broken down. For example, mail-order houses now operate large department stores and vice versa. Department stores have become chain stores. In addition, many department stores have set up boutiques or specialty shops within their stores. As retailing becomes more scientific, there will be a continuing need for skilled personnel in all phases.

REVIEW QUESTIONS AND DISCUSSION

1. Name at least five types of retail stores, and give an example of each type.
2. What are the major tools retail stores use to sell merchandise?
3. What is meant by image, with relation to stores?
4. What are some problems that retailers face in selling fashion?
5. Should merchandise be presented by price, by size, or by category?
6. Discuss what you look for when you shop for apparel in a retail store.
7. Discuss the types of stores you patronize consistently.

12

ADVERTISING, PROMOTION, AND PUBLICITY

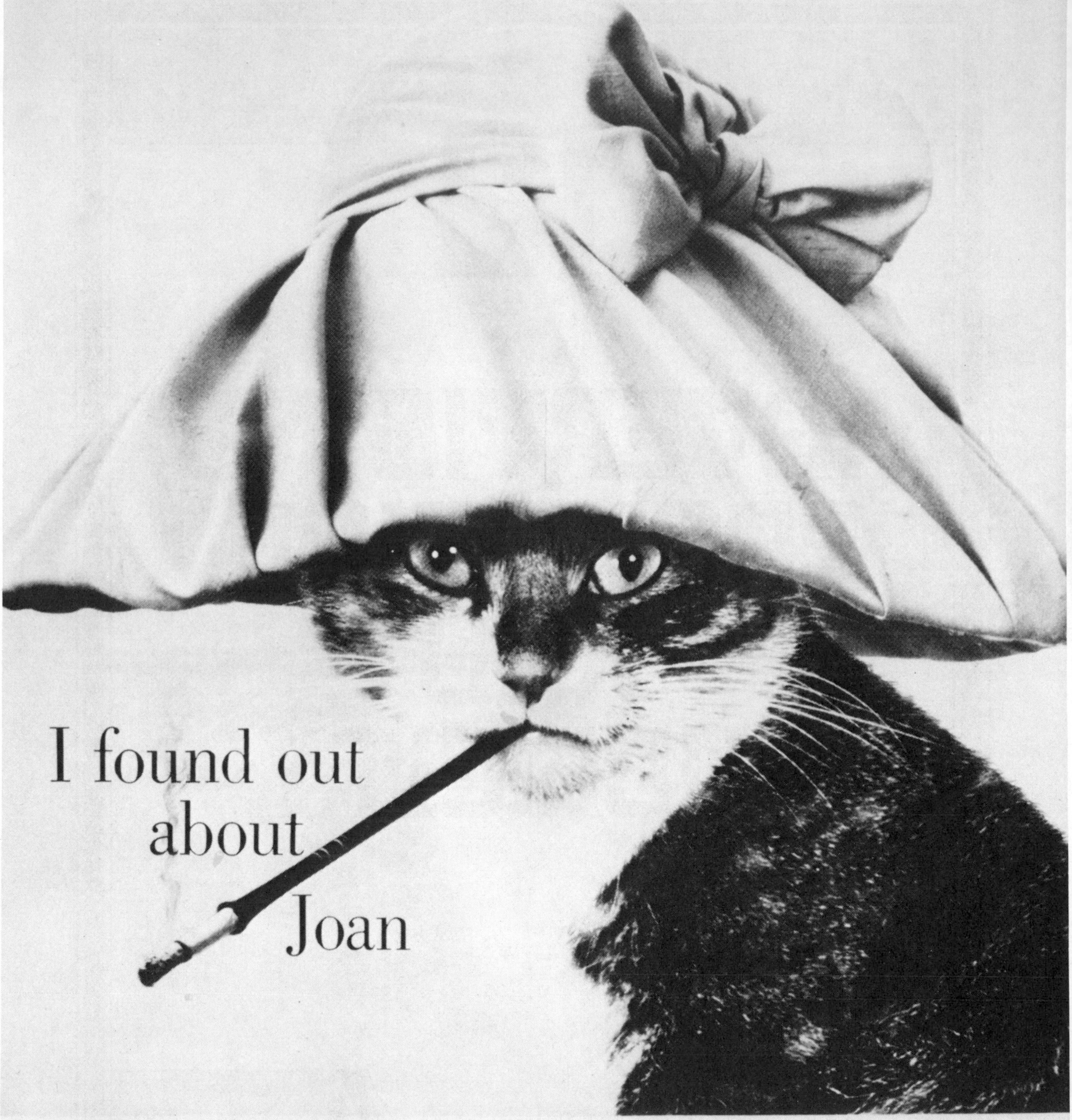

The way she talks, you'd think she was in Who's Who. Well! I found out what's what with *her*. Her husband own a bank? Sweetie, not even a bank *account*. Why that palace of theirs has wall-to-wall *mortgages!* And that car? Darling, that's horsepower, *not* earning power. They won it in a fifty-cent raffle! Can you imagine? And those clothes! Of course she *does* dress divinely. But really…a mink stole, and Paris suits, and all those dresses…on *his* income? Well darling, I found out about that too. I just happened to be going her way and *I saw Joan come out of Ohrbach's!*

Ohrbach's

34TH ST. OPP. EMPIRE STATE BLDG. · **NEWARK** MARKET & HALSEY · "A BUSINESS IN MILLIONS, A PROFIT IN PENNIES"™

Fashion is a visual art, and advertising plays a very important role in the fashion business. The greatest part of all newspaper advertising space is used by retail stores and the largest portion of this space is devoted to fashion advertising. This means that day after day the consumer who reads the paper is exposed to fashion presentations. In addition to newspapers, fashion is prominently featured in a large number of magazines and on TV.

THE MEDIA

Before we look at advertising, let's examine the various media used in transmitting fashion trends and ideas.

The term media means methods of transmission or communication; thus newspapers, magazines, radio, TV, billboards, and direct mail are all media. Because fashion is constantly changing, it relies on the media to convey its story. Without newspapers, magazines, and TV, fashions would sell and change more slowly. Through mass communication, women all over the world can be made aware literally overnight of what is fashion news. Fashion communication takes many forms in order to reach different audiences.

TRADE PAPERS AND JOURNALS

Every business and profession has its own publications, aimed at those employed in that particular business or profession. The fashion industry is no different. It, too, has a number of papers and journals intended to reach manufacturers, buyers, retailers, and others in the industry. Probably the most important is the Fairchild group, which includes, among others, *Women's Wear Daily, Home Furnishings Daily,* and *Men's Wear.* This is without a doubt the most influential group of publications in the field because all but *Men's Wear,* which is a monthly, are published five days a week. Most of the other trade publications in the fashion and home-furnishings field are published monthly and cover specific segments of the apparel market.

These publications can be very influential in their respective fields because they reach the management of an entire industry. Often they do research in their special fields, advising about market trends, merchandising, and other essentials. At times they can be controversial, advocating steps for an industry that are not universally popular. Generally, *trade publications* are a "must" reading for decisionmakers in their respective fields.

THE RETAILERS DAILY NEWSPAPER   A FAIRCHILD PUBLICATION
WOMEN'S WEAR DAILY ®
WEDNESDAY, APRIL 16, 1975
Vol. 130 No. 74   *25 CENTS*   One Year $36 Payable in Advance

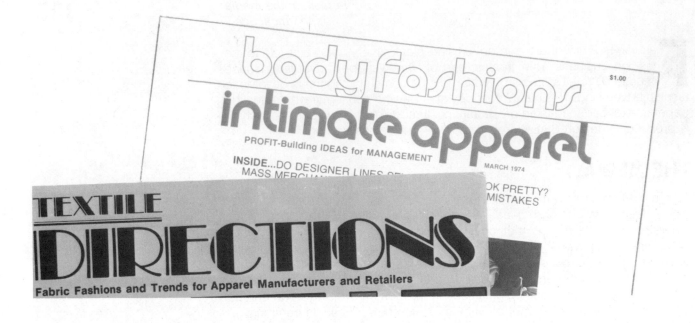

TRADE PUBLICATIONS: THE BUYER'S AID

Advertising Age
American Fabrics
American Textile Reporter
Apparel Manufacturer
Body Fashions
Boot and Shoe Recorder
Boutique Magazine
California Apparel News
California Men's Stylist
California Stylist
Chain Store Age
China, Glass, and Tablewares
Clothes
Curtain and Drapery Magazine
Daily News Record (men's)
Department Store Management
Discount Merchandiser
Display World
Earnshaw's Review (children's apparel)
Fabricnews
Fashion Week
Femme Line
Footwear News
Fur Age Weekly

Gift and Decorative Accessories
Handbags and Accessories
Homefurnishings Daily
Homesewing Trade News
Hosiery and Underwear Review
Housewares Review
Intimate Fashion News
Jewelers Circular–Keystone
Juvenile Merchandising
Knitted Outerwear Times
Linens and Domestics
Masculines
Men's Wear
Modern Textiles
Small World
Stores Magazine
Style
Supermarket News
Teens and Boys Outfitter
Texas Fashions
Variety Department Stores
Western Apparel Industry
Women's Wear Daily

The magazines that reach the customer are called consumer magazines. Like the trade publications, they are classified by major categories. Let's briefly examine each classification.

Fashion Magazines. First come the fashion magazines. Each of these magazines tries to aim at a particular segment of the women's or girls' audience. The circulation of these magazines is not great, but their influence is.

Vogue and *Harper's Bazaar* are the "high-fashion" magazines aimed at the more mature, well-to-do woman. They try to be pacesetters and direct attention to new fashion trends. Although their circulation is not large, it is selective, and the magazines are influential and widely read by the trade and by those who create fashion news.

Glamour aims at the career woman and the average college girl. It is down-to-earth and shows many moderately priced clothes. *Glamour* has the largest circulation of the fashion magazines.

Mademoiselle aims at the prosperous college girl and young married woman. It features clothes priced a notch or two above *Glamour*. It is interesting to note that *Vogue, Glamour,* and *Mademoiselle* are all owned by Condé Nast, which is in turn owned by the Newhouse interests. These three magazines attempt to maintain different audiences to avoid competing with each other.

Seventeen, Co-ed, Teen, and *Ingenue* aim at the younger audience—high school and college girls.

Brides and *Modern Bride* aim for the woman about to be married. In addition to bridal gowns, they also feature home furnishings. Their readership is relatively stable, because the number of marriages in this country remains at about 250,000 each year.

American Girl is directed at the subteenager and is published by the Girl Scouts of America.

The hair-style publications, like *Hair Trend* and *Hair-Do,* are generally quarterly and appeal to all those interested in the newest hair styles.

Service Magazines. The next classification is called service magazines because the publications feature articles on cooking, decorating, home furnishings, fashion, child care, housekeeping, and related subjects.

All of these magazines have far greater circulation than do any of the fashion magazines, mostly between six and eight million readers or more.

Family Circle and *Woman's Day* receive especially wide circulation because they are sold at the checkout counters of most supermarkets. They are aimed at the average homemaker and offer housekeeping ideas and budget suggestions, as well as fashion news.

Ladies' Home Journal, Good Housekeeping, and *McCall's* are aimed at a somewhat more affluent reader than *Woman's Day* and *Family Circle* and usually contain some fictional entertainment or nonfiction articles. These three cost much more per copy than *Family Circle* and *Woman's Day.*

Shelter Books. The next important category of magazines for women is the shelter books. The magazines in this group such as *House Beautiful, House and Gardens,* and *Better Homes and Gardens* deal with homes, gardens, and fashions in home furnishings.

In addition to the magazines previously mentioned, such general publications as *Cosmopolitan, Redbook,* and *Ms* are aimed at the women's market.

Men's Magazines. Magazines for men offer possibilities for reaching a diverse audience through advertising. They usually run feature articles on the latest men's fashions. *Esquire* caters to the more intellectual man; *Argosy* and *True* are adventure magazines; and *Playboy* and *Penthouse* and similar publications aim for the younger male audience. *Boy's Life* is published by the Boy Scouts of America for the subteenage boy. There are also a number of military publications for servicemen.

General Magazines. We must not forget the great general magazines such as *Time, Newsweek, Reader's Digest, Holiday, Ebony,* and *Essence.* While they do not feature fashions constantly, they do carry fashion and home-furnishing news when they consider it appropriate. These magazines reach a wide national audience.

Add to these publications romance magazines, true story and confession magazines, sports such as *Sports Illustrated* and recreation magazines such as boating, skiing, bowling, golf, mystery, adventure, fiction, and many regional *(Sunset),* specialized *(Weight Watchers),* and foreign *(Elle)* magazines and you have some idea of the enormous scope of the periodical field.

All these magazines, of course, show people wearing clothes and in home environments. They influence the consumer and stimulate the desire to imitate people in the magazines and to decorate homes the way they look in the color pictures. Most have fashion editors or home-furnishings editors who report the newest happenings in the world of fashion.

NEWSPAPERS

The most important medium for communicating fashion news is the newspaper. The newspaper is a daily organ, so it can transmit news quickly. Most magazines are weekly or monthly so they cannot possibly match newspapers in *timeliness*. The newspaper is the chief medium used by retail stores which features fashions day after day. These great department stores and ready-to-wear specialty stores are anxious to let the consumer know the latest fashion news.

Then too, many of the big metropolitan papers have special women's sections in their Sunday editions covering fashions, home furnishings, and society news. In addition, many of these same papers have important Sunday magazine sections with extensive fashion advertising both from apparel manufacturers and retail stores. The *New York Times* also publishes special men's and women's fashion supplements each spring and fall. These influence the entire market. Fashion editors try to help their readers by stressing in their columns what they believe is important, from the hundreds of fashion stories that flood into the newspaper offices.

A leading retailer's advertising often sets the fashion climate. The fact that such stores feature particular fashions makes those fashions important. When a number of fashion-conscious retail stores all show particular trends, you may be sure that these are the important current fashions.

The Miami Herald

ST. LOUIS POST-DISPATCH

The New York Times

Detroit Free Press

Los Angeles Times

San Francisco Chronicle
THE VOICE OF THE WEST

Chicago Tribune

The Evening Bulletin

San Francisco Examiner

THE SUN

NONNEWSPAPER READERS

There's a growing group of customers that's hard to reach with newspapers—younger customers. In short, *radio can reach people you've never reached before* with your messages. New customers you can keep for life. And at the same time talk to your present customers about store news.

TELEVISION AND RADIO

Because fashion is largely visual, radio has not and cannot be an important medium for fashion news. However, it can be important in backing up store sales or fashion features by reminding people to come to the store.

Television, on the other hand, is growing in importance in fashion presentation. Fashion news can be transmitted quickly and excitingly via the color TV tube. Retail stores, too, are making greater use of television. Many fashions, especially sportswear, are best shown in motion, as they have fluid or interesting lines when the wearer is moving. In such cases TV is particularly effective.

However, television production is expensive and complicated. It is much more difficult to make a live or motion-picture film of fashions than to take a still photograph. So, while advertising fashion on TV is extremely effective, its cost often makes it prohibitive. A number of people in the fashion industry are working on this problem, and it is hoped that the costs for TV production can be reduced to make its wider use possible.

There are many popular local women's TV shows. These shows are often built around a local TV "personality." The format is oriented to traditional "women's interests"—fashions, cooking, and beauty. Some of these shows have store sponsorship, or the stores buy time on them to show fashions. The national network shows such as the *Today* show occasionally cover fashions, fashion designers, and new ideas in home furnishings and life styles.

PERCENT OF STORES THAT WILL INCREASE ADVERTISING IN EACH MEDIUM

Newspapers	20%
Circulars	21%
Direct Mail	30%
Television	35%
Radio	43%

Source: 1975 Media Survey, National Retail Merchants Association.

A network show that interviews a leading designer and shows the newest fashions reaches millions of women across the nation in moments. Needless to say, this can be a very influential medium. If consumers see a woman or women they respect attired a certain way during an interview, it can touch off an instant trend. Even a newscast that shows momentary flashes of social events or news events can set style trends. The Miss America contests and the awarding of Oscars in Hollywood each year can alert millions of women to current fashion ideas. Television is indeed a potent force in the transmission of fashion concepts.

DIRECT MAIL

We often take for granted what we receive in the mail without fully realizing its force. The catalogs of such firms as Sears Roebuck, Montgomery Ward, Spiegel's, Aldens, and J. C. Penney are all direct mail, as are the monthly-statement enclosures and other circulars, folders, and brochures we receive from stores where we have charge accounts or are on mailing lists.

Millions of dollars' worth of merchandise is sold each year through direct mail. Direct mail has been used extensively to sell fashion and home-furnishings merchandise. Today color printing is used more than ever before, making it still easier to transmit and sell fashion concepts.

At Christmas time many of the large stores issue a holiday catalog covering gift ideas, in which fashion plays a large part. A great store in a major city may have as many as half a million or more names on its mailing list. When you multiply this by hundreds of stores, you can easily see how millions of consumers are reached by direct mail.

Fashion manufacturers also use direct mail at the trade level, sending brochures to store buyers to alert them to their new fashion lines. Many firms issue two catalogs or brochures a year, covering their spring and fall lines and giving style numbers, colors, and sizes, so that store buyers may order directly on order forms provided.

WOODWARD & LOTHROP
A CHRISTMAS TRADITION

The letter or postal card can also be an important selling tool to the consumer. Many stores invite charge customers to special advance sales by letter or card. As part of trade advertising, apparel manufacturers invite store buyers and merchandise managers to their special showings. These are usually sent as invitations and require an RSVP. Direct mail is indeed an important method of getting the fashion story across at all levels—to the consumer, to the retail buyer from the garment manufacturers, and to the apparel manufacturer from the fiber and textile firms.

Large department stores have from 200,000 to 800,000 or more active charge accounts. Each month *every active charge customer* receives from two to six statement enclosures. The response to these "stuffers" amounts to billions of dollars each year.

Because direct mail is so lucrative, many nonretail firms use their own or purchased mailing lists to solicit business. Typical examples of such firms are American Express, Shell Oil, Diners Club, Franklin Mint, and Trans World Airlines.

MISCELLANEOUS MEDIA

Outdoor.

America's fastest-growing medium
Institute of Outdoor Advertising

In addition to the recognized media, we must not omit specialized ways of transmitting ideas. Posters, car cards, handbills, displays, show windows, telephones, and telegrams are all media.

Many stores use telephones very effectively in soliciting phone orders for items advertised in newspapers and other media. Some even have their telephone operators call names on their charge lists and call attention to special sales and fashion events. Occasionally telegrams are sent to customers of stores to invite them to come to the store for special events. Manufacturers also use telegrams to dramatically call attention to new activities.

Both stores and manufacturers use posters or "blow-ups" of ads, photos, or fashion sketches. These large-size posters are used in store windows, on the selling floor, or perhaps in manufacturers' showrooms. Fashion magazines also make blow-ups of their covers for use in stores and showrooms.

Media experts agree that there is no one consumer group, but hundreds of segments. Each group has its own tastes, ideas, and interests and responds to particular media. It is up to the people in the fashion business to put together the best possible combination of media to achieve their goals.

With this brief outline of the various media as a background, let us examine the three main categories of planned exposure of fashion to the public—advertising, publicity, and promotion. All three are closely related in that they all attempt to familiarize consumers with particular products for sale.

ADVERTISING

Advertising is paid space or time in media. It is divided into two major classifications.

National advertising is just what the name implies. If an advertiser decides to run the same ad in 20 to 50 newspapers across the country, that is national advertising. An ad in a magazine with national coverage, meaning it is circulated in most states, is national advertising. An advertisement appearing on network TV or broadcast on network radio is national advertising.

National advertising's main purpose is to build *brand* identity. The manufacturer hopes that through national advertising a product will be so well known that the consumer will ask for the product by brand name.

PRE-WASHED

Denim blue zips up
for some soft skirting.
The bib shows her
name or 3 initials
in red, gold or green;
suspenders adjust
when she grows.
4-6x, <u>13.00</u>;
7-14, <u>15.00</u>.
Her red plaid
shirt's flannel-warm.
4-6x, <u>8.00</u>;
7-14, <u>9.00</u>.
All cotton,
by Bobbie Lane.
Shops for Girls
on two, Fifth
Avenue and
branches.

B Altman & Co

Allow three weeks for delivery

Local advertising, or retail advertising, as it is sometimes called, differs from national advertising in that it is run locally. An ad appearing only in the *New York Times* is a local ad aimed at the people of New York City. If a spot advertisement appears only on WGN-TV in Chicago, it is a local TV ad. Most retailers use only local advertising and pay the local rate, which is substantially lower than the national rate. In other words, a national advertiser pays more for a page of advertising in the newspaper than does the local retailer using the same space. Most retailers have a bulk linage contract. This means that the more space a retail store uses, the less per line it costs. The same rate structure generally applies to other media as well. There are bulk discounts for an increasing usage of space, or frequency in the case of radio or TV.

Local advertising is aimed at immediate consumer response—the same morning the ad appears in the newspaper or within the next few days. While a store may feature brand name merchandise, it also features its own services, conveniences, and assortments of merchandise. This means that even if the merchandise in a particular ad does not appeal to a customer, the store tells the customer it has a great assortment of similar or related merchandise from which to select.

in a class by itself.

Tropical rains won't wilt the elegance that is Arthur Richards...the lapel-vested Harrison and the peaked lapel Laughton of 65% Fortrel Polyester and 35% Flax, both from $135 to $185. At the discriminating stores below or write to us.

FORTREL FOR FASHION

Arthur Richards

THIRTY ONE WEST FIFTY SIXTH STREET, NEW YORK, NEW YORK 10019 (212) 247-2300

Juster	Minneapolis	May D & F	Denver, Colorado	Redwood and Ross	Kalamazoo, Mich.
Louis	Boston, Mass	Mister Guy	Kansas City, Mo.	Rich's	Atlanta, Ga
Miltons	Quincy, Mass	Neiman Marcus	All Stores	Sakowitz	Houston, Texas
Maas Bros	Tampa, Fla	Nordstrom	Seattle, Wash	Union Co	Columbus, Ohio
I Magnin	San Francisco	Perkins Shearer	Colorado Springs, Colo	Woolf Bros	Kansas City, Mo

Fortrel® is a trademark of Fiber Industries, Inc., a subsidiary of Celanese Corporation   Celanese®

Every fashion advertiser must analyze which media are best to reach the particular audience desired. There are two major fashion advertisers: manufacturers of fashion merchandise and retail stores that sell the merchandise. Manufacturers usually advertise nationally, placing ads in fashion magazines that are circulated nationwide and in the Sunday magazine supplements of all the leading newspapers in the United States. They also use network television.

Retailers, on the other hand, are only interested in the local audience. Here, too, there are a number of choices. For example, a retail store in New York has three important daily newspapers to choose from—the *Times,* the *Post,* and the *Daily News.* Each has its own audience of readers. Many cities and towns in the United States have more than one paper, usually a morning and an evening publication. Most cities have at least two TV stations and three or four radio stations. In addition, there may be billboards and bus or car cards posted in local transportation. There may be outlying suburban newspapers and foreign language or ethnic publications to consider. And, of course, there is direct mail. Retailers must decide which combinations of these media will best reach an intended audience.

ADVERTISING BUDGETS

There are a number of decisions to be made regarding how money is to be spent in presenting fashions to a predetermined audience. Let us take several examples of fashion advertisers and see how they might budget their advertising funds.

Fashion Manufacturer. Suppose a manufacturer of junior sportswear does an annual volume of five million dollars. Typically, the manufacturer appropriates 5 percent of sales revenue for advertising, in this case creating a budget of $250,000.

This allocation is broken up into two seasons—spring and fall. Because fall is the more important season for this firm's line, the manufacturer decides to spend $150,000 of the budget for fall and $100,000 for spring. The next decision is what media to use. This manufacturer, like most others, uses the services of an advertising agency. The agency recommends budgets and media, makes up the suggested advertising schedule, and prepares the advertisements.

Retail Store. Now let us take a typical retail store with an annual volume of $10 million. Most nonpromotional stores allocate 2.5 to 3 percent for advertising. This means this store has $300,000 to spend for advertising. The first step for a retailer is to look at last year's records. If March does 10 percent of the total year's business, it is entitled to 10 percent of the advertising budget, or $30,000.

The next step is to allocate, by department, the $30,000 to be spent in the month of March. The junior sportswear department does 8 percent of the store's total March business, so it is entitled to 8 percent of the $30,000 advertising budget for March, or $2,400. The buyer and ready-to-wear merchandise manager agree to divide it evenly for the four-week period—$600 each week. They will also use co-op advertising from the manufacturer mentioned above, thus adding $400 to their budget. This co-op allocation is based on the amount of merchandise the store has purchased from the manufacturer.

This is a typical retail plan; the only remaining duty is to select the merchandise to be featured in each of the ads. If a store uses radio and TV, some of the

A TYPICAL ADVERTISING BUDGET

ADVERTISING			SPACE COST
Seventeen			
	Spring	1 color page	$ 9,500
	Fall	2 color pages	19,000
Ingenue			
	Spring	1 color page	7,800
	Fall	2 color pages	15,600
Co-Ed			
	Fall	1 color page	6,500
Teen			
	Fall	1 color page	5,500
Spring and Fall color statement enclosures free to retail stores			60,100
Co-op advertising with stores on a 50-50 basis in local papers up to 4 percent of net purchases			65,000
Production and miscellaneous			61,000
	Total		$250,000

budget would be allocated to these media as well as to newspapers. The advertising manager of the store decides which media to use on the basis of past performances and results.

CO-OP ADVERTISING

From time to time in the fashion business you will hear of "co-op advertising." This is short for *cooperative advertising,* meaning that a manufacturer shares the cost of advertising with a retail store. If a particular store does a total volume of $100,000 yearly with a manufacturer, that apparel firm may have a standard practice of allowing 4 percent of net purchases—in this case $4,000—which the store may use provided it matches the manufacturer's $4,000 with an equal amount of its own money. Usually a manufacturer of apparel or related products allows the store to decide on media.

Most retailers count heavily on co-op to augment their own budgets. It is standard practice with most toiletry and cosmetic firms, undergarment manufacturers, and many others to allocate co-op advertising funds to retailers. Most large men's shirt, sportswear, and clothing firms also have a co-op advertising policy.

Under the Robinson-Patman Act (a federal law governing trade practices), a manufacturer may choose any cooperative policy as long as it is standard for all of his or her customers. Co-op advertising figures are rarely discussed or publicized. However, co-op advertising is very important for both manufacturers and retailers.

Planning, creating, and preparing advertising is a specialized business requiring trained personnel. Retail stores have found that it is economical to have their own advertising departments. For ready-to-wear manufacturers, it is more economical to have an advertising agency and maintain only a small internal staff for advertising and sales promotion.

The Retail Advertising Department. The size of the store usually determines the size of the advertising budget and the department. Large stores may have as many as fifty persons in their advertising department, smaller stores as few as three or four people. A major store's advertising staff is headed by an advertising or sales promotion manager who supervises three divisions—the advertising production department, the art department, and the copy department.

The *production department* is concerned with traffic and detail. The production manager is often the chief assistant to the advertising manager. A busy retail advertising department deals with newspapers, radio stations, and television stations, as well as direct-mail printers, engravers, typographers, mat makers, photostat houses, and other suppliers such as photographers and freelance artists.

The *art department* is responsible for all layouts and sketches for newspapers. When photography is used, the art department makes layouts for the photographer to follow. It may also make "story-boards" for television spots. Often the artists specialize in categories: women's fashions, men's fashions, or home furnishings.

The *copy department,* as the name implies, is concerned with writing the copy that appears in the store's newspaper advertising or on radio or television. There is a copy chief and various copywriters, who are specialists in different merchandise categories.

Media decisions are generally made by a committee of the buyer, merchandise manager, and advertising manager. The decision is based on what will be most productive and balanced, giving the store representation in different media.

It is the task of the retail advertising department to prepare the best possible advertising for the store and give it personality and character. Each store is said to have its "format." This means that all the advertising should be related and have a consistent, overall look and concept. Most television material requires entirely different production techniques from those necessary for preparing a newspaper ad. If a retail store does not need a full television staff, it may hire an outside agency to help produce the television material.

The Advertising Agency. Unlike local or retail advertising, a 15 percent agency commission is standard for *national* newspaper advertising, for trade publications, consumer magazines, radio, and television. If a firm spends $100,000 for *national* advertising in media through an advertising agency, that agency collects $15,000 in commissions by deducting the amount from the gross media invoice. In addition fees and other charges may be billed to the client.

For this reason most retailers have their own advertising departments, while most ready-to-wear manufacturers with reasonable advertising budgets use advertising agencies.

Advertising agencies have the same breakdown as the retail advertising department: production, art, and copy. In large agencies, groups of people are assigned to particular accounts. In addition, agencies must have account executives who act as liaisons between the advertising agency and the client accounts. Not many years ago, most apparel firms were small companies with no advertising budgets. Today there are many large apparel manufacturers, and most owe their success to a national reputation and brand image of some stature, built through advertising.

Firms such as Jonathan Logan, Russ Togs, Bobbie Brooks, Leslie Fay, White Stag, Jantzen, London Fog and their subsidiaries have become relatively large users of advertising, particularly in fashion magazines. The advertising agencies who handle these accounts try to build an image and brand consciousness in the consumer's mind similar to the image built by food, cosmetic, and detergent firms. However, as an industry group, national fashion advertising is a small fraction of the nation's total advertising expenditures.

PUBLICITY AND PUBLIC RELATIONS

The large advertising agencies may have publicity departments that help their clients get publicity in various media. These departments may have fashion-oriented personnel who help their clients with shows, color, and fabric trends. Public relations and publicity is the effort to get products mentioned in the *news columns* or *editorial* portions of publications. It should *never* be referred to as "free advertising," because it is not advertising but editorial matter. No publication's editorial columns are or should be "for sale."

Large ready-to-wear manufacturers may have their own public relations or publicity departments. These internal departments function the same as an outside agency. The public relations agencies who specialize in this phase of business do not usually also do advertising. There are a number of freelance public relations people who have previously worked for a major ready-to-wear firm and are able to get this firm and others as clients on a consulting fee basis.

The most important rule in public relations is that what is offered to the publication must be *newsworthy*. Good publications are not interested in material that does nothing but serve the interests of retail stores or ready-to-wear manufacturers. "Releases," as they are called, should contain information of interest to readers of the publication, often with accompanying photographs.

Skilled public relations people often try to find out what interests editors at particular times. With this information they try to slant their material toward the current interests of the publication. After a time certain public relations people win the confidence of the publications in the area in which they work and are even called by editors to find out "what's new."

For Release: On or after Nov.16,17, 1974

On Behalf of: THE DENIM COUNCIL

DENIM AMERICAN STYLE...to jog, sail, bike or take a stroll beautifully.
Hooded sweatshirt zips and drawstrings to a blouson, Matching
drawstring pant ties up the message in indigo blue cotton denim.
By Landlubber. Shirt: #912, S,M,L, $14.00. Drawstring pant: #310,
S,M;L, $14.00. To be shown in the "Yankee Denim Dandies" fashion
show at NYC's Hotel Plaza, Nov. 20th during American Designer Week.

CONTACT: TERRY MAYER 165 East 35th Street, New York City 10016 — Tel. (212) 685-6561,9819

SALES PROMOTION

Sales promotion is still another phase of fashion presentation. Sometimes this is defined as the overall effort to promote sales, including advertising and publicity. In that case, the sales promotion manager has an advertising manager and a publicity person reporting to him or her.

Sales promotion also means the efforts that are not strictly advertising or publicity. Thus a fashion show or fashion movie fall under the heading of sales promotion. Sales promotion is not advertising, although it may make a product, label, or store well-known. It may get publicity, but it is not publicity in itself. Beauty demonstrations and modeling on the floor also fall into this category. Macy's Thanksgiving Day Parade is a sales promotion event.

Sales promotion also includes proper display of the product. Store shopping bags are promotional material. Posters, display cards, props, and even store fixtures are used. The cosmetic industry, for example, spends millions of dollars a year working out displays for stores.

Packaging is another area of sales promotion. Here again in the field of cosmetics and toiletries, packaging is a vital part of selling the product.

Sales training is another important part of selling. Manufacturers have discovered that sales people sell better when they are familiar with and understand their particular product. Thus many apparel manufacturers make an effort to train store sales personnel. This is often done with booklets about the products, slides, or motion pictures, plus a talk by a representative of the manufacturing firm.

CONCLUSION

Most apparel firms and related businesses make efforts and spend money for advertising, public relations, and sales promotion. Each industry may have somewhat different problems. For example, while packaging plays an essential part in the toiletry and cosmetic field, it plays only a small role in apparel. While fashion shows play a large role in apparel, they are relatively unimportant to the cosmetic and toiletry business.

Behind Every Great Man... There's A Great Promotion

MICKEY MOUSE IS SELLING BETTER THAN EVER!

Each type of business must determine its own needs with respect to advertising, public relations, and sales promotion. One firm may spend the largest part of its budget on public relations, another on sales promotion, and still another on advertising.

Fashion manufacturers advertise in trade publications to reach retailers. Retailers advertise in consumer media to reach the public. Suppliers to manufacturers, such as textile firms, also advertise in trade publications. Both apparel manufacturers and retailers may use sales promotion to reach their respective audiences.

Those in the fashion business learn by experience how to use the various tools of communication most effectively.

REVIEW QUESTIONS AND DISCUSSION

1. What is the difference between a trade publication and a consumer publication?
2. What is a women's service magazine? a shelter magazine?
3. Define *media* and name the four major media.
4. What media might you use to promote women's fashions for a retail store? for a manufacturer?
5. Explain the difference between advertising, public relations, and sales promotion.
6. What is local or retail advertising? How does it differ from national advertising?
7. Outline the structure of a retail store's advertising department. Discuss the function of each division.
8. What does an advertising agency do? Do most retail stores use them? Why or why not?
9. Discuss how you would plan an entire program to promote apparel if you were a retail promotion executive.

13

HOME SEWING

Announcing
THE GREATEST SEW ON EARTH
Altman's
Great Sewing Seminar
will have you on pins and needles

Be here. 3 days only,
May 15, 16, 17
in our Fifth Avenue store

There's no business like sew business • For fun & R & R (Rest & Relaxation) • For fit • For fine quality • For fashion (and let's not forget good old thrift)

Dresses are coming back. Now's the time to see the beautiful new Burlington Klopman dress fabrics, of Bright Cloud®, a Qiana® nylon, and Suraline®, a textured Dacron® polyester gabardine.

• DEMONSTRATIONS • FASHION SHOWS
• LECTURES • GUEST PERSONALITIES
• SPECIAL EVENTS EVERY DAY
• SECRETS & INSIDE TIPS
from the experts on all phases of home sewing

There's no people like sew people.
Meet designers • Carol Horn and • Stan Herman for Vogue Patterns
• Evelyn De Jonge for Liberty of London • and Kleibacker
• Plus experts from leading fabric mills & McCalls Pattern Co.

Burlington/Klopman —new fashion fabric directions
• Logantex—how to sew with chiffons and voiles
• Master Knitters—how to sew on boucle knits
• Apsco—how to sew the fluid jerseys
• Loomskill—how to sew on Nyesta® nylon crepe and Qiana® nylon jersey
• McCalls—how to do the new "lettuce edging" on Nyesta® nylon crepe

SCHEDULE OF APPEARANCES

Thursday, May 15	Friday, May 16	Saturday, May 17
11:00 am Burlington/Klopman	11:00 pm Loomskill	10:30 am Loomskill
12:00 noon Carol Horn	12:00 noon Burlington/Klopman	11:30 am Burlington/Klopman
1:00 pm Logantex	1:00 pm Stan Herman	12:30 pm Apsco
2:00 pm Apsco	2:00 pm Evelyn De Jonge	1:30 pm Master Knitters
3:00 pm Master Knitters	3:00 pm Logantex	2:30 pm Logantex
4:00 pm Loomskill	4:00 pm Apsco	3:30 pm Fit in Fashion
5:00 pm Burlington/Klopman	5:00 pm Master Knitters	4:30 pm Kleibacker
6:00 pm Kleibacker		

CHECK THE SCHEDULE, CHOOSE WHAT YOU WANT TO LEARN, THEN ON WITH THE SEW!
All in a special 'theatre' on our fifth floor, New York only.

B Altman & Co

Long before there was ready-to-wear as we know it today, there were homemade clothes. In cold climates people wore clothes to protect themselves from the elements, but in warmer areas clothing served as adornment or badges of rank or office. For example, the chief of the Bear Tribe probably had a more beautiful and luxurious bear skin than anyone else in his tribe. Chiefs, kings, and rulers wore splendid robes designating their high rank.

All these clothes were made by members of the household. They spun the yarns, wove the fabrics, and created the garments according to the styles of their times. In the households of rulers, there were persons assigned to make clothes just as there were persons to cook, clean, fetch water, and do other household chores. So down through the years, the making of apparel was a home art, like cooking. Clothing was always needed, and each household took care of its own needs.

A HISTORY OF HOME SEWING

The first fashions were probably developed as a result of the tastes of the ruling households. Others copied their garments, and these became the styles of that period. Later there were to be laws that prevented "lower classes" from imitating the dress of the nobility or the affluent.

Other styles developed as functional necessities; one woman would show another a garment that proved practical and useful. Another would tell of how wool proved warmer than cotton, or how a certain fabric made in strips wound around the legs would protect the wearer from cold and underbrush.

The main source of all fabrics and apparel was the home. Until 1850 virtually all clothing was made in the home or by individual dressmakers or tailors hired by the more well-to-do.

In the early 1850s probably an all-time high was reached in the amount of yardage a woman wore. It was the era of crinoline, and women's costumes billowed to unprecedented proportions. A single outfit might require as much as 40 yards of fabric! All this required a great deal of sewing.

In addition to a muslin shift or knitted undergarment and corset, the proper woman wore a flannel petticoat, a muslin petticoat, a padded petticoat reaching to the knees, then a white, starched petticoat, plus two or three additional muslin petticoats each three or four yards wide, and—finally—her full-skirted gown.

There was much construction work as well as sewing. Since starched pads did not hold up such layers of cloth properly, steel hoops covered with cotton cloth laced together with tapes were used. When it was discovered that tilting hoop skirts could be revealing, the ladies sheathed their legs with pantalets trimmed with flounces or lace. Parties had to become smaller as most living rooms could not accommodate many hoop-skirted women at the same time!

The home sewing machines developed in the mid-1800s were so inexpensive that almost every middle-class family could own one. Women's magazines gave instructions for home dressmaking and also issued patterns.

As we have seen in previous chapters, the invention of the sewing machine changed the entire concept of making clothing. It ultimately led to the creation of ready-to-wear. However, the sewing machine also went into the home, and through the years home sewing has supported a large retail piece goods business, also referred to as the over-the-counter fabric industry.

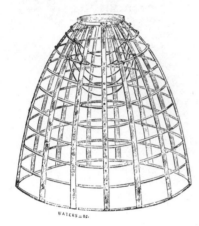

REASONS FOR THE HOME-SEWING BOOM

The boom in home sewing is on, and for many good reasons:

1. Women of all ages desire individuality and fashion in their apparel, and they find enjoyment in the creative expression of home sewing.
2. The cost of ready-to-wear gets higher and higher; at the same time the quality for the price seems to get lower and lower. This alone has convinced many to make all or part of their wardrobes at home.
3. A woman's clothing needs are greater and more varied than ever before in history. The day of the basic black dress, dressed up or down for any occasion, is gone forever. Now pants, tunics, culottes, shorts, shifts, and at-home-wear are as necessary as dresses in a woman's life. For most women on a fixed clothing budget, the only way to have more of the kinds of clothes they need and more individuality is to make them.
4. Sewing is now fun and socially "in," especially among the young. Simplicity pattern company estimates 6 out of 7 teenagers sew.
5. More leisure time means women are doing more kinds of things. This requires more kinds of clothing. By the same token, they have more time to sew and create apparel at home.
6. Sewing is easier and more fun to do now than ever before. Patterns are simpler to work with and are as current and fashionable as ready-to-wear. Fabrics have more variety, are more appealing, and more practical than ever. Sewing machines are easier to operate and do more finishing and detailing automatically.

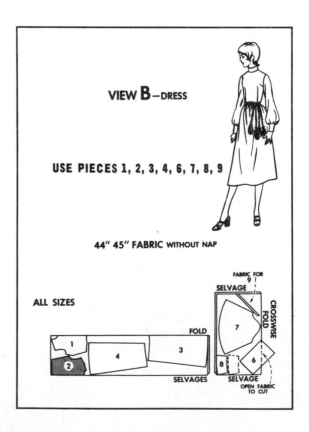

6887 Simplicity $1.50
IN S.A. & CANADA
1.50

Sample

6779 Simplicity $1.00
IN S.A. & CANADA
1.10

Sample

6808 Simplicity $1.25
IN S.A. & CANADA
1.25

Sample

'HOW TO SEW' FASHION BASIC SEPARATES
Including a Tissue Lesson Chart On "How to set in sleeves."

2 FIGURE TYPES / 8 SIZES • Young Junior-Teens' / Misses'

6836 Simplicity $1.25
IN S.A. & CANADA
1.25

Sample

'HOW TO SEW' FASHION BASIC SHIRT
Including a Tissue Lesson Chart On "How to set in shirt sleeves."

2 FIGURE TYPES / 7 SIZES • Teen-Boys' / Men's

HOME SEWERS

Among the total sample of home sewers surveyed, the majority (54%) considered themselves "About Average" in terms of sewing ability. A sizeable portion (28%) said they were "Beginning Home Sewers," while 12% considered their skills "Better Than Average." Only 4% of those surveyed rated themselves as "Much Better Than Average."

The majority of home sewers (58%) sew between 1 and 4 garments per year. However, 26% sew between 5 and 10 garments and 11% sew over 11 per year. Those sewing 9 or more garments per year were considered "heavy" sewers, and these women tend to have distinctive characteristics. Heavy home sewers tend to be younger than average, better-educated, and are more likely to come from larger families (4 or more people).

TYPE OF STORE SHOPPED FOR PATTERNS, FABRICS, AND NOTIONS

TYPE OF STORE	PATTERN	FABRICS	NOTIONS
Fabric store	43%	46%	32%
National mercantile chain	32	27	35
Department store	16	22	20
Discount store	9	12	19

AVERAGE NUMBER OF GARMENTS MADE IN PAST YEAR

"Better Than Average" sewers	5.4
"Average" or "Beginner" sewers	2.7
Home sewers 24 years old or less	4.8
Home sewers 25–44	2.6
Home sewers 45 and over	2.6
Total Sample	3.4

Source: *Simplicity Annual Report 1972*. Courtesy of Simplicity Pattern Company.

McCall Pattern Company points out that the woman who sews is more affluent than the average woman. The income of the average sewing family is $9,500, well above the national average. Today's home sewer doesn't sew because she has to, but because she wants to. She's looking for value in all aspects of her life, and she demands value in the clothing she needs for herself and her family. Instead of one dress, for example, she can have three—if she sews. For $50 she can create a fashionable garment that might cost $200 off the rack.

Sewing is no longer the province of the older, economy-minded woman. The average age of the home sewer has gotten younger and younger each year. In 1975 it was down to 23. As a group, 55 percent of all sewing machine owners are under 40.

Patterns have become simpler than ever, with some designs requiring only two main pattern pieces. All the major pattern companies—McCall's, Simplicity, Butterick, and Vogue—publish seasonal catalogs, as well as numerous supplements. Those who sew at home can browse through these pattern books in the piece goods department of most stores and choose pattern, fabric, and notions in one shopping trip. Sizing for patterns was recently revised to become more standard, and many patterns are now multi-sized to insure better fit. "Jiffy" patterns now allow a woman to make a simple outfit in as little as two hours or less!

THE HOME-SEWING INDUSTRY

According to reports from the Simplicity Pattern Company (the largest in terms of volume), the fastest-growing segment of this market is the teenager, who wants to "do her own thing," have outstanding apparel and who is attracted by the excitement of creative sewing.

The Vogue-Butterick Pattern Company says the home sewer today can generally find excellent local fabric shops. As a result of the growing interest, hundreds of boutique-type fabric specialty stores and fabric chain stores have opened up in recent years. Leading department stores promote home sewing on a continuing basis. Today, the home-sewing industry is the third largest industry in the United States. Millions of dollars' worth of buttons, braids, trimmings, ribbons, belt buckles, and other sewing accessories are sold, in addition

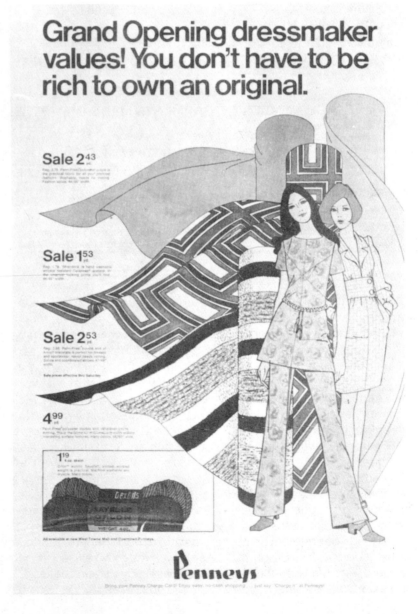

to fabrics. Boards of education statistics show that more than six million girls are taking sewing courses in school home economics classes or under the sponsorship of youth clubs. This indicates that millions of women will continue to make their clothes at home.

It is estimated that the average person spends about 10 to 20 percent of his or her income on clothing. Therefore, good planning and budgeting are generally necessary. So, whatever you make or buy, it is wise to have a plan and stick to it. Ingenious girls and women can often make older garments in their wardrobe look new by adding accessory touches. These accessories can be made at home more easily than garments. Collars, cuffs, kerchiefs, belts, appliqués, and other detail can be added to last season's dress to update it.

STATISTICS ON THE HOME-SEWING INDUSTRY

Number of women who sew	44 million
Number of garments made at home	300 million
Fabrics sold, in retail dollars	$2.5 billion
Notions, findings, buttons, zippers, trimmings, in retail dollars	$400 million
Patterns sold	
Dollars	$150 million
Units	200 million

Source: *Simplicity Annual Report 1974.* Courtesy of Simplicity Pattern Company.

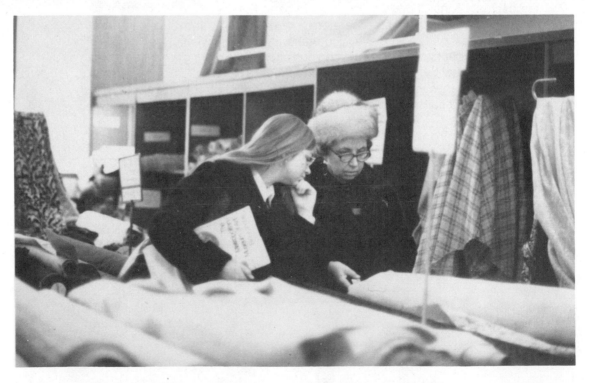

HERE ARE SOME OF TODAY'S MEASURING AIDS

1. *Hem Gauge.* Made of special light-weight metal, for quick, easy, and accurate hems and turned edges. All necessary measurements for straight and curved hems are marked on both sides of the gauge, which can be used to mark a hem from ¼" to 4" on a straight edge and from ¼" to 2½" on a curved edge.

2. *Sewing Gauge.* 6" long, slotted down the vertical center. A smooth-moving nylon slide can be set for quick, accurate, repetitive measurements, whether you're marking pleats, tucks, a hem, or the space between buttonholes.

3. *Dressmaker's Ruler.* Of transparent plastic, with 6 parallel slots for precision markings from ¼" to 1" wide. One edge of the ruler is calibrated in inches and eighths thereof, the opposite is in yard fractions from ⅛ to ⅜. A great help in marking chalk or pencil lines for many sewing purposes. 15" long.

4. *Dressmaker's Gauge.* 6" long, for accuracy in marking and measuring important sewing details. Clear plastic. Scalloped edge marks scallops from ½" to 2" wide. Perforations every ½" along the center are to mark placement of braid, trimmings, buttons, buttonholes.

5. *Dressmaker Guide.* Of aluminum, 6" long, printed on both sides, and deeply notched at each inch mark. It has different scallop gauges ranging from ½" to 2", and variously shaped holes that act as stencils for marking embroidery details such as dots, arrows, crescents, squares.

6. *Skirt Marker.* To let you mark your own hem. The lever clamps to the fabric at each marking position on the hem. A pin is inserted though a slot in the lever. Other skirt markers use chalk. Heavy base holds ruler measuring from 2" to 30" off the floor. Small bottle holds powdered chalk. Set the marker at the desired height, squeeze the bulb, and air in the tube puffs chalk onto the fabric.

7. *T-Square.* Of clear plastic, 9" × 4", with marking holes in the center of each vertical inch. Marks true right angles, measures two areas at once, squares off straight edges. Use the crosswise rule to measure length of buttonholes and vertical rule for positioning accurately.

8. *Right-Angle Ruler.* Of light-weight metal, 12" × 6", has inch and inch-fraction subdivisions on the long edge, center-point marking on shorter surface, with inch and inch-fraction calibrations on either side of it. Especially useful for marking centers of fabric areas.

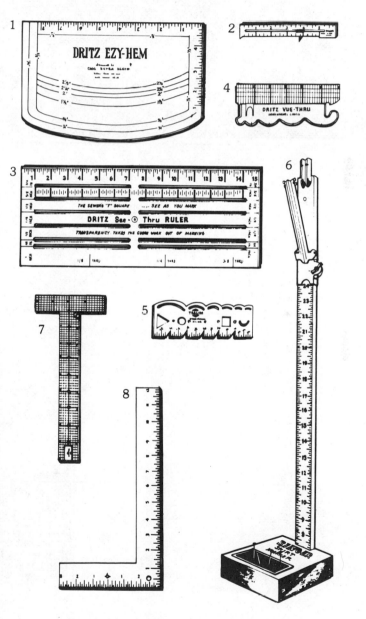

Many of the leading department stores got their start by dealing in fabrics. Most of the great stores of today that are more than 70 to 80 years old had huge main floor departments with hundreds of bolts of fabrics on display. Their customers could choose from huge assortments of textiles, many of which were imported from England, France, and other countries. After the turn of the century, fine silks from the Orient were added to the foreign and domestic selections.

Today the piece goods department in most stores all over the world is still one of the most important in the store.

As we move into the age of technology, methods of sewing at home, easy-to-use patterns, and precut, planned garments packaged with all the findings, will make it easier to sew at home. All indications point to a growing interest in home-made fashions. For the foreseeable future, this sector of the fashion business will maintain its share of the total apparel market.

4587

4633

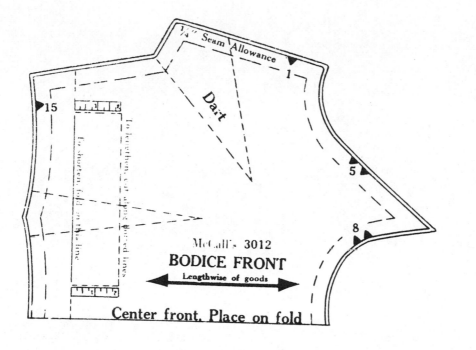

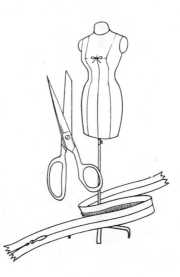

CONCLUSION

Home sewing will continue to grow because it is *creative*. Individuals can make clothes exactly the way they want them, to fit their exact tastes and moods. In addition to the self-expression possible, apparel made at home can be distinctive and often considerably less expensive than the same type of garment purchased in a retail store. Furthermore, the same creativity can be carried out in home furnishings. It all adds up to continued and growing interest in home sewing.

REVIEW QUESTIONS AND DISCUSSION

1. Before the introduction of ready-to-wear, why was the making of apparel solely a "home art"?
2. Keeping in mind the availability of ready-to-wear clothes, list some reasons why today's woman still would choose home sewing.
3. Which is the largest pattern company, in terms of volume?
4. What are two names given to the retail department that sells fabrics?

14

FASHION AND CHANGE

CHANGING IMAGES, CHANGING CONSUMER TASTES

Tyrone Power

Dustin Hoffman

More
Realism!

More Like
Average
People!

Jean Harlow

Barbra Streisand

Clark Gable

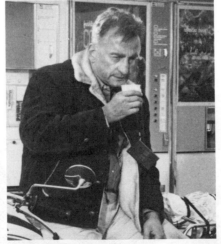

George C. Scott

More Typical
Situations!

Change is inherent in the concept of fashion. Each season fashion is *expected* to change to fit the new ideas that seem to be "in the air." Apparel is the constant creation of artificial obsolescence—fashions must not be *worn out,* they must be *discarded* as obsolete.

The relationship between fashion and change has long been recognized. Shakespeare commented on artificial obsolescence in *As You Like It* by saying, "The fashion wears out more apparel than the man."

In his famous book *The Theory of the Leisure Class,* Thorstein Veblen sets forth the idea of fashion changes as "conspicuous waste." In a chapter entitled "Dress as an Expression of the Pecuniary Culture," he says:

> It is also true that admitted expenditure for display is more obviously present, and is perhaps, more universally practised in the matter of dress than in any other line of consumption . . . Dress must not only be conspicuously expensive and inconvenient, it must at the same time be up-to-date. No explanation at all satisfactory has hitherto been offered of the phenomenon of changing fashions.

It is understandable that the question of changing fashions has puzzled social commentators through the ages.

Why is change an integral part of fashion? In one sense, it is simple—when a man or woman buys a new article of apparel, why duplicate an old garment? So, starting from the premise that people want something new when they buy apparel, fashion becomes a symbol for change.

On the other hand, changing fashion is extremely complex, reflecting changes in the society as a whole. Many economic, social, and psychological factors create the climate for fashion change.

Changes in the fashion world fall into three categories—trends, cycles, and fads. *Trends* are usually gradual and one-directional. The word trend is most often used in the long term or long range sense of fashion. An example of a major trend is the elimination of corsets and more complex underpinnings—garters, girdles, and slips—in favor of more natural, less restricting undergarments.

Crisp as lettuce
green-and-white dotted
rayon chiffon dress, $35.
Straw bowler, $20.
All, Bonwit Teller

Engaging pink Valentines
on turquoise rayon crêpe.
Two-piece dress, $35. Hat, $20.
Hattie Carnegie,
Jeune Fille Salon

Pretty pink carnations
on a black dress of
Crown-Tested rayon crêpe, $40.
Milan hat, $23.
All, Saks-Fifth Avenue

J. may 15, 1942

Bamboo stalks on a
black-and-white
linen-like rayon
for this two-piece dress, $50.
Hat, $19. All, Bergdorf Goodman

Coming June 1
101 Ideas for a healthy,
well-spent summer

Although this trend may not seem so significant to many people, it coincides with women's demands for more freedom and less restrictions in their lives. This is a good example of how changes in society are reflected in fashion.

A *cycle* is generally described in the fashion business as a repetitive or recurring sequence of events, lasting a few seasons or perhaps even a few years. For example, hemlines follow a cycle—they are raised for a number of years, then lowered, and later raised again. Another example of a cycle is the recurrence of a "look" from a different era—the 1930s look, or the look of the 1940s or even the 1950s.

While trends and cycles are either long-lasting or recurring, a *fad* is a quick burgeoning of any particular interest and then its quick demise. Put another way, a fashion fad is a very short-lived trend that suddenly appears on the scene and just as suddenly disappears. Hot pants, T-shirts with particular themes, and the "string" bikini are recent fads in the fashion field. Fads, of course, also appear in hobbies, games, sports, and entertainment.

Who is responsible for fashion changes? Again, the answer is complex. There are at least three interacting groups involved in fashion changes—the "select few," or those few people who create new fashions; the manufacturers, buyers, retailers, and others involved in the business of selling to consumers; and ultimately, consumers themselves, who can make or break a new fashion by their willingness or refusal to buy. Let's briefly discuss each group.

THE SELECT FEW

The author spent numerous days over a six month period researching the answer to the question: Who decides what *is* fashion and what is *not*? If there are such people, who are they and how do they decide and then make the decision stick?

For many years (1900 to 1960) it was generally conceded that a handful of great designers in Paris had more to say about what people wore than anyone else in the world. Their influence dominated fashion thinking and fashion trends from top to bottom.

242

THE FASHION DECISION MAKERS

PLACE	MEN	WOMEN	TOTAL
Paris	9	3	12
London	5	2	7
Italy	2	2	4
New York	50	40	90
Chicago	12	8	20
Texas	2	2	4
California	6	2	8
Oregon	4	2	6
North Carolina	2	—	2
Florida	3	1	4
Total	95	62	157

In the 1970s and going into the 1980s all that is changed. Paris no longer dominates the fashion world. The author's research indicates that a relatively small group of people meeting over cocktails and luncheon tables, mostly in New York, make crucial decisions concerning fabrics, colors, and fashion trends.

It may seem strange that perhaps about 150 persons decide what millions of men and women will wear and how they will furnish their homes. True, three to four hundred more persons help the "decision makers," but relatively few actually decide matters that involve billions of dollars in fibers, fabrics, and apparel.

Of course, these decisions made by a few people do not determine the whole fashion story. The main problem with this secretive process is that these influential few cannot always predict what will sell. The fashion business, like any other, is set up to make a profit. A fashion firm must operate as any other profit-making company with plans, budgets, and projections for the coming seasons. Those in the business must attempt to meet consumer demands by staying on top of the various styles that people are following in any given season.

The majority of the decisions are made over cocktails and lunch in New York. Similar meetings in Paris, London, Los Angeles, Chicago, Rome, or Florence pretty much take care of the remaining decisions. Chicago and High Point, North Carolina, are involved in home-furnishing decisions, and Chicago is involved in men's apparel decisions.

Let's drop in on a number of "typical" lunches and find out what happens.

LUNCHEON #1
Location: New York City, Orsini's, October.
Cast: Editor, women's fashion magazine; key fashion executive in major retail organization.
Conclusion: At end of lunch, the fashion editor has found out the direction the powerful retail organization is moving with respect to a fashion trend for spring of the following year. The magazine editor assures retail executive that the magazine "will be on the bandwagon in the same direction."

LUNCHEON #2
Location: New York City, Grenouille, November.
Cast: Key executive of major apparel firm; editor of fashion magazine.
Conclusion: At conclusion of lunch, apparel executive and editor agree on position their respective firms will take on important fashion trends.

LUNCHEON #3
Location: Paris, Maxim's, April (where they can watch passersby).
Cast: Famous couture designer; owner of textile firm; designer for textile firm.
Conclusion: When leisurely lunch is over, the three walk to a secluded bench in the Bois. There the textile executive and designer show swatches of fabric to couturier that they developed from idea they saw on a Ukrainian peasant during a recent trip to the Soviet Union. The couturier "flips." It will be a featured fabric in the fall line.

LUNCHEON #4
Location: New York, Four Seasons, January.
Cast: Key executive of major textile firm; top executive of major apparel manufacturing company.
Conclusion: As they leave the table, direction that textile firm will take as supplier of major apparel company is pretty well decided.

LUNCHEON #5
Location: Chicago, Wrigley's Restaurant, December.
Cast: Vice president of leading men's apparel firm; fashion editor of leading men's magazine; president of major textile company, important supplier to clothing firm.
Conclusion: As the three walk out of the restaurant, the "ball game" is decided. Each of the three organizations will reinforce the others on their positions on fabrics, looks, and trends for fall of the following year.

LUNCHEON #6
Location: New York, Private Dining Room of Leading Apparel Manufacturer, October.
Cast: President of apparel firm; editor of leading fashion magazine; vice president of important textile firm, supplier to apparel firm; top designer for apparel firm.
Conclusion: After they compliment the host on the superb lunch, everyone agrees on the important fabrics, colors, and fashion looks for the coming spring season. Each commits his or

her organization to support the others on these points. *Note:* Women will read the magazine and learn the fashion trends which will just happen to have featured the fabrics and trends discussed at this luncheon.

LUNCHEON #7

Location: Hollywood, California, Brown Derby, June.

Cast: Chief designer for major film which is set in the 1930s; West Coast editor of leading East Coast trade paper.

Conclusion: As they powder their noses in the ladies room after a chatty two-and-a-half-hour lunch, it is agreed the designer will send over sketches of the costumes to be worn by stars of film which will be prominently featured in trade paper along with article explaining importance of the 1930s look on the current fashion scene. Article will also have current pictures of stars and gossip of the forthcoming film.

LUNCHEON #8

Location: Chicago, McCormick Place Restaurant, June.

Cast: Vice president of major home-furnishings manufacturing company; executive of leading fiber firm; executive of leading textile firm.

Conclusion: As they walk toward the exhibits in the convention hall, it is agreed that the home-furnishings firm will manufacture products using the textile firm's fabric which will feature the fiber of the leading fiber firm.

LUNCHEON #9

Location: New York, Private Dining Room in Textile Firm, September.

Cast: Vice president of textile firm; key executive of major fiber firm; president of major apparel manufacturing company; vice president of major retailing organization.

Conclusion: As the napkins are placed on the table after a superb five-course lunch, it is "understood" that the fiber firm will give advertising support for a program featuring its fibers in the fabrics which the fabric firm will produce, the apparel manufacturer will make, and the retail store will feature prominently in its own advertising and windows, for spring of the following year.

Multiply these lunches by twenty or thirty, slightly varying the casts and locations, and it becomes clear how many important decisions are made and reinforced. Manufacturers of garments and home furnishings can only make products from textiles that are available, containing certain fibers. Trade and consumer publications are important because they "predict" trends. However, they can only predict trends of merchandise that will actually be manufactured, as it antagonizes everyone to read about merchandise that never comes on the market. Consumer publications must report what is available in the stores so they must consult manufacturers and retailers before they can write their articles.

Where did the ideas come from that were discussed at the luncheons? From everywhere—Ukrainian peasants, movies about the 1920s and 1930s, the theater, Moroccan bazaars, ski resorts, famous personalities, important dates such as a bicentennial, new books, presidents' wives, television—the list is endless. The textile executive bought a dancer's skirt in Spain, and it is turning into a great fabric. The president of an apparel firm bought a caftan in an Algerian bazaar that is the basis for a new fashion in his forthcoming line. The editors see some of these ideas at the lunches and say it looks "divine," and soon it appears in the trade and consumer publications.

PANDORA GOES PERUVIAN IN ORLON.

Pandora®

The Serape in all its Peruvian-patterned brilliance. Sleeveless and side-tied over a turtletop the color of denim.
Keeping them both in enviable shape: easy-care Orlon® acrylic that's beautifully machine-wash-and-dryable.

The Serape, about $16. Long-sleeved turtle, about $13. In junior sizes.
For your Pandora store, write to Pandora Industries, Inc., 1407 Broadway, New York, N.Y. 10018.

*Du Pont registered trademark.

DU PONT
Orlon®
ACRYLIC

MANUFACTURERS, RETAILERS, AND OTHERS

The best that can be done to find out what people may want is to set certain common denominators each season. This is generally done in New York by a consensus of opinion. The fabric designers discuss trends with the fiber manufacturers, and both speak with fashion magazine editors who report from Paris, London, Rome, and other fashion centers. The leading trendsetting fashion manufacturers discuss with all of these people their ideas for the coming season.

Finally the buyers of the major stores "vote," with their purchases, what their customers will buy. These people are motivated by what has happened in recent seasons. However, each particular institution—fiber manufacturers, textile manufacturers, fashion magazines, trade publications, and ready-to-wear manufacturers and retailers—has its particular image and point of view, depending upon the segment of the market that it is trying to reach.

For example, one magazine may direct its publication to young girls, while another aims for the more mature woman. One textile manufacturer may make knit fabrics that are appropriate for certain apparel, while another makes flat woven goods for a different market. Retail establishments such as Bergdorf Goodman in New York, Nieman Marcus in Dallas, or I. Magnin in California may direct their attention to the affluent, high-fashion customer. Other stores, such as Macy's in New York, Filene's in Boston, Weiboldts in Chicago, or Gimbels in Philadelphia may direct their appeal to the middle-income and career woman.

The pattern of change is planned months and even a year in advance and usually on at least a twice a year basis—spring and fall. In recent years many large apparel firms have adopted a system of constantly adding to their lines between these major seasons, while others develop transitional lines between seasons. Successful manufacturers must be aware of changing consumer demands. As an example, let us take a manufacturer of women's dresses. A few years ago he was making garments from wool and polyester, woven cloth. In the space of a year or two, customers' tastes changed. They wanted knit fabrics. This entirely changed his pattern of doing business because knit fabrics are made in different mills and must be worked differently from flat woven goods.

EVERYONE IS WEARING THEM!

Amos Parrish, one of America's greatest fashion merchandising-marketing authorities, whose fashion clinics in the 1940s and 1950s were attended by most leading retailers, has a simple theory of fashion. He observed that fashion leaders often used the expression "Everyone is wearing them."

His idea was *count them*! Send out a number of reporters and have them go to different locations and actually count the number of mini skirts, maxi skirts, knickers, hot pants, bell-bottom trousers, peasant looks, or any other fashions that "everyone is wearing." He observes that often the big surprise is the small percentage of women who are wearing what everyone is supposed to be wearing. Perhaps fashion authorities should take Mr. Parrish's advice and do more counting.

An alert manufacturer, aware of the changing market, may jump in with a new look or idea and achieve success. Older firms, doing what they did the year before, may have declining sales or even go out of business.

Thus fashion is change and change creates major challenges to manufacturers. What particular manufacturers did right last year could be wrong this year.

This brings us to the consumer's role in fashion changes. The consumer is the recipient of new products or styles; therefore the success or failure of any new fashion must ultimately rest with customers. If they will not buy a particular fashion, it is a failure, no matter how ingeniously conceived, created, and promoted.

FASHION SUCCESSES AND FAILURES

There is no *one* reason for fashion successes or failures. Let's examine a few of each and analyze, if we can, what was behind them.

Some years ago Paris came out with the "shift dress." It was a simple concept, an "A" line with no belt or narrowing at the waist. Everyone in the fashion business was convinced this was the new look. Thousands and thousands of these garments were made. For the most part they remained on the racks in the stores. The American woman was not ready for the "new look."

A number of smaller, ready-to-wear stores and some dress manufacturers failed because of this disastrous season. A few seasons later, the same concept was reintroduced and ultimately became one of the basic new looks and a best seller.

This particular failure was one of timing. The fashion concept was sound; however, it was too sharp a break from the past. The American woman was not conditioned for this completely new idea. As it gradually was introduced, she accepted the look.

Now let's take a case from the men's field—the Nehru suit. A few men's suit manufacturers thought that a completely new look might be accepted. Instead of lapels, a high collar that buttoned to the neck would be used. Taking its name from the Indian prime minister who always wore this style, it would be popular and perhaps replace the old lapeled suit.

Many manufacturers and retail stores liked the idea, and it then became band-wagon psychology; thousands of Nehru suits were made. The stores were loaded with them. The customers began buying them. Then suddenly the customer lost interest just as manufacturers were producing still more and more. It was a fad that had burned itself out in a short time. As a result, thousands of Nehru suits were marked down and some perhaps shipped to India where they could be sold if priced reasonably. The Nehru suit disappeared almost as quickly as it appeared.

Why this failure? Apparently the idea was good in the sense of a variation of a new look. It came in a spring season but was not cool or comfortable for summer because of its high, buttoned collar. It could not be worn over the shirts men had in their drawers at home. It needed a turtleneck shirt or light sweater. Men were not about to discard a whole wardrobe of shirts and wear a hot, restricting style for summer. All these things together created a fashion failure.

Let's take another case—the maxi look. Again it was Paris that introduced the longer look for women's fashions. It was first shown in the fall of 1967, which made it too late to be introduced in America for that season. It appeared in the spring of 1968 and was an indifferent success; a limited number of maxi styles were sold. A long coat or dress that would be uncomfortable in the spring or summer did not make much sense.

By the fall of 1968 raincoat manufacturers decided it did make sense for them; it protected the wearer from head to toe. Also, coat manufacturers decided that if a coat was to keep you warm, the maxi was a great idea. The maxi began to catch on, representing a fair percentage of coat and raincoat sales, particularly to the young markets. Then function and practicality began to work. The millions of women living in cities found them clumsy for getting on and off buses, or going up and down stairs. There might be a few die-hards who continued to wear a maxi, but the maxi was dead. It was dramatic, it was different, but it didn't work for the long run. It got dirty and ragged at the bottom and was difficult to wear.

These examples give you some idea of the potential power that consumers have in determining what is, or is not, fashion.

CONSUMER INFLUENCE

As with most other phases of the market place, buying patterns of the consumer have changed considerably in recent years. These changing habits have affected all categories of merchandise, but particularly food and clothing.

Before the late 1960s and 1970s, fashion in the western countries moved according to definite patterns of styles, colors, and looks. Fashion writers, pattern companies, and fashion trade publications could all point out and follow definite trends. It was "the full skirt," "the shorter look," "the chemise look," "the new long look," "the Chanel look," "the vamp look," "the return to the 1930s," or "the Dior look," among others. An individual man or woman who was popular and well publicized could set a fashion image that millions would follow. Famous motion pictures, television shows, and their stars could touch off trends in apparel or home furnishings.

In the past both the consumer and the retail stores had definite categories of merchandise in mind—sportswear, dresses, lingerie, coats, or accessories. Such merchandise was purchased mainly in department stores from specific departments labeled "Misses Sportswear," "Junior Coats," "Women's Dresses," "Intimate Apparel," "Bridal Department," and other designations.

As with women's apparel, men's and children's patterns of manufacturing and retailing followed similar patterns of nomenclature and selling. Stores pushed "Elvis Presley looks," "Western looks," "007 looks," and similar apparel concepts from current heroes, real and fictional. Millions of older men wore business suits. Casual clothes were worn mostly for weekends and informal occasions. All this is changing in the 1970s, which might well be called "the age of the consumer."

Consumers have become much more individualistic in their tastes and expect more from manufacturers and retail stores. Changes in consumer attitudes and life styles have changed the entire pattern of marketing, and there is new respect for consumers and their needs. In the 1950s and 1960s particularly, manufacturers produced and stores sold pretty much what they pleased and the public bought, without too much questioning, what they produced and advertised. In the late 1950s a man named Ernest Dichter worked out research theories concerning the consumer called "motivation research." These theories analyzed what motivated the consumer when he or she made a purchase. Packaging, label color, container shape, and all related matters were carefully examined to determine what made the consumer buy product A instead of product B, if they were directly competitive. Dichter was primarily a consultant to manufacturers who wanted to outdistance their competitors. The idea behind this concept was to attract and tempt the buying public, not necessarily to give more satisfaction to the consumer.

250

GIMBELS

the look is you!

the now
pioneers
blaze new
fashion trails
...a mix of
patchwork,
smocking, fringe,
with a
western accent

prairie shirt + vest + rodeo midi
Brown mini-plaided shirt of Fortrel® polyester/cotton by Lady Arrow. 8-16 . . $11
Buckskin vest, long, long fringe; by Rose Leather. Chocolate, rust, cocoa. S, M, L $17
Buckskin A-Line midi zipped up with a shiny brass ring. By Rose Leather. Cocoa, rust, in sizes 5-13 . . $26

smocked shirt + vest + gaucho pants
smocked country girl blouse in Kodel® polyester/cotton. Red or brown. 8-16. By Lady Arrow $11
Suede vest lit with rings of brass. Rust. One size fits all $28
Suede gaucho pants for fashionable cowgirls. Rust, chocolate, navy. By Rose Leather. Sizes 5-13 . . $38

patchwork shirt + laced front pants
Patches get together on a multi-color cotton shirt. Sizes 8, 10, 12 . . . . $24
Suede pants with front crisscross tie closing. Brown or buck. 8-14 . . . . . $60

add:
gaucho belt
Contour shaped suede with brass studs and fringed ties by Miss Dior. Black, dark brown, cranberry, navy, rust, gold. One size . . $16
felt cowboy hat
Deep crown, broad brim, trimmed in leather polished off with a brass buckle. White, black, beige, brown, rust, red, navy, forest green. By Betmar $11

Leather and Suede,
Jr. Sportswear
Place on
3rd floor,
Gimbels, N.Y.;
also at
all suburban stores.
Better Blouses,
3rd floor.
Belts, street floor.
Millinery,
4th floor,
Gimbels, N.Y.;
also
at Westchester, Paramus,
Valley Stream and Roosevelt Field;
Belt,
also at Bridgeport.

smocked shirt + vest + gaucho pants

prairie shirt + vest + rodeo midi

patchwork shirt + laced front pants

new fashion frontiers...pulled-together prairie looks

Who was concerned with consumers and their needs? Not many, aside from Better Business Bureaus and these had a good many limitations. These bureaus were sponsored and supported by retail stores and their main target was unethical competition.

A few manufacturers and retail stores seemed to be genuinely concerned about the consumer and maintained high standards and quality controls through the years. On the whole, however, the attitude seemed to be to satisfy the consumer only in superficial ways, and artificial obsolescence was taken for granted.

CONSUMERISM

Then in the late 1960s along came a man who had more to do with what we call "consumerism" than any other individual in history—Ralph Nader. He questioned everything about what was produced and offered to the public. He began with the most important and expensive item purchased by millions of consumers—the automobile. He took on America's biggest corporate giant, General Motors, singlehandedly. He indicated that many cars produced by all the auto companies were "unsafe at any speed." General Motors attempted to intimidate him by having him privately investigated. He discovered that this was being done, sued General Motors, and won over $300,000 in damages. Since that time many of the automobile firms have recalled particular models from time to time, for "adjustments and modifications" at no cost to the consumer.

Now in the 1970s and looking toward the 1980s we are entering a period in which city, state, and federal governments are expected to aid and protect the consumer by enacting laws that will set minimum standards and insure that the customer gets a fair shake. Misrepresentation, false advertising, and improper labeling will be punished much more severely than in the past. Labeling laws are becoming much more stringent. Textile labeling laws now require that garment labels include exact fiber content and basic care information. Labels now read "65% polyester 35% cotton" or "50% acrylic, 50% nylon." In addition, labels must be sewn in the garment. This is important, because once the attached paper tag is thrown away, the consumer has no way of remembering just what was purchased.

New laws requiring flame-retardant fabrics for children's sleepwear were recently passed. Eventually this concept may be expanded to include all children's apparel. This and other moves in the direction of consumer protection indicate a more conscious attitude by government agencies of the need for such laws. The growing use of synthetic fibers has made the whole area of textiles very confusing to the consumer.

There is a great deal of confusion about the generic names of fibers and the brand names of leading synthetic fibers. For example, du Pont's "Dacron," Eastman's "Kodel," American Enka's "Encron," Hystron's "Trevira," and Phillips' "Quintess" are all *polyester* fibers. Monsanto's "Acrilan," du Pont's "Orlon," and Dow-Badische's "Zefran" are all *acrylic* fibers.

And there are hundreds of other trade names for nylons, acetates, rayons, and other synthetic fibers and blends. Eventually, labeling laws will probably insist on simplifying this type of information so the consumer will be able to differentiate between trade and generic names.

THE "NEW" CONSUMER

The consumer is constantly becoming more discriminating. There is less susceptibility to the influence of mass media and more individuality. Patterns are not being followed as in the past; consumers are "doing their own thing." This is as it should be. When it comes to apparel, each individual should wear what is becoming to him or her rather than what is supposed to be "the latest thing."

Consumerism of the 1960s and 1970s has produced the following:

1. Demand for the satisfaction of individualized tastes and needs particularly suited to personal life style
2. Demand for better quality and durability
3. Greater interest in classic styles and reduction of artificial obsolescence
4. Demand for better labeling and information for the consumer
5. More honest advertising and elimination of exaggeration and false claims
6. Demand for new consumer protection laws
7. Trends toward putting consumer representatives on the boards of leading manufacturers and retailers

All this adds up to trouble for the retailers and manufacturers who continue to ignore the fair demands of the consumer. There have already been a number of "class action" suits against some manufacturers and retailers. This means that a group can sue a manufacturer or retailer who has misled and deceived the consumer. All those who bought such a product can recover damages from the retailer and/or the manufacturer. Millions of dollars have been returned to consumers on the basis of such suits. No longer will the phrase *caveat emptor* ("let the buyer beware") be the theme of the market place. In the next few years it may well become "let the *seller* beware."

Products must be properly labeled, and they must meet all legal requirements. While mass production is still the basis of our technologically oriented society, more variety and individualization of products will be the order of the future. The customer will express his or her individuality and will not wish to look like hundreds of others. The present and future generations will want to express themselves in distinctive styles of dress and furnish their homes according to their specialized tastes and ideas.

It has been interesting to note, that since retailers often ignored the ideas of young people, youth began making beaded items, jewelry, belts, flowers, blouses, macrame items, and other merchandise and sold these wares on the streets, often outside some of America's greatest department stores!

MARKET RESEARCH

In many consumer markets—foods, drugs, soaps, detergents—a great amount of market research is done before a product is brought out and advertised on a large scale. However, in the apparel field to date very little research has been and is being done. There seems to be a critical need for data in this area.

A company that plans to come out with a new detergent first has marketing people prepare questionnaires to be filled out by the consumer about likes and dislikes, needs and comments on existing products. When the thrust of the answers is apparent, the new product is developed to meet these requirements. It is then tried in a test market, and only if it proves itself is it produced in large quantity and widely advertised.

In the fashion field there are many reports of what is currently selling but little or no research in projecting *future trends*. Such firms as RAM and Neustadt furnish reports to retailers and manufacturers about what are best sellers in the various sectors of the apparel market. While this informs retailers and manufacturers about current sales, it does very little to indicate what the consumer will want next season.

In the future through research perhaps the consumer may decide just what is fashionable for wear and the home, and the fashion trade press will report the consumer decision rather than tell the consumer what the manufacturers say is the latest style.

The customer will demand that the right fiber and fabric be used in the end product and that the manufactured product be made properly. A good fabric can be used poorly and made into poor garments and home-furnishing items.

Each step toward the finished product must be checked. The fiber must be good and appropriate for the fabric for which it is used; the fabric must be woven properly to give it maximum durability and end use adaptability. The garment or finished item must be put together for wear, durability, and easy care. When this entire chain is properly completed, then and then only has the consumer been delivered a good product. If each party to the transaction holds the previous party responsible, it will form a chain of responsibility that cannot be broken.

In this way, everyone is protected and the consumer will get a good end product. If each step along the way sets standards of quality and maintains them, there will be accountability and responsibility—each firm stands behind its product and guarantees performance.

When the consumer rejects shoddy, poorly made merchandise and it remains unsold, it will automatically punish the retailer and the manufacturer who made it. Discriminating and demanding consumers are the best insurance for better quality and fair prices.

Many manufacturers and retailers will have to reorder their priorities to meet the demands of the contemporary consumer. As travel, motion pictures, television, and mass communication broaden the horizons of the consumers, retailers and manufacturers will have to keep pace. They will have to do more market research in life styles. It will no longer be a matter of selling what you have or can make. Retailers and manufacturers must find out what the consumer wants and deliver it.

The American blue jean or "Levi" is an example. It provided an inexpensive, basic garment that fulfilled a need. It was durable, classic, easily washed, and even got better with wear. As a result, it became a worldwide mode of dress. In the beginning no one pushed it or made it a fashionable thing to wear. Only when young people throughout the world demanded and wore it, did fashion "recognize it."

No longer can the fashion and home-furnishings trade press and consumer magazines dictate what is fashionable and what is not.

While in the world of fashion, style plays an important role and there is a certain amount of inherent obsolescence, quality and durability must be emphasized. There will be fewer slaves to style and more pragmatic consumers who will buy apparel and home furnishings that are durable and perform well. The era of the consumer is at hand—let the retailer and manufacturer beware!

LIFE STYLES

All the changes we have been discussing in this chapter have taken place because of changes in the way we live. The overall trend toward more casual life styles demands more casual dress. We have mentioned life styles briefly. Now let's look at this phenomenon in more detail. What do we mean by life style, and why are life styles such an important determinant of the clothes we wear and the way we furnish our homes?

We have recently become more conscious of the way people live throughout the world—the way they dress, the houses they live in, the food they eat, their beliefs and opinions, and the patterns of their lives. We use the term "life style" to label and describe this aspect of society.

Another term used in connection with the way groups of people live is *sub-culture*. The dictionary defines this term as: "A group (within a society) of persons of the same age, social or economic status, ethnic background, and having its own interests and goals." Such widely diverse groups as hippies, suburbanites, artists, ethnic groups, and college students fall into this category. Each subculture has its own life style and therefore, its own distinct patterns of dressing and home furnishing. To the fashion industry this means that there is always more than one prevailing style.

Until fairly recently, life styles in the western world followed a formal pattern. Dress indicated a person's position in society. Today dress as a status symbol or indication of rank has gradually disappeared. Dress has become much more casual and, in fact, more democratic. For example, in the business world, the "business suit" is a uniform that seldom indicates rank or position. In today's society a senator or top corporate executive can pass unnoticed anywhere unless his or her face is recognized. It is difficult to equate wealth with apparel.

A person's income used to be the major factor in determining life style. However, it has become less important, and in many cases has disappeared as a determinant of how people live. It has been humorously asked, "How do you tell the rich hippies from the poor ones?"

What factors are responsible for the trend toward more casual life styles? There are many reasons, but they probably all have to do with people's growing awareness of themselves and the world around them. Broadening education, increased leisure time, travel, and exposure to the mass media have brought people in contact with the world.

Student rates and charter flights have put travel within the reach of most young people. Once travel abroad was possible only for the well-to-do. Now thousands upon thousands of youngsters of modest means with small packs on their backs are roaming the world. They hike, ride bicycles, sleep in their sleeping bags or hostels as they visit far off cities and historic places from Katmandu to London, from Singapore to Hawaii, from Labrador to the Cape of Good Hope.

Working 49 or 50 weeks a year and taking a short vacation was also a way of life until recently for all except school teachers, students, and retired people. Now, many young people work for a while until they have enough money and then play or travel until their money runs out. Today there is much more freedom of choice for life styles.

Changing life styles affect the way people dress and furnish their homes. Only a few years ago a young man or woman who was planning a trip to Europe took a large wardrobe filling several suitcases and perhaps even a trunk. Today perhaps a pair or two of blue jeans, a few shirts or tops, a bathing suit, a few undergarments, and socks in a back pack along with a sleeping bag are all that may be needed for a summer in Europe or anywhere else. Of course, not everyone likes to travel this way. Many wish to have attractive clothes, particularly when they go out in the evening.

It is up to contemporary creators of apparel and home furnishings to be aware of these new trends and design and plan products to fit new life styles. The days are gone when designers can lump together millions of persons and assume they will all be satisfied with the same type clothing or home furnishings. Statistics show that the better the education, the more variable the tastes and ideas of the individual.

For example, young people constantly on the go may wish to have simply furnished homes as they do not want to spend a great deal of time with cleaning and maintenance. They are no longer interested in emulating their parents' way of dressing or furnishing their homes or, for that matter, their parents' way of life. Their much more casual approach to living has influenced much of the world.

Young people have pushed fashion apparel manufacturers into making garments appropriate to these new life styles. For example, the young American woman pushed the manufacturers into making more pants, not vice versa.

With respect to apparel, American sportswear has created a demand throughout the world, which indicates that everywhere there is a more casual approach to ways of living. Even in such faraway places as Asia or Africa, the American blue jean and other items of American sportswear come more and more into prominence. A major trend in all apparel seems to be an approach to functionalism. This means that selections are made on the basis of end use. This same concept applies to home furnishings as well. What is the purpose of the item purchased? The contemporary consumer makes a purchase that best fulfills the requirements of function and practicality.

Leading business schools in the field of marketing soon may have classes in life styles. Manufacturers and retailers will have to do their homework and research to discover what the new directions of apparel and home furnishings will take. The past will be an unreliable source of information for indications of new trends and markets.

Each person can and will fashion a personal life style to suit his or her particular tastes. Such life styles in the aggregate will determine what we put on our bodies and in our homes. Life styles must be thought of in their *totality*. The way we live and dress is part of a pattern that must make sense in its *entirety*. In the future, work, leisure, travel, and homemaking may not be such segmented and isolated entities. They may run together and form new patterns of life styles unknown today. We will think of life styles as part of an integrated pattern in which all aspects come together—our way of dressing, furnishing our homes, working, and spending our leisure time.

CONCLUSION

New life styles and practicality demand creative thinking. We must free our minds from the yesterdays and think of the tomorrows. The future will call for greater flexibility, quality, comfort, and classic durability. Millions will be seeking and finding new and satisfactory life styles, each perhaps needing completely different combinations of apparel, home furnishings, and accessories for both.

In the apparel business particularly, there has been predominantly short-range thinking—almost from day to day, month to month, season to season. This will have to change.

Life styles of the future offer exciting possibilities for creative minds in retailing and manufacturing of apparel and home furnishings. When all the new possibilities of life styles are considered, they are virtually endless. Catering to all these people with their individual tastes and ways of life offers challenges undreamed of today.

1. Define *trend, cycle,* and *fad,* and give examples of each.
2. Where do new ideas for fashions come from?
3. Name three groups of people who make fashion changes, and tell how each group is responsible for change.
4. How does consumerism affect the fashion industry?
5. If you were a designer, what factors would you take into consideration in planning a new fashion look?
6. What is meant by *life style*? What does this term have to do with fashion?
7. Why do some fashions succeed and others fail?

15

FASHION CAREERS

"In Shakespeare's time, 'The play's the thing.'
In our time, 'The job's the thing.'"

Most students who choose fashion courses in school or attend institutions related to the fashion business expect to find jobs in the fashion world. Like any other profession or occupation, there are hundreds of different jobs in the fashion business. Those who desire jobs in this industry must analyze the particular business and the classification of jobs in their chosen areas of the fashion world. Then the particular skills required for those jobs must be considered. To demonstrate the scope of this field, following is a discussion and listing of some of the jobs available in fashion.

MANUFACTURING

Manufacturing firms are divided into major categories according to the products they manufacture. Included under this heading are the manufacturers of women's, men's, and children's wear, as well as home furnishings. When you consider all the different types and sizes of apparel and home furnishings, you can begin to realize what a large field this encompasses. Apparel manufacturers in all categories need:

1. Sales personnel
2. Showroom personnel
3. Administrative personnel
4. Designers and patternmakers
5. Stylists
6. Models
7. Samplehands

Home-furnishings jobs include:

1. Colorists
2. Designers
3. Decorators and coordinators
4. Sales, showroom, and administrative personnel

RETAILING

There are numerous categories of retailing (See Chapter 11). Retailing jobs for fashion-trained personnel include:

1. Sales clerks
2. Buyers and assistant buyers
3. Merchandise managers
4. Copywriters
5. Artists
6. Advertising production personnel
7. Display personnel
8. Sales promotion personnel
9. Administrative personnel
10. Fashion stylists, coordinators
11. Publicity people
12. Models

HOW THE MAGIC "YOU" AND OTHER PERSONAL PRONOUNS MADE SHIRLEY POLYKOFF RICH

The copywriter who wrote "Does she . . . or doesn't she" is rich and a legend in her own time. All because she knows how to make personal pronouns more personal than anybody—but anybody. Her first job at furrier I. J. Fox paid her $85 per week. At Bamberger's she did better. But she struck it rich at Foote, Cone & Belding, Clairol's agency. Her salary jumped from $25,000 to $50,000 and skyrocketed to $100,000.

"She Reached Into Her Own Life to create headlines (and copy) that had emotional truth. Her secrets were every woman's secrets." Because she approached the woman "as an informed consumer and as an intelligent, interest-ing human being," she helped women change their self-image. Here are a few of the headlines that made hair coloring respectable and boosted Clairol's ad budget from $400,000 to $33 million a year:

"To know *you're* the best *you* can be."

"The closer he gets the better *you* look."

"How long has it been since *your* husband brought *you* flowers?"

"What would *your* husband do if suddenly *you* looked 10 years younger?"

"If *I've* only one life, let *me* live it as a blonde." (Rollo May called this "the ultimate existential statement.")

Source: Quoted from Shirley Polykoff, *Does She . . . or Doesn't She? And How She Did It* (New York: Doubleday, 1975), in *Hear, There & Everywhere,* No. 96 (September 1975), a newsletter for retail executives. Courtesy of Harrison Services, Inc.

ADVERTISING AND PUBLICITY

As discussed in Chapter 12, many advertising agencies and public relations firms handle fashion accounts. Following are some of the jobs available in this field:

1. Writers
2. Artists
3. Photographers
4. Models
5. Advertising production personnel
6. Advertising and publicity liaison personnel

PUBLICATIONS CAREERS

Under the heading of publications fall the various media discussed in Chapter 12—fashion consumer publications, trade publications, newspapers, and newspaper magazine supplements. Some of the jobs available in this category are:

1. Writers and editors
2. Artists
3. Photographers
4. Production personnel
5. Promotion personnel
6. Advertising salespersons

PIONEER GIRLS....

WERE NEVER LIKE THIS!

CLEAN AND PRETTY COLORS, SOFT FABRICS,
MIDI LENGTHS, BRING WELCOME NOSTALGIA
AND FEMININITY TO THE SEVENTIES.

INNOCENT VERSIONS FOR THE YOUNG AND
MORE SOPHISTICATED STYLES FOR THE
NOT SO YOUNG.

WINDOW DISPLAYS COULD INCLUDE OLD
WAGON WHEELS, WOODEN BARRELS AND
ONE DIMENSIONAL COVERED WAGONS AND
HORSES MADE OF BROWN PAPER PASTED
TO BURLAP.

PRETTY PROVINCIAL

LOOKS ARE INSPIRED BY THE DRESSES
OF SCANDINAVIAN PEASANTS, GYPSIES
AND PIONEER WOMEN.

COARSE OR HOMESPUN FABRICS ARE
INTENDED FOR COUNTRY WEAR,
VACATIONS AND HER OWN BACK YARD

THE PERFECT ACCESSORY IS A PAIR
OF DUTCH SHOES OR FLAT DANCING
PUMPS.

PROM DRESSES IN THE SAME MOODS
OF ORGANDY OR DOTTED SWISS ARE
A NEW EXPERIENCE FOR JUNIORS.

RESIDENT BUYING OFFICES AND OTHER ORGANIZATIONS

Resident buying offices need buyers and assistant buyers, administrative personnel, fashion coordinators, and fashion reporters. Television and radio programs with women's fashion news offer opportunities for writers, announcers, and production, camera, and stage personnel. Fashion consultant firms have openings for writers, artists, photographers, and administrative personnel. Fashion photography studios need photographers, stylists, and models. Model agencies hire administrative personnel and models.

FASHION JOB DESCRIPTIONS

The following job descriptions come from the *Occupational Outlook Handbook,* 1974–1975 edition, published by the United States Department of Labor, Bureau of Labor Statistics. Most of the jobs described apply to many fields, including fashion.

Practically all manufacturers—whether they make computers or fabrics—employ salesworkers. Manufacturers' salesworkers sell mainly to other businesses—factories, apparel firms, home-furnishing firms, wholesalers, and retailers.

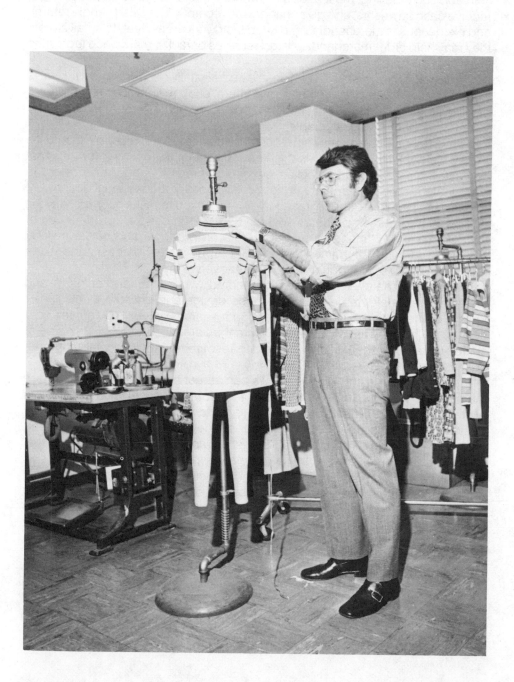

Most manufacturers' salesworkers sell nontechnical products. They must be well informed about their firms' products and also about the special requirements of their customers.

The success of any retail business depends largely on its salesworkers. Courteous and efficient service from behind the counter or on the sales floor does much to satisfy customers and build a store's reputation. Even though contact with customers is a part of all sales jobs, the duties, skills, and responsibilities of salesworkers are as different as the kinds of merchandise they sell.

In selling items such as furniture or clothing, the salesworker's primary job is to create an interest in the merchandise. The salesman or saleswoman may answer questions about the construction of an article, demonstrate its use, and show various styles and colors.

In addition to selling, most retail salesworkers make out sales or charge slips, receive cash payments, and give change and receipts. They also handle returns and exchanges of merchandise and keep their work areas neat. In small stores, they may help order merchandise, stock shelves or racks, mark price tags, take inventory, and prepare displays.

Credit managers in retail and wholesale trade usually cooperate with the sales department in developing credit policies liberal enough to allow the company's sales to increase and yet strict enough to deny credit to customers whose ability to pay their debts is questionable.

A credit manager frequently must contact a customer who is unable or refuses to pay his debt. He or she does this through writing, telephoning, or personal contact. If these attempts at collection fail, the credit manager may refer the account to a collection agency or assign an attorney to take legal action.

Business people require a great deal of information to make sound decisions on how to market their products. Marketing research people provide much of this information by analyzing available data on products and sales, making surveys, and conducting interviews. They prepare sales forecasts and make recommendations on product design and advertising.

Marketing researchers are often concerned with customers' opinions and tastes. For example, to help decide on the design and price of a new line of towels, drapes, and bedspreads marketing research workers may survey consumers to find out what styles and price ranges are most popular. This type of survey usually is supervised by marketing researchers who specialize in consumer goods.

Displays in stores and store windows can attract customers and encourage them to buy. Knowing the effectiveness of this form of advertising, some stores allot a large share of their promotion budget to displays. Display specialists design and install such exhibits. Their goal is to develop attractive, eye-catching ways of showing store merchandise to best advantage. To create a setting that enhances the merchandise, these specialists need imagination as well as knowledge of color harmony, composition, and other fundamentals of art. They may, for example, choose a theme—a beach setting to advertise swimming suits and surfing equipment—and design an eye-catching display around this theme. After the design has been approved by the store's management, display people obtain the props and other accessories needed for the display.

Courses that provide helpful training for display work include art, woodworking, mechanical drawing, and merchandising. Some employers prefer applicants who have completed college courses in art, interior decorating, fashion design, advertising, and related subjects.

A team of commercial artists often creates the artwork in newspapers and magazines and on billboards, brochures, catalogs, and television commercials.

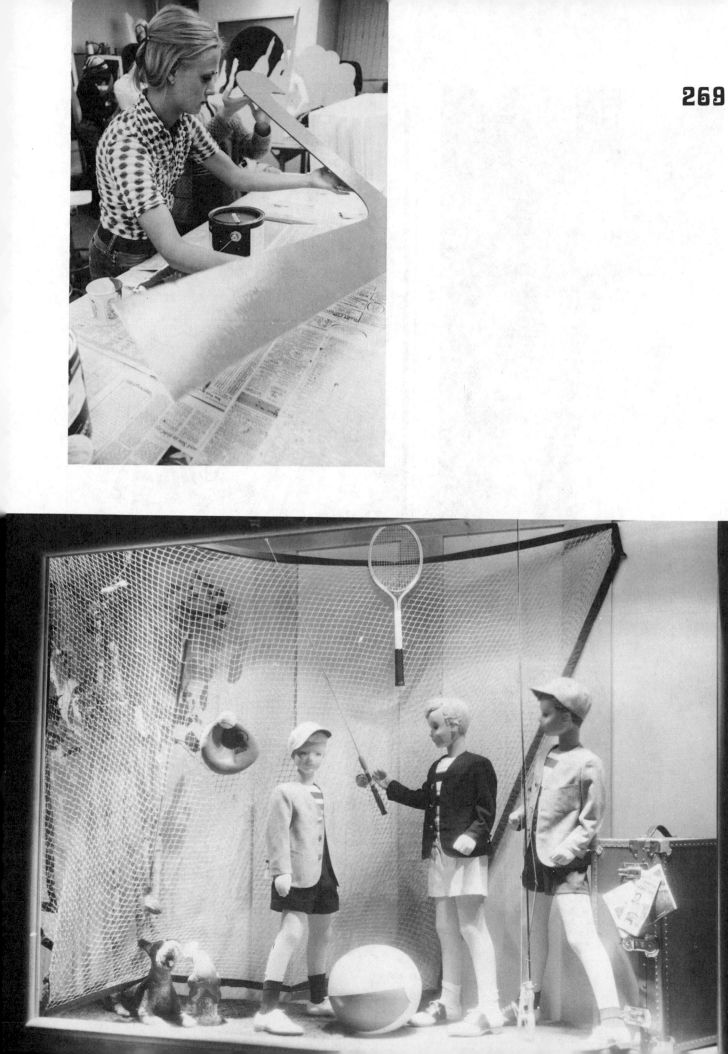

The art director supervises this team of artists with varying skills and specializations. The director develops the artistic aspects of an advertising plan, then turns it over to a layout artist for further refinement. The layout artist constructs or arranges elements of the advertisement. The artist may also select and lay out illustrations and photographs, plan use of typography, and determine color and other elements of design. Then the layout artist prepares a "rough visual" or sketch. After consulting with the director, the layout artist may change the visual and complete a more comprehensive layout for the customer.

In a small office, the art director may perform the layout and boardwork with the aid of apprentices. In a large office, the art director develops concepts with the copywriter; sets standards; deals with clients; and purchases needed photographs, illustrations, lettering, and other art work from staff or freelancers.

Advertising artists create the concept and artwork for a wide variety of items. These include direct-mail advertising, catalogs, counter displays, slides, and film strips. They also design or lay out the editorial pages and features and produce or purchase the necessary illustrations or artwork.

Advertising copywriters create the headlines, slogans, and text that attract buyers. They collect information about products and potential customers. Copywriters use a knowledge of psychology and writing to prepare copy especially suited for the particular readers or listeners sought as buyers and for the advertising medium used. They may specialize in a type of copy that appeals to certain groups—housewives, businesswomen, businessmen, retailers, manufacturers—or that deals with a class of items such as packaged goods or apparel products. In advertising agencies, copywriters work closely with account executives, although they may also be under the supervision of a copy chief.

Advertising production managers arrange to have the copy and artwork converted into print. They deal with typography, printing, engraving, filming, recording, and other firms involved in the reproduction of advertisements. The production manager needs a thorough knowledge of printing, photography, reproduction techniques, paper and inks, and related technical materials and processes.

Public relations workers gather and give out information that keeps the public aware of their employer's projects and accomplishments. They prepare and assemble information and contact the people who may be interested in publicizing their information. Many newspaper items, magazine articles, and pamphlets about a company start at public relations workers' desks.

Public relations workers also arrange and conduct direct public contact programs. Such work includes setting up speaking engagements for executives and writing the speeches they deliver. These workers often serve as an employer's representative during community projects and occasionally show films at school assemblies, plan conventions, or manage fund-raising campaigns.

Photographers use their cameras and other equipment to portray merchandise, people, and events on film. Skillful portrait photographers, for example, take pictures that are natural looking, attractive, and expressive of an individual's personality. Those who photograph fashion try to show the exciting merchandise in action.

Most models specialize in some line of live or photographic work. Some fashion models work before an audience, often by participating in style shows. Models walk past customers and pause to exhibit favorable features of the clothes they are wearing. On some jobs they may stop to tell individual customers a garment's price and style number. Fashion models who work for clothing designers, manufacturers, and distributors are called showroom or wholesale models. They work constantly during peak seasons, but during slack times they may have clerical duties such as typing.

INTERVIEW JUNE GRADS NOW!

- • • Showroom Assistant
- • • Fashion and Color Coordinator and Assistant
- • • Shopper/Stylist and Assistant
- • • Sales Trainee
- • • Merchandising Assistant
- • • Assistant Piece Goods Buyer
- • • Assistant Converter
- • • Sales Promotion Assistant
- • • Advertising Assistant
- • • Publicity Assistant
- • • Quality Control Assistant
- • • Junior Engineer
- • • Assistant Production Manager
- • • Production Assistant

Please call Ms. Phyllis Madan, Placement Office 239-7654, or mail the details requested below:

Name of Firm: _____

Address: _____

Person to Call: _____

Tel. # _____

Sponsored by the Board of Education of the City of New York with the cooperation of the Educational Foundation for the Fashion Industries under the program of the State University of New York.

PLACEMENT DEPARTMENT

Fashion Institute of Technology, 227 West 27 Street, New York, N.Y. 10001

Source: Fashion Institute of Technology. By permission.

Informal models work in department stores and custom salons where the pace is more leisurely than in showrooms. Still others may demonstrate new products and services at manufacturers' exhibits and trade shows.

Photographic models usually are hired on an assignment basis. After arriving for an assignment, the model changes into the appropriate clothing. The photographer then decides on poses, adjusts lights, and takes several pictures. Most fashion models display fashions, but some pose with other merchandise such as china, towels, or home furnishings.

The creative work of interior designers helps make living, working, and playing areas more attractive and useful. Interior designers plan and supervise the design and arrangement of building interiors and furnishings. They help clients select furniture, draperies, other fabrics, floor coverings, and accessories. They also estimate what any work or furnishings will cost. Interior designers may do "boardwork," particularly on large assignments. This boardwork includes work on floor plans and elevations and the preparation of sketches or other perspective drawings so clients can visualize their plans. After the client approves both the plans and the cost, the designer may make arrangements for buying the furnishings; for supervising the work of painters, floor finishers, cabinet makers, carpet layers, and other craftsmen; and for installing and arranging the furnishings.

Many large department and furniture stores have separate design departments to advise their customers on decorating and design plans. The main purpose of the designers in these departments is to help sell the store's merchandise, although materials from outside sources may be used occasionally when they are essential to the plans developed for the customer. Department store designers frequently advise the store's buyers and executives about style and color trends in interior furnishings.

MOVIES, THEATER, AND TELEVISION

Each film, theatrical production, and television show must have the actors properly clothed for their roles. For this reason, each film or show has its costume designer. If the film or show is a period piece, a great deal of research must often be done to make the costumes authentic. Well-designed fashions for an important film or Broadway show have often resulted in a new fashion trend. *My Fair*

STUART, CHARLES I
1625-1649

CAPES

Lady touched off a trend for turn-of-the-century influences. Western movies have created a big demand for frontier, western, and American Indian looks. The movie *Bonnie and Clyde* touched off a 1930s "gangster look."

All the clothes for these shows were carefully designed by leading apparel creators. Cecil Beaton created the *My Fair Lady* costumes. He is one of England's leading apparel designers. A leading American designer for the films is Edith Head, who has won many design awards.

MUSEUMS AND LIBRARIES

There are several important museums in the United States that have costume collections. The Metropolitan Museum of New York has one of the best collec-

tions. The Brooklyn Museum also has a costume and textile collection. The Smithsonian Institution has fashions worn by presidents and their wives through our country's history. In England, Madam Tussaud's Exhibition features a collection of life-size wax figures of famous personalities in appropriate costumes.

The New York Public Library has an extensive collection of costume pictures in its picture collection. Other museums and libraries have collections that help fashion people get ideas from the past.

CONCLUSION

All of the various fields of the fashion industry have job opportunities for fashion-minded people. Some require artistic talent, ability to take exciting photographs, or some writing ability. Some fashion jobs require knowledge of designing, merchandising and buying, or perhaps selling in a store and stocking fashion merchandise. There are jobs in bookkeeping, accounting, statistics, and unit control, all related to fashion.

Fashion Points

SPORTSWEAR The Chameleon of Fashion

The chameleon, a creature frequently seen near lakes and streams is notorious for changing colors, pale salmon to bright orange to drab green.

Only sportswear fashion can be likened to the changeability of the chameleon. Since woman and capriciousness are synonymous nothing compliments her more than a fickle and changeable wardrobe. There is however, a very practical quality to woman, thus emphasizing the importance of sportswear as your most functional apparel.

For a romp through the woods, horseback riding, gardening or cycling through the park, jeans earn the leading role. More flattering than ever, for work or play — in the very-now tie-dyed water colors, stripes or prints, in a variety of sturdy fabrics, or blended to stretch and come back again with great resiliency . . . styled with fly-front, hip-huggers and swinging bell bottoms. Contrast them with the new ranch shirt in cool cotton easy-care blends, in plaids, stripes or solids — can be worn over the ribbed athletic shirt reminiscent of the undershirt.

Or be subtle, accentuate your femininity by alternating with the body-conforming boyish knickers or dashing midi-gaucho pants.

To further enhance your sportswear wardrobe, this is the year that sportswear has gone feminine. The very casual, carefree nature of sportswear reflects the quick-changing spontaneity of woman.

As the chameleon changes its hue, you will enjoy your garden party most in your sheer embroidered peasant blouse worn over your graceful midi-skirt — or in the fitted, laced bodice, full-skirted midi peasant dress with ruffled petticoat showing —in a kaleidescopic variety of prints and colors; nostalgic with the glow of innocence of the milk-maid in time gone-by.

For more information and tips on accessorizing *"The Many Looks of Sportswear"* title of exciting illustrated 16pp fashion booklet, based on a designer's sketchbook — simply write to the Consumer Service Division, Union Label Department, International Ladies' Garment Workers' Union, 275 Seventh Avenue, New York, New York 10001. You'll be glad you did.

There are jobs for those who know textiles, fabrics, and colors, and jobs for people with scientific background for research in fibers and chemicals that go into textiles.

Almost all kinds of talents and abilities are needed in the fashion business. If you can speak well and face an audience, you may be a commentator at fashion shows. If you can put together smart looking ensembles and accessorize them properly, you may be a fashion coordinator or stylist. If you can trim a window or create a display, you may work for a fashion store's display department.

There is almost no limit to the job opportunities in the fashion world. It is important to evaluate your talents and see how they best fit into this vast and many-faceted enterprise. There are now and for the foreseeable future thousands of jobs for talented people who think creatively and understand the business of fashion. Those who wish to enter will find it an exciting world.

REVIEW QUESTIONS AND DISCUSSION

1. Besides apparel firms, name four other types of business firms involved in fashion. How does fashion relate to these fields?
2. How do theater, motion pictures, museums, and television relate to fashions?
3. Discuss the different career possibilities in the fashion world. At this point in time, analyze your own talents. Which area interests you most? Why? Is it accessible to you?

GLOSSARY

A-LINE   Silhouette flaring to the hem.

ACWU   Amalgamated Clothing Workers' Union.

ABRASION-RESISTANCE   Resistance to wearing away by scraping or rubbing.

ACCESSORIES   Articles worn or carried to complete one's costume, such as jewelry, neckwear, scarves, handbags, shoes, millinery.

ACCORDION PLEATS   Narrow pleats folding together, resembling an accordion.

ACETATE   Generic term for a cellulose fiber.

ACRYLIC   Generic term for a major synthetic-fiber group derived from a compound of hydrogen cyanide and acetylene.

ADAM   Relating to a style of English furniture and architecture with straight lines and ornamentation of garlands; after Robert and James Adam, eighteenth-century British architects.

ADAPTATION   A copy of a design, with outstanding features of the original.

ADVERTISING   Paid space or time in media.

ADVERTISING MANAGER   Supervisor of all printed and broadcast media presentations.

AFGHAN   Soft knitted or crocheted wool blanket, sometimes worn as a cape.

AGATE LINE   Measure of advertising space in newspapers, 1 column wide and $\frac{1}{14}$ inch deep; used for rate purposes.

ALENÇON   Type of lace, solid design on net.

ALL-OVER   Relating to a print that covers the entire fabric, as opposed to a border print along the edge.

ALPACA   Fleecy, woollike hair of the South American alpaca, related to the llama.

AMULET   Good-luck charm.

ANGORA   Soft yarn from the hair of the angora rabbit; often used for sweaters. Also, the hair of the angora goat, woven into mohair.

ANILINE   Chemical used as basis of coal-tar dyes.

ANTIMACASSAR   Small covering to protect the back and arms of upholstered furniture.

APPLIQUÉ   Decoration in which material is cut out and sewn, embroidered, or pasted on another material.

ART-DECO   Ornate style of interior design and architecture of the 1920s and 1930s.

ASCOT   Scarf or tie, one end tied over the other, falling from the neck.

ASSISTANT BUYER   Person responsible for a department's merchandise operations when the buyer is in market; filling merchandise requisites for branch stores; analyzing inventory statistics for flagship and each branch store; checking and pricing merchandise in receiving and marking department; followthrough on advertising details and approving copy and illustrations from merchandise viewpoint.

ASSOCIATION OF BUYING OFFICES (ABO)   Organization of New York buying-office executives to standardize and unify services available to stores; traditionally, the manager of the NRMA merchandise division is ABO executive secretary.

ATHLETIC SHIRT   Sleeveless shirt; tank top; man's undershirt.

AU COURANT   French for "up-to-date."

AUTOMATIC MARKDOWN   System of reducing the price of merchandise that does not sell on scheduled basis; originated by Filene's of Boston.

AVERAGING OUT   Marking merchandise at different prices to come out at required margin of profit.

BABUSHKA   Scarf covering the head and tied under the chin.

BACK ORDER   Shipping merchandise ordered, omitting some items that are to be shipped later.

BACKED   Relating to a fabric having two-ply construction.

BACKUP STOCK   Additional merchandise in warehouse supplementing the retail store's floor stock.

BALANCED STOCK   Merchandise available throughout all price zones or ranges in proportion to demand.

BALBRIGGAN   Cotton fabric with fine-knit surface; used for undergarments.

BALMACAAN   Overcoat of loose, flaring style.

BAND   Strip of fabric, such as a hat band.

BANDANA   Large, brightly colored kerchief worn on neck or head; also describes print.

BANDED   Having one or more bands.

BANGLE   Jewelry, pendant on necklace or bracelet.

BAR TACK   Small, stitched bar to finish and hold pleat or provide reinforcement.

BARGAIN STORE OR BASEMENT   Where off-price merchandise is sold.

BARGAIN TABLE   Usually main-floor table in a retail store reserved for off-price merchandise.

BASIC DRESS   Classic style that can be accessorized "up" or "down."

BASIC STOCK   Staple merchandise to be in stock at all times.

BASTE   Sew temporarily to hold in place.

BATIK   Method of dyeing designs on cloth by coating with removable wax the parts not to be dyed (Malay); cloth made in this way.

BATISTE   Sheer, soft, plainweave cotton or linen fabric; used for summer shirts, blouses, and handkerchiefs.

BATWING   Sleeve with deep armholes.

BAZAAR   Marketplace of many shops.

BEAU BRUMMEL   Dandy, well-dressed man; after a nineteenth-century Englishman.

BELL BOTTOMS   Sailorlike trousers flared at bottom.

BERET   Round, soft hat, like the Scottish tam-o-shanter.

BIAS   Diagonally cut fabric.

BIKINI   Abbreviated two-piece swimsuit.

BLAZER   Jacket, often with embroidered motif and brass buttons; sports jacket.

BLAZER STRIPES   Bright stripes, sometimes multicolor.

BLINDSTITCH   Sew in such a way that no stitching shows on front side of garment.

BLOCK   To put shape into apparel, particularly knits and hats.

BLOOMER   Pantaloon formerly worn by women as undergarment.

BLUE JEANS   Denim pants, Levi's.

BOA   Long, snake-shaped scarf of silk or feathers.

BOBBIN   Spool on which thread is wound.

BODICE   Women's laced outergarment covering waist and bust; peasant dress.

BODYSUIT   Close-fitting stretch-type undergarment; body stocking.

BOLERO   Short Spanish jacket, generally worn open.

BOLT   Length of cloth rolled on tube or board, double-folded before rolling.

BOUDOIR   Private room of ladies of yesteryear.

BOUDOIR LOOK   Lingerie look in apparel.

BOUTIQUE   Small shop specializing in particular merchandise.

BRAID   Intertwined strands forming a narrow strip.

BREECHES   Trousers especially for horseback riding.

BROADCLOTH   Closely woven fabric, mostly cotton, but could be any fiber.

BROADLOOM   Carpeting in wide widths.

BROCADE   Fabric of Jacquard weave having raised figures.

BUCKLE   Frame device, usually metal, to close a belt or shoe, or for decoration.

BUCKSKIN   Skin of deer or buck; soft, strong yellowish tan; worn by frontiersmen.

BUDGET STORE   Store carrying modestly priced merchandise.

BURNOOSE   Hooded cape from North Africa.

BUSH COAT   Safari jacket from the African bush, generally with multiple pockets.

BUSTLE   Frame or pad, worn below the waist at the back to extend the skirt.

BUYER   Person who buys merchandise for a retail store; supervisor of salespeople; source of merchandise information. A department store generally has a buyer for each department.

BUYING OFFICE   Resident buying office serving retail stores in major markets.

C.O.D.   Cash on Delivery.

CABLE KNIT   A knit producing heavy cord, often in raised loop stripe.

CAFTAN   Long, full, slipover garment with long sleeves; from the Middle East.

CALENDERING   Fabric finishing process in which heated rollers smoothe the fabric.

CALL SYSTEM   Arrangement in a retail store to give each salesperson numerical rotation.

CAMISOLE   Woman's sleeveless, often lace-trimmed underwaist; originally a corset cover, now worn under a sheer blouse.

CANDLEWICK   Thread tuftings to give napped surface, usually forming a design; used for bedspreads.

CANVAS   Strong, heavy, plain, woven fabric generally of cotton; sometimes called sailcloth; also used for interlinings, art needlework, and stiffener for shaped clothing.

CAP SLEEVE   Sleeve just covering the shoulder.

CAPE   Sleeveless outergarment hanging from shoulders, any length.

CARAT   Unit of weight for precious stones and metals.

CARDED   Relating to rough arrangement of fibers in parallel formation; not as finished as COMBED.

CARDIGAN   Collarless, front-closing sweater; high, collarless neckline.

CASHMERE   Fiber from the cashmere goat; from Kashmir, India.

CASSOCK   Long, close-fitting garment worn by clergy in Middle Ages.

CAUTION   Advance payment for admission to French couture houses.

CHAINSE   Ancient ankle-length garment similar to the Roman toga.

CHALLIS   Light-weight, soft fabric of wool, cotton, or synthetics.

CHAMBRAY   Fine-quality gingham; formerly only of cotton, now also in synthetics.

CHAMBRE SYNDICALE DE LA COUTURE PARISIENNE   Trade association representing the haute couture houses in Paris.

CHAMOIS   Goatlike antelope whose yellow-colored skin is used for apparel.

CHANTILLY   Lace from the town of that name in France.

CHAPEAU   French for "hat."

CHECK   Criss-cross square pattern of any size.

CHECK OUT   Usually used with "number"; indicating a garment that sold quickly at retail.

CHECKERBOARD   Alternating dark and light squares.

CHEMISE   Formerly loose woman's undergarment; now loose-fitting look, hung straight.

CHENILLE   Fabric of any fiber with velvetlike pile.

CHEVIOT   Rough-surfaced wool fabric, closely napped, for suits and coats.

CHEVRON   V-shaped design or zig-zag; sergeant's stripes.

CHIC   Cleverly attractive, fashionable.

CHIFFON   Sheer, soft fabric of any fiber.

CHINCHILLA   Fur-bearing South American rodent; high-value fur.

CHINO   Soft twill fabric, usually light tan; pants made of this fabric.

CHINTZ   Plain or printed fabric with glaze; widely used for draperies and slipcovers.

CHIPPENDALE   Relating to an English style of furniture characterized by graceful lines and, often, rococo ornamentation; after Thomas Chippendale, an eighteenth-century English cabinetmaker.

CHITON   Ancient tunic or gown.

CHOKER   Necklace or band worn closely around the neck.

CLASSIC   Simple, graceful apparel not quickly dated or out of style.

CLEARANCE   Retail-store sale to clear out merchandise that hasn't sold.

CLIP   Fastening; piece of jewelry with hinged clasp worn on any part of a garment.

CLOAK   Loose outer garment; cape, wrap.

CLOCHE   Close-fitting hat.

CLOCK   Decoration on sides of stockings.

CLOSE OUT   Price merchandise so as to sell it all; cut price.

COAT OF ARMS   Heraldic shield with family design worn by knights; now symbol of schools, worn on blazers.

COLLECTION   Designer's or manufacturer's group of garments for a particular season.

COMBED   Relating to yarn; twisted tightly; smoothed by combing; fine-textured.

COMPARISON-SHOPPER   Retail-store employee who shops competitors to compare prices and merchandise.

CONE   Bobbin to wind thread.

CONFINED   Relating to brand or label sold to limited number of stores, usually in one city.

CONTOUR   Shape or outline.

CONTRACTOR   Firm doing sewing for apparel manufacturer; term derived because the work is done under contract.

CONVERTER   Textile firm that buys plain or grey (greige) goods and prints or converts for final use.

COORDINATES   Apparel made to go together; mix or match separates.

COPY   Written material for advertising; duplicate.

CORDED   Ribbed as if with cords.

CORDOVAN   Nonporous horsehide leather.

CORSELET   Undergarment with few supports; armor for body; breast plate.

CORSET   Tight-fitting, smooth undergarment to support and mold the figure.

COST PRICE   Cost of manufacturing product to which profit must be added.

COSTUME   Complete dress; all outer garments and accessories; special fancy dress.

COSTUME JEWELRY   Fabricated of nonprecious stones or metals.

COSTUME SUIT   Dress including jacket or coat to be worn together.

COUTURE   French for "needlework" or "sewing"; applied to high fashion.

COUTURIER   French designer, owner of dressmaking firm; generally leading Paris names (fem. COUTURIÈRE).

COVERALLS   One-piece garment worn over other garment to protect the latter or as casual garment worn alone; jump suit.

COVERT   Diagonal twill fabric of medium weight.

COWHIDE   Rough leather used for belts, handbags, jackets.

COWL   Hood, generally attached to a garment, which may be dropped; draped neck or sleeve.

CRAVAT   French for "necktie."

CREPE   Crinkle-faced fabric; crepe de chine; originally Chinese.

CRETONNE   Strong, medium-weight fabric with different weaves and finishes, generally cotton or linen.

CREWEL   Loosely twisted yarn; needlework with yarn.

CRINOLINE   Stiffened silk or cotton fabric used as support or to shape garments.

CROSS MERCHANDISING   Displaying merchandise from one area in another area of a retail store; for example, cutlery, china, and glassware in the table-linen department; belts in the separates department; shoes in the hosiery department.

CROSS SELLING   Selling a customer merchandise from several departments.

CROWN   Headdress worn by royalty; upper part of hat.

CULOTTE   Full, trouser-legged garment that looks like a skirt.

CUT   Style or line of garment; in advertising, engraving.

CUTTER   Trade name for garment manufacturer; garment worker who does actual cutting.

CUTTING-UP TRADE   Same as CUTTER, referring to garment industry.

CYCLE BILLING   Correlation of alphabetical breakdowns to specific days of month to equalize retail billing-department work load.

DACRON   Du Pont's trade name for its polyester fiber.

DAMASK   Heavy, reversible, glossy fabric in any fiber, usually woven on Jacquard looms to bring out design.

DÉCOLLETAGE   Revealing, low-cut neckline exposing shoulders, neck, and back.

DECOR   Home furnishing with particular reference to overall design or plan.

DEMODÉ   Passé, outdated, out of fashion.

DEMONSTRATOR   Salesperson who devotes all of his or her time to a particular manufacturer's products, usually requiring application, such as cosmetics.

DENIER   From French, unit indicating fineness or coarseness of threads.

DENIM   Strong, rough, cotton fabric; from French "de Nîmes," from the city of Nîmes.

DEPARTMENT MANAGER   In branch stores, takes over buyer's function as supervisor of salespersons and source of merchandise information; responsible for sales.

DEPARTMENT STORE   Retail store with various departments usually covering all merchandise.

DEPARTMENTALIZING   Organization of related merchandise and subsequent identification as a department; arranging by category.

DE-SIZED   Cloth given finish to reduce starch and chemicals.

DIRECT MAIL   Use of mails to make announcements, sell merchandise, sell services, sell a store's image, character, and way of doing business; used by apparel manufacturers, mail-order firms, and retail stores.

DIRECTOIRE   Relating to French period 1795–1799, when long, flowing garments were worn.

DIRNDL   Gathered skirt fitting at the waist; bodice-type dress; peasant look.

DISCOUNT MERCHANDISING   Low-margin retailing, generally self-service; selling goods at less than list price.

DISCOUNT STORE   Store operating on lower overall margin than conventional store selling same type of merchandise; generally offering less service.

DISCOUNTER   Retailer who sells at lower prices.

DISPLAY   Visual presentation of merchandise, usually with signs. Most stores have window displays and interior displays.

DISPLAY MANAGER   Supervisor of all window and interior displays, signs, and props.

DISTRESS MERCHANDISE   Merchandise which, for any reason, must be sold at a sacrifice (at either wholesale or retail level).

DOLMAN   Wide sleeve with wide armhole.

DOMESTICS   Cotton goods, such as muslin sheeting or print cloth; term for sheets, towels, pillow cases, and bedding.

DONEGAL   Tweed originally from Ireland.

DOOR-TO-DOOR   Shipping term denoting consignment of goods to be picked up at vendor's place of business and delivered directly to store's place of business; also selling from house to house.

DOTTED SWISS   Fine fabric with small embroidered or appliquéd dots.

DOUBLE-TICKET   Tag same merchandise for misses and juniors. Such as 7/8, 11/12.

DOUBLE-TRUCK OR DOUBLE-SPREAD   Two-page advertisement utilizing "gutter" space to make advertisement appear as a unit, as opposed to two facing pages; center-spread.

DOUBLET   Tunic, overlapping in part; man's jacketlike garment.

DRAPER   Formerly, British dressmaker or piece-goods vendor.

DRILL   Firm, coarse cotton or linen cloth.

DRIVER ACCEPT   Written instructions on C.O.D. salescheck for driver to accept an article of merchandise as an even-exchange additional C.O.D. charge, or refund to customer upon delivery of new purchase.

DROP SHIP   Merchandise shipped directly to branch store, saving time and expense of shipping to central warehouse and having store ship to branch; ship directly to customer.

DRY GOODS   Yard goods, bedding, textiles, apparel.

DUCK   Closely woven strong cotton or linen fabric often used for sportswear, lighter than canvas.

DUNGAREE   Pants of heavy fabric; coarse East Indian cotton fabric.

E.O.M.   End of Month; indicates time allowance for discount is reckoned from the end of the month during which goods were bought, not from the date of invoice; for example, 10 days E.O.M.

EDWARDIAN   Relating to styles of British period 1900–1910, during the reign of Edward VII.

ELIZABETHAN   Relating to the reign of Elizabeth I of England, 1558–1603.

EMBOSSING   Raised design; stands out in relief.

EMBROIDERY   Needlework stitching done by hand or machine.

EMPIRE   Relating to French Napoleonic period 1804–1814; in fashion, high-waisted under bustline.

EPAULET   Shoulder ornament or trim, military.

EXECUTIVE TRAINEE   Generally, college graduate with specialized training who works in various divisions of store while receiving on-the-job training for an executive position.

EXTRA SIZES   Large sizes, sometimes designated XL, XXL.

EXTRUDE   Force out synthetics through small holes to make fibers.

F.O.B.   Free on Board; shipping term signifying that vendor or shipper retains title and pays all charges to F.O.B. point.

FACING   Finished edge of another fabric or extra fabric applied to raw edge.

FACT TAG   Conveys product information and consumer benefits to salespeople and customers at point of sale.

FAD   Minor or short-lived fashion.

FAILLE   Slightly glossy fabric with bias grain.

FALL   Small, independent hairpiece; cascade of ruffles or lace.

FASHION COORDINATOR   Person who puts together fashion concepts and ideas.

FASHION GROUP   International association of women involved in fashion, headquartered in New York City.

FASTENERS   Devices that hold together or close separate parts; hook and eye, snap.

FELT   Thick, heavy, matted fabric used for hats and table coverings.

FIBULA   Ornamented pin clasp from the Roman era.

FILL IN   Buy merchandise to round out gaps in stock.

FINDINGS   Buttons, decorations, braids; used to complete garments.

FINISHING   Last process applied to fabrics to complete them.

FLANNEL   Light-weight wool or cotton, soft and napped; used for sleepwear, shirts, and pants.

FLAX   Fiber from which linen is made, from flax plant.

FLEECE   Sheep's covering; fabric with soft pile.

FLOUNCE   Strips sewn to garment causing it to flare.

FLYING SQUAD   Group of salespeople with exceptional selling ability and flexibility who can be added to departmental sales staff when needed; also used in sales-supporting and nonselling areas during peak load periods.

FORMAT   General arrangement or plan, having continuity, as in advertising.

FORTREL   Celanese Corporation's trade name for its polyester.

FOUR-AND-A-HALF-SECOND STOP AVERAGE   Average length of time customer inspects visual merchandising display.

FOUR-IN-HAND   Way of knotting a man's tie.

FROCK   Any type of dress.

FROCK COAT   Man's long coat, usually double-breasted.

FROG   Loop closing, Chinese influence.

FULL DRESS   Formal attire for men.

FULL LINE   Stock of any given classification of goods that includes every variety of style, color, size, and material; consists of four definite categories: (1) staples, (2) style merchandise, (3) novelties, and (4) outsizes (for stocks that have size element).

FUSED   Stuck together by high temperature.

GABARDINE   Firm, durable cloth, showing a diagonal line on the face of the goods; used for pants, skirts, and jackets.

GAITER   Covering for leg or ankle.

GAMINE   French for "street urchin"; used to describe a woman of elfin appeal.

GARTER   Stocking supporter.

GATHER   Draw fabric together; also called shirring.

GAUCHO   South American cowboy style.

GAUGE   Describing fineness or closeness of threads, particularly in hosiery.

GAUNTLET   Glove with fabric covering wrist and above.

GAUZE   Light, thin, transparent fabric; often used in layers.

GENERAL MERCHANDISE MANAGER   Person who participates in major policy making and administers policy for entire merchandise division; liaison executive between merchandise division and all other major store divisions; responsible for total merchandising operation.

GEOMETRIC   Design having precise geometrical appearance rather than a random print of various design.

GEORGIAN   Relating to furniture and apparel styles, 1714–1830, during the reigns of King George I, II, III, and IV.

GIBSON GIRL   Style and silhouette, 1890–1900, created by Charles David Gibson.

GINGHAM   Light, firm, cotton fabric; woven in solids, stripes, checks, or plaids; often yarn-dyed; from Malayan "ginggang," meaning striped.

GORES   Fabric inserts; skirts described as having "seven gores."

GOSSAMER   Filmy, sheer.

GREY (GRAY, GREIGE) GOODS   Fabric in its natural form from weaving looms.

GROSGRAIN   Silk or silklike fabric with heavy crosswise ribs; used for ribbon.

GROUP MANAGER   Supervisor in branch store responsible for stocks, signing, and salespeople selling merchandise from several flagship, or main, store departments;

usually does no buying, unless reordering staples; keeps "parent" department informed concerning what is selling, what is needed, and what is not selling; manager of a group of units.

GUSSET   Triangular, tapered piece of fabric inserted in accessory or garment for reinforcement or better fit.

GYPSY   Nomad; in fashion, a rag-tag look.

HABERDASHER   Keeper of small shop; dealer in men's clothing.

HABIT   Costume, dress, indicating occupation; for example, nun's habit, riding habit.

HALF-SIZE   Size scale for larger women, such as 22½, 24½.

HALF-SLEEVE   Sleeve halfway up forearm.

HALF SLIP   Petticoat.

HALTER   Strap supporting front of backless apparel, looped around neck.

HAND   Feel of a fabric.

HANGER SHOW   Fashion show with garments shown on hangers, not models.

HARD GOODS   Housewares, china, glassware, cutlery. *See also* SOFT GOODS.

HARD SURFACE   Linoleum or tile floor covering.

HARLEQUIN   Alternating colored panels or diamond shapes, multicolored.

HEAD OF STOCK   Junior executive responsible for arrangement and identification of reserve and forward stocks in a retail store.

HEADRAIL   Head covering wrapping around the face.

HEMSTITCH   Sewing process, drawing out and stitching threads; decorative finish.

HENNIN   Long, conical, pointed headdress, ancient.

HEPPLEWHITE   Relating to style of furniture originating in late eighteenth-century England, after George Hepplewhite.

HIGH FASHION   Couture design, limited acceptance; exclusive.

HIMATION   Greek mantle like a shawl.

HOME ECONOMICS   Science of home management, including domestic arts and sciences.

HOMESPUN   Strong, loose, durable, rough-surfaced, woolen fabric; used for drapery and upholstery.

HOOP   Round band or frame for skirts in seventeenth and eighteenth centuries; frame to hold embroidery.

HOSE   Covering for foot and leg; stockings, socks, pantyhose.

HOSTESS GOWN   At-home, full-length costume, formal or informal.

HOUNDSTOOTH   Irregular check having toothy look.

ILGWU   International Ladies' Garment Workers' Union.

IMAGE   Reputation of store; particular look or character; feelings of customers toward store. Also, appearance of art or photography in visual terms.

IMPORT   Merchandise from foreign country.

IMPULSE MERCHANDISE   Merchandise purchased by consumer on spur of moment without predetermined consideration.

INCENTIVE PAY   Bonus or commission paid to salespeople for exceeding their production quotas; bonus pay for performance.

INTERLINING   Layer of fabric between lining and outside of garment to hold shape.

INTIMATE APPAREL   Corsets, brassieres, underwear, slips, sleepwear, lounging apparel.

INVENTORY   Total stock of merchandise; take inventory—count the stock.

INVOICE   Itemized statement showing merchandise sent to store by supplier; bill for services rendered.

IRREGULAR   Relating to imperfect merchandise.

JABOT   Scarf tie or ruffle on shirt or blouse front.

JACQUARD   Figured weave done on Jacquard loom, generally intricate design; pattern loom for weaving of elaborate design.

JERSEY   Stretchable, plain, knitted fabric in all fibers.

JOB LOT   Miscellaneous group or assortment of styles, sizes, and colors purchased by store as a "lot" at a reduced price.
JOBBER   Wholesaler; go-between for manufacturer and retailer.
JUMP SUIT   One-piece coverall.
JUMPER   Loose slip-on garment, usually sleeveless.
JUNIORS   Size scale for younger women, odd numbers 5–17.
JUTE   Fiber used for burlap, sacking, twine; from East India jute plant.

KALASIRIS   Draped Egyptian garment; Greek sheath.
KAPOK   Fiber from ceiba tree; used to stuff pillows, cushions, and mattresses.
KEYHOLE   Round neckline with wedge-shaped opening.
KHAKI   Sturdy twill fabric often in olive drab, dull yellow-brown; pants made of this fabric.
KILT   Short, pleated skirt, Scottish.
KIMONO   Japanese-style robe with full sleeve.
KNICKERS   Short pants banded below the knee.
KNIT   Process of making fabric by interlocking a series of loops of continuous yarn, by hand or machine; knits may be single, double, tricot, raschel, warp, weft.
KNOCK OFF   Slang for a copy of a high-priced garment to be sold at a lower price.
KNOCKED DOWN   Reduced in price.
KODEL   Eastman's trade name for its polyester.

LACE   Open-work fabric with design.
LAMÉ   Cloth woven of gold or silver threads, often brocaded.
LAMINATED   Two or more layers glued together, fabric or wood; backed.
LAPEL   Part of neckline that folds over; usually front of jacket or coat.
LAST   Form for making a shoe.
LATEX   Liquid rubber or plastic used for stretch in swimsuits and foundation garments.
LAWN   Light, thin cloth made of combed cotton.
LAY-AWAY   Method of deferred payments in which merchandise is held by store for the customer until completely paid for.
LAYERED LOOK   Garments over garments—blouse, vest, jacket, coat.
LAYOUT   Sketch or diagram showing arrangement; advertising preliminary.
LEOTARD   Short, fitted garment worn by dancers; sometimes called bodysuit; now top or outergarment.
LEVI'S   Blue denim pants; from Levi Strauss, original maker of these pants.
LINE   Group of items prepared for season—"spring line"; cut of garment.
LINE-FOR-LINE   Relating to an exact copy of garment, usually couture.
LINENS   Collective name for sheets, towels, bedding; fabrics of flax.
LINGERIE   Intimate apparel—slips, nightgowns, robes, underwear.
LINING   Cloth covering inside of garment.
LIRIPIPE   Long, pointed hood.
LONGUETTE   French for "long," referring to dress length.
LOSS LEADER   Special item, specially purchased or drastically reduced in price, used to draw traffic into department or store.
LOW END   Least expensive merchandise in a classification.
LUREX   Trade name for metallic fabric; metallic thread.

M.O.R.   Monthly Operating Report; store report compiled by statistical, research, or accounting department showing operating results for each department.
MACKINAW CLOTH   Heavy, napped fabric, usually wool; used for jackets and coats.
MACRAMÉ   Fine, twisted cord used to make knotted lace and objects.
MADE-TO-ORDER   Specially made, not ready-to-wear; custom-made.
MADRAS   Firm, cotton fabric, usually striped or corded; from Madras, India.
MAIN STORE   Downtown store, not branch stores; also known as flagship store.
MAN-MADE   Relating to synthetic fibers.
MANDARIN COAT OR COLLAR   Chinese style; long; embroidered; narrow stand-up collar; often with frog closings.

MANNEQUIN   Model, display figure for garments; also spelled "mannikin."

MANTEAU   Cape, cloak, wrap mantle.

MANTLE   Loose garment, cloak, or wrap.

MANUFACTURER'S REPRESENTATIVE   Selling agent who gives informative talks to sales personnel about manufacturer's products.

MARK   Price merchandise; put price ticket on merchandise.

MARK DOWN   Reduce price from original selling price.

MARKET   Where retailers buy merchandise.

MARKET REPORT   Detailed report of merchandise from buying office to retail store.

MARKETING   Program and plan for selling products; includes advertising, public relations, sales promotion, research, and distribution.

MARKING ROOM   Room in retail store where prices are marked on merchandise.

MARQUISETTE   Light-weight, soft, open-mesh fabric, usually of cotton, silk, or rayon.

MAXI   Ankle-length or floor-length garment.

MECHANICAL   Final assembly of components of advertisement for reproduction.

MEDIA   Means of communication—newspaper, magazine, radio, TV; in advertising: direct mail, signs, skywriting, motion pictures, programs, or broadcasts.

MELTON   Smooth, heavy, woolen cloth for overcoats and jackets; from Melton, England.

MERCERIZE   Treat cotton threads or fabric to strengthen, using soda and caustic.

MERCHANDISE MANAGER   Often synonymous with divisional merchandise manager; sometimes a separate executive responsibility, under divisional merchandise manager, for merchandising activities of one or more selling departments.

MERINO   Fine, soft wool from merino sheep.

MESH   Any fabric, knitted or woven, with open texture.

MIDI   Mid-length; mid-calf skirt.

MILL RUN   Run of the mill, fabric not inspected; ordinary, sometimes poor quality.

MINI   Short skirt, three or four inches above knee or higher.

MISSES   Sizes for women, even-numbered 8–18.

MODE   Short for "a la mode," in style.

MODEL   Original design that serves as a pattern for making copies; mannequin.

MODEL STOCK   How much of what to have, good balance of merchandise in different size and price categories.

MOHAIR   Hair of angora goat.

MOIRÉ   Silk or taffeta watered or clouded to give shimmery effect under light.

MOTIF   Print of various designs or themes; unit of design; separate figure; subject for development or treatment; dominant idea or feature.

MOUSSELINE DE SOIR   Gauzelike, sheer fabric, usually silk.

MUSLIN   Soft, cotton fabric, plain bleached or unbleached; used for model garments, pillow cases and sheets, under covering of upholstered furniture.

MUTED   Relating to color, toned down or subdued.

NRMA   National Retail Merchants Association; the only national retail trade group specifically functioning in the interests of department, chain, and specialty stores.

NAP   Downy or hairy surface of cloth formed by short hairs or fibers, as in pile of velvet.

NATIONAL BRANDS   Nationally advertised merchandise, as opposed to local brands or private brands.

NEEDLETRADE   Clothing manufacturing.

NEGLIGEE   Soft dressing gown, generally loose-flowing.

NET   Open-work cloth with mesh of varying sizes and fibers; for example, cable, fish, and tulle.

"NEW LOOK" Dior silhouette of 1947; long, full skirt instead of short, tight-fitting skirt.

NINON   Smooth, transparent, voile fabric, French chiffon; used for curtains.

O.T.B.   Open-to-buy; buyer has money to spend.

OBI   Broad Japanese sash with large bow in back.

ODD LOT   Incomplete assortment.

OFF PRICE   Below normal selling price.

OILSKIN   Fabric treated with oil and chemicals to make waterproof.

ON ORDER   Relating to merchandise purchased but not yet received.

OPENING   First showing of new apparel line; part of garment that opens to put it on.

OPENWORK   Fabric or garment having small openings; drawn, punched, or lace effect.

ORGANDY   Fine, crisp, muslin-type fabric, plain or figured, often stiffened.

ORGANZA   Crisp, sheer fabric used under other fabrics.

ORIGINAL   Couture model created and worn at showing; others are "repeats," "copies," or "duplicates."

ORLON   Du Pont's trade name for its acrylic fiber.

OTTOMAN   Heavy, firm, ribbed fabric of cotton, wool, silk, or synthetic fibers. Also, footstool.

OUTERWEAR   Coats, suits, sweaters, usually worn over other clothing.

OVER-THE-COUNTER   Relating to fabric sold by the yard at retail.

OVERALLS   Outer garment worn over others for protection; coverall; trousers with bib and straps over shoulders.

OVERBLOUSE   Blouse or shirt worn outside skirt or pants.

OVERPRICED   Relating to merchandise priced too high to sell readily.

PAISLEY   Irregular, colorful, pear-shaped design in numerous versions; from Paisley, Scotland.

PALLA   Fabric head covering from ancient Rome.

PALLIUM   Outer garment; cloak; rectangular mantle.

PANE   Slit in garment showing contrasting cloth beneath.

PANEL   Front or back gore of dress or skirt.

PANNIER   Light framework for extending a woman's dress or skirt at the hipline.

PASTEUP   See MECHANICAL.

PATTERN   Model or guide for making clothes; design.

PEASANT   Cloth, usually dyed muslin; look, typical dress of rural Europeans.

PEAU DE SOIE   Soft, firm, durable, silk fabric with dull satin finish.

PEBBLE   Give rough texture to cloth or leather.

PELISSON   Fur-lined outer garment, 1200–1300.

PEPLUM   Small flounce at waist, flared extension on hips; short skirt attached to bodice.

PERCALE   Plain, woven, cotton sheeting, solid color or print.

PERUKE   Same as "periwig"; wig of the type worn by men in the seventeenth and eighteenth centuries; usually powdered and having the hair gathered together at back with a ribbon.

PETER PAN   Round, turned-down collar.

PETITE   French for "small"; in clothing, small sizes, as in junior petite.

PICK   Number of threads per inch in fabric warp and weft.

PIECE   Put together, join parts; specific length of goods from loom.

PIECE DYE   Dye fabrics by individual lots, many yards at a time.

PILE   Fabric surface where threads stand up, as in fake furs, velvet, cut pile, or looped pile.

PILOT NUMBER   First completed model; trial model of style.

PIMA   Fine, long-strand cotton grown in Arizona and New Mexico.

PIN TUCK   Very narrow tuck.

PINWALE   Narrow-ribbed corduroy.

PIPE   Decorate with narrow, tube-shaped edging.

PIQUÉ   Corded, waffle-surfaced fabric, usually cotton.

PLACKET   Opening in skirt or at neck, usually buttoned or zipped.

PLAINS   Abbreviation for plain fabrics or solid colors.

PLEAT   Flat double-fold in cloth, of uniform width and pressed or stitched in place; for example, accordion, box, inverted, unpressed.

PLY   Layer or thickness, as in two-ply; to bend or mold.

POINT OF PURCHASE (P.O.P.)   Retail counter where sale is made.

POLYESTER   Synthetic fiber from polymeric resins, formed chiefly by condensing polyhydric alcohols with dibasic acids.

POLYURETHANE   Imitation leather used for handbags, luggage.

PONGEE   Shantung or slub-weave fabric, usually silk or rayon.

POPLIN   Durable, medium-weight, plain-woven fabric of cotton, silk, or wool.

PREMIER First showing, opening.

PRÊT-À-PORTER French for "ready-to-wear"; literally, "ready to carry," as opposed to couture.

PRETICKETED Relating to merchandise bearing retail price tag when shipped to retailer.

PRICE BRACKET Definite price zones or levels at which merchandise is sold.

PRICE RANGE Approximate price with top and bottom limitation.

PRIMARY MARKET Manufacturers of raw materials such as textiles.

PRINT Fabrics stamped with design by various means, including rollers, heat transfer, discharge, screen, stencil, and hand block. Also, media printed matter.

PRIVATE BRANDS Brand names owned by retailers.

PROMOTION To sell by advertising, display, and other means.

PUBLICITY Editorial or news appearing as result of effort to expose in media; usually done by public relations director.

PUBLICITY DIRECTOR Sometimes called sales promotion manager; in large retail store, publicity director supervises advertising, display, special events, press and/or public relations managers, fashion coordinators, and comparison-shoppers.

QIANA Du Pont's trade name for its nylon.

QUILLS Small spools of synthetic yarns.

QUILTING Stitching through two thicknesses of cloth with padding between.

QUOTA Figure establishing goal of daily or weekly sales to be obtained by salespeople, individually or by department; also set for manufacturer's salespeople.

RAGLAN Sleeve style used on coats, in which armhole joins neckline.

RASCHEL Type of knitting similar to tricot.

RAYON Synthetic, cellulose-based fiber.

READY-TO-WEAR Mass-produced apparel, as opposed to custom-made.

REDINGOTE One-piece garment with the look of a coat over a dress.

REGALIA Emblems, insignia of rank or royalty.

REGIONAL SHOPPING CENTER Shopping center having 50 to 100 stores, including at least one major department-store branch.

RELEASES Publicity or news releases.

REORDER NUMBER Item that continues to be ordered by retailers.

RESOURCE Retailer's term for manufacturer or wholesale supplier.

RETAIL FRANCHISE Exclusive ownership by store in trading area of prestige manufacturer's line; frequently a line selectively distributed.

RETAILING The business of buying for resale; also known as "acting as customer's agent."

REVOLVING CREDIT System developed by department stores whereby a given amount of credit is available to a customer, who can charge up to that amount and make monthly payments.

RIBBING Raised ridge in cloth, especially in knits.

ROCOCO Ornate, extravagant style.

ROVING Collecting loose strands of fiber prior to spinning; form slivers.

RUNNER Style that keeps selling over a period of time.

SALES PROMOTION MANAGER See PUBLICITY DIRECTOR.

SAMPLE First or trial garment made, often shown to trade.

SANFORIZED Trade name for shrink-tested.

SATIN Shiny, high-gloss fabric, usually silk or rayon.

SCHENTI Egyptian for "loin cloth."

SEAM Joining line where parts of garment are sewn together.

SEASONAL MERCHANDISE Merchandise purchased to meet demands of specific periods or seasons.

SECONDS Articles of merchandise that fall below standards set for first quality.

SECTION MANAGER Executive in operating division as management representative with disciplinary and adjustment jurisdiction; budgeting and staffing responsibility within departments under his or her supervision.

SELLING AREA Part of sales floor devoted exclusively to selling (shoe and ready-to-wear stock rooms, fitting rooms, and wrapping stations are considered part of selling area when sales could not be consummated without them).

SEPARATES Individual apparel items often planned to coordinate.

SERGE Soft, durable, woolen fabric.

SERVICE AREA Part of sales floor devoted to servicing the selling area (such as escalators, elevators, stairways, freight landings, restrooms, and shop windows).

SEVENTH AVENUE Synonym for New York garment district.

SHANTUNG Slub-weave fabric, originally silk.

SHARKSKIN Pebbly grained, woven fabric.

SHIFT Simple, slipover undergarment; shirt, chemise.

SHIRRING Stitching fabric so that it gathers.

SHUTTLE Used in weaving loom; passes back and forth, creating "weft."

SIGNING Writing and using signs for retail point of sale and display (manufacturers supply factual information and consumer benefits that make signing easy).

SILHOUETTE Outline; contour of figure or garment; profile.

SILK-SCREEN Hand method of applying prints to fabric or paper using silk fabric.

SISAL Smooth straw used for rugs.

SIZING Additive to fabric to give body, stiffness, smoothness; usually starch, gum, wax, or casein.

SLEEPER Good item if properly promoted; steady seller; sells slowly but is important.

SLIVER Rope or continuous strand of fiber prior to spinning; end product of roving process.

SLUB Yarn made with bunches of untwisted threads at irregular intervals.

SMOCKING Decorative stitching.

SOFT GOODS Textiles, apparel, curtains, draperies, bedding. *See also* HARD GOODS.

SOUTACHE Narrow, corded braid.

SPECIAL EVENTS DIRECTOR Reports to sales promotion manager; cooperates with advertising departments in activating promotions; supervises special events, such as demonstrations and parades.

SPECIALTY STORE Store concentrating on specific merchandise classification.

SPINNING Process of making thread or yarn by twisting fibers together.

SPOT CHECK Inspection and count of small, random amount of goods in large shipments.

STAPLE Item of merchandise for which there is a steady demand, usually nonfashion item; basic fiber, as in staple yarn.

STENCIL Paper or thin metal cut out to form motif or pattern to be transferred to another surface.

STOMACHER Apparel covering stomach and chest.

STORY BOARD Small series of sketches showing story line of TV spot.

STUFFER Enclosure sent to charge customer in bill envelope.

STYLE Cut, design, type of article, particular number; current fashion.

STYLIST Person who styles and accessorizes garments.

SUBTEEN (GIRLS) DEPARTMENT Separate department for girls 9–13 years old, one of the fastest-growing departments in retail stores.

SUEDE Soft leather with napped surface; used for gloves, jackets, belts.

SWATCH Small sample of a fabric.

SYNTHETIC Man-made, not natural.

TAFFETA Glossy, smooth silk or silklike fabric.

TAPESTRY Woven fabric of colored threads used as wall hanging or upholstery fabric.

TENSILE STRENGTH Breaking strength of fabric or thread; tested in terms of pounds.

TERRY Fabric with raised loop and uncut pile for toweling, usually cotton; also called turkish toweling.

TEXTILE Cloth or fabric.

THREAD   Filament, fiber, cord, of various degrees of fineness, produced by extrusion (synthetics) or twisting together fibers (spinning); used for constructing fabrics, sewing, stitching.

TIE-DYE   Tying together portions of fabric so that the fabric will not take dye evenly.

TOGA   Loose, Roman wrap robe or mantle draped around body.

TOILE   Any of various linen or sheer cotton fabrics.

TOOLING   Decorative work on leather or wood, often done by hand.

TONE ON TONE   Color superimposed on a closely related color.

TRADE PAPER   Publication aimed at specific trades, such as apparel, shoes, supermarket.

TRADEMARK   Trade name; symbol or word by which source or product is identified.

TRADING AREA   Surrounding area from which most of store's trade is drawn; each main branch store needs to know to what extent and from what directions it draws customers.

TRAFFIC   Number of persons, both prospective and actual customers, who enter a store or department.

TRICOT   Fabric knitted or woven to give knitted appearance.

TRUNK SHOW   Complete collection of a manufacturer or designer brought into retail store.

TUCK   Folded or gathered fabric stitched in place, used also to shape garment.

TUDOR   Relating to style of furniture and apparel, 1485-1603, during the reign of the Tudors in England—Henry VII, Henry VIII, Mary, Elizabeth I.

TULLE   Small-mesh net fabric.

TUNIC   Overblouse or coat, usually to hipline.

TURNOVER   Total number of times, within given period, that stock of goods is sold and replaced.

TURTLENECK   High, rolled collar.

TUSSAH   Shantung-type fabric, soft, strong, light-weight; pongee.

TWEED   Homespun-effect fabric originating in Scotland; rough-surfaced woolen.

TWILL   Weave producing ridges.

UNDERPRICED   Relating to merchandise that should be priced higher.

UNISEXUAL   Relating to items that can be worn by both men and women.

UNIT CONTROL   Inventory system, checking each item sold.

VELOUR   General term for cut-pile cloth; fabric with fine, raised finish; velvetlike.

VELVET   Thick piled fabric with plain back; originally cotton or silk, now also crush-resistant synthetics.

VELVETEEN   Cotton pile fabric; short, close pile.

VENDOR   Seller, manufacturer, resource.

VICTORIAN   Relating to the style of furniture and apparel, 1850-1900, during the reign of Victoria in England.

VIGNETTE   Process of deleting background in a photograph used in advertisement; in display, small suggestion of a room setting using complete furnishings but not setting up as a room; gradual shading off.

VIRGIN WOOL   Wool that has never before been processed.

VOGUE   Fashion, mode, what is in style.

VOILE   Transparent or semitransparent fabric of cotton, silk, or synthetics; used for apparel and curtains.

WALE   Vertical ridge formed in cloth, as in corduroy.

WARP   Yarns running the length of the fabric. *See also* WOOF.

WASH 'N WEAR   Relating to garments that need no ironing.

WEAVE   To form fabric by interlacing threads on looms; examples include basket, twill, diagonal, dobby, Jacquard, herringbone, plain, pile.

WEIGHTING   Adding chemical additives to fabric for more body; sizing.

WELT Strip of material, border edge or over seam, used for trimming or reinforcement; raised portion.

WHIPCORD Twill-type fabric, diagonal weave.

WHITE GOODS *See* LINENS.

WHOLESALE Price to retailer to which markup is added to get retail selling price.

WILL CALL Relating to merchandise to be picked up at a later date.

WOOF Yarns running crosswise in fabric, now called filling. *See also* WARP.

WORK DOWN Reduce inventory or stock.

WORK ROOMS Behind-the-scenes rooms for sales-supporting services, such as alterations and repairs.

WORK SHEET Form for recording key figures or records for one's own use.

WORSTED Strong yarn from long wool fibers; strong wool fabric made from yarn.

WRITE OFF Loss; to consider a purchase almost worthless.

YARN Thread, fiber, product of spinning and spinning mills; wool, cotton, silk, linen, or synthetic fibers.

YARN DYE Dye yarn instead of fabric; most sweaters are yarn-dyed.

ZIG ZAG Angular back-and-forth turns.

ZIP Close with slide fastener.

ZIPPER Slide-fastener closing.

SUGGESTED READINGS

296 Adams, James D. *Naked We Came*. New York: Holt, Rinehart and Winston, 1967. Interesting and humorous account of apparel.

Arnold, Pauline, and Percival White. *Clothes and Cloth*. New York: Holiday House, 1961. Serious analysis of apparel and of the material from which it is made.

Beaton, Cecil. *The Best of Beaton*. New York: Macmillan, 1968. The notable costume designer shows his best, including *My Fair Lady*.

Bender, Marylin. *Beautiful People*. New York: Coward, McCann, 1967. Society, fashion, and our times; the jet set is explained.

Benedict, Ruth. *Patterns of Culture*. Boston: Houghton Mifflin, 1934. Great classic about different peoples from an anthropological view.

Bennett-England, Rodney. *Dress Optional: The Revolution in Menswear*. Chester Springs, Pa.: Dufour, 1968. The changing picture in men's apparel.

Bigelow, Marybelle S. *Fashion in History*. St. Paul: Minnesota Business Publishing, 1970. Good supplemental reading on fashions through the years.

Bradley, Carolyn. *Western World Costume*. New York: Appleton-Century-Crofts, 1954. Interesting narrative with pictures of apparel in our society.

Brenner, Barbara. *Careers and Opportunities in Fashion*. New York: Dutton, 1964. Good analysis of the various career possibilities in fashion.

Brenninkmeyer, E. *Sociology of Fashion*. New York: Corner, 1969. Fashion analyzed from the standpoint of its role in society.

Brooke, Iris, and James Laver. *English Costume from the Fourteenth through the Nineteenth Century*. New York: Macmillan, 1937. Well-illustrated, intelligently approached review of fashions in Great Britain and the Western world.

Clarke, Leslie J. *Craftsman in Textiles*. New York: Praeger, 1968. Interesting exposition of the leaders of textile manufacture and design.

Cobrin, Harry. *Men's Clothing Industry: Colonial through Modern Times*. New York: Fairchild, 1970. Good history of the men's clothing industry.

Collier, Ann M. *A Handbook of Textiles*. New York: Pergamon, 1970. For textile students only.

Corinth, Kay. *Fashion Showmanship*. New York: Wiley, 1970. Former *Seventeen* editor tells how to promote fashions.

Crawford, M. C. *One World of Fashion*. 3rd ed. by Beatrice Zelin *et al.* New York: Fairchild, 1946. The interrelation of the various aspects of the fashion business.

Daves, Jessica. *Ready-Made Miracle*. New York: Putnam, 1967. Fashion's role in our society and its great contribution.

Epstein, Beryl. *Fashion Is Our Business*. Philadelphia: Lippincott, 1945. Discussion of the fashion business as an industry.

Esquire Magazine Editors. *Esquire Fashions for Men*. New York: Harper & Row, 1966. Taken from the pages of the leading men's magazine.

Fairchild, John. *Fashionable Savages*. New York: Doubleday, 1965. Observations of a fashion trade editor–publisher on people of his times.

Finley, Ruth. *The Lady of Godeys—Sarah Josepha Hale*. Philadelphia: Lippincott, 1941. History of early pioneer in fashion.

Fitz-Gibbon, Bernice. *Macy's, Gimbels, and Me*. New York: Simon and Schuster. The highest-paid copywriter and ad woman tells her story.

Fried, Eleanor. *Is the Fashion Business Your Business?* New York: Fairchild, 1958. Helpful for those thinking about making a career in fashion.

Galbraith, John Kenneth. *The Affluent Society*. Boston: Houghton Mifflin, 1958. Important study of our society from an economist's view.

Gorsline, Douglas. *What People Wore*. New York: Viking, 1952. Excellent pictorial history of fashion.

Hamburger, Estelle. *It's a Woman's Business*. New York: Vanguard, 1939. A brilliant mind gives you much to think about even though written more than thirty years ago.

Hansen, Henry H. *Costumes and Styles*. New York: Dutton, 1956. A somewhat different viewpoint on fashion and its effect on people.

Head, Edith. *Fashion As a Career*. New York: Messner, 1966. Excellent study of why to make fashion a career.

Hill, Margot H., and Peter A. Bucknell. *Evolution of Fashion*. New York: Van Nostrand, Reinhold, 1968. A thoughtful analysis of how previous fashions affect later concepts.

Horn, Marilyn. *Second Skin*. Boston: Houghton Mifflin, 1968. Contemporary thinking about fashion and its motivation.

Kybalova, Ludmila, *et al.* *Pictorial Encyclopedia of Fashion*. New York: Crown, 1969. Beautiful and comprehensive pictorial coverage of fashion through the years.

Laver, James. *Concise History of Costume and Fashion*. New York: Abrams, 1969. This British authority brings great knowledge of costume to bear on the subject.

Laver, James. *Costume through the Ages*. New York: Simon and Schuster, 1968. Interesting and penetrating analysis of apparel through the years.

Laver, James. *Dandies*. London: Weidenfeld and Nicholson, 1968. The expert talks about Beau Brummel and other famous dandies.

Laver, James. *Modesty in Dress*. Boston: Houghton Mifflin, 1969. Explanation of apparel as body covering.

Levin, Phyllis L. *Wheels of Fashion*. New York: Doubleday, 1965. An analysis of what makes fashion tick and who its leaders are.

Linton, George E. *Natural and Man-Made Textile Fibers*. New York: Hawthorn, 1966. An excellent summary of textiles, from fiber to finished product.

McCardell, Claire. *What Shall I Wear?* New York: Simon and Schuster, 1956. A famous designer discusses what to wear when and why.

Merriam, Eve. *Figleaf: The Business of Being in Fashion*. Philadelphia: Lippincott, 1960. Light-hearted and sometimes humorous analysis of fashion as occupation.

Mills, C. Wright. *White Collar*. New York: Oxford, 1951. Sociological study of economic classes, particularly the upper-middle class.

Payne, Blanche. *History of Costume*. New York: Harper & Row, 1965. A good recapitulation of apparel history to the present.

Picken, Mary B. *Fashion Dictionary*. New York: Funk & Wagnalls, 1956. Excellent reference for fashion vocabulary and terminology.

Quennell, Peter. *On Human Finery*. Newell, CA: Hogarth, 1945. Interesting analysis of apparel through the ages.

Richards, Florence. *The Ready-to-Wear Industry*. New York: Fairchild, 1951. A sensible explanation of New York's garment industry.

Roshko, Bernard. *The Rag Race*. New York: Funk & Wagnalls, 1962. The story of competitiveness in the garment industry.

Ryan, Mildred G. *Dress Smartly*. New York: Scribner's, 1967. Straightforward basic advice on how to make the most of yourself.

Stein, Leon. *The Triangle Fire*. Philadelphia: Lippincott, 1968. A reporter's approach to a tragic episode that changed many laws and regulations pertaining to the fashion industry.

Sices, Murray. *Seventh Avenue*. New York: Fairchild, 1953. A realistic explanation of the garment industry of New York City.

Toffler, Alvin. *Future Shock*. New York: Random House, 1970. Excellent analysis of the future from the standpoint of society and technology.

Troxel, M.D., and B. Judelle. *Fashion Merchandising*. New York: McGraw-Hill, 1971. Up-to-date, detailed picture of current merchandising practices.

Veblen, Thorstein. *The Theory of the Leisure Class*. New York: Macmillan, 1912. A brilliant thinker introduces a new economic viewpoint and theory.

Vecchio, Walter, and Robert Riley. *The Fashion Makers: A Photographic Record*. New York: Crown, 1968. Just what its title claims.

Wilcox, R. Turner. *Mode in Costume*. New York: Scribner's, 1942. Pictorial exposition of contemporary apparel.

Wilcox, R. Turner. *Five Centuries of American Costume*. New York: Scribner's, 1963. A pictorial history, including military fashion.

Wilcox, R. Turner. *Mode in Costume*. New York: Scribner's, 1942. Pictorial exposition of contemporary apparel.

Women's Wear Daily. *Seventy-Five Years of Fashion*. New York: Textile Book Service, 1975. Summary of the past seventy-five years of fashion by the leading fashion trade journal.

Young, Agatha. *Recurring Cycles of Fashion: 1760–1937*. New York: Harper & Row, 1937. Interesting analysis of fashion cycles and how they repeat themselves.

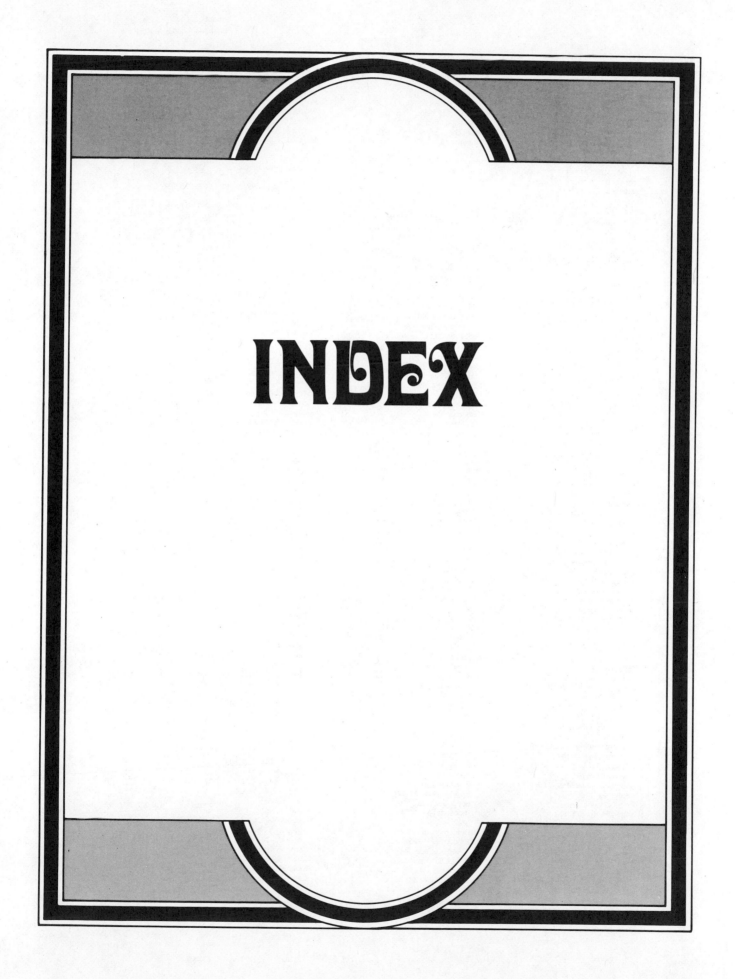

INDEX

ACKNOWLEDGMENTS

In addition to the illustrations itemized by page number, grateful acknowledgment is also made to the firms and associations whose trademarks have been reproduced in this book.

Abraham & Strauss: 203. *Aileen:* 54, 57, 59 left and right, 263,267. *Amalgamated Clothing Workers of America, AFL-CIO, CLC:* 155 bottom left and right, 163, 164. *American Trade & Industrial Development with Israel, Inc.:* 144 bottom left. *Apparel Mart, Chicago:* 136. *B. Altman:* 76 bottom, 89, 115 bottom, 118 bottom, 203, 207, 220. *Baker Furniture:* 119. *Aubrey Beardsley:* 241 top left. *Bergdorf Goodman:* 209, 240. *Bergner's:* 92. *Bloomingdale's, Wagner International Photos, Inc.:* 108, 120 top, 122 bottom, 123 top, 125, 203. *Bonwit Teller:* 240. *Brothers II:* 102 right. *Burlington Industries, Inc.:* 120 bottom, 121 top, 124 right, 270 bottom right. *Condé Nast Publications Inc.:* 126 left (Copyright © 1975 by The Condé Nast Publications Inc.), 197 (*Glamour,* Copyright © 1973 by The Condé Nast Publications Inc.; *Mademoiselle,* Copyright © 1975 by The Condé Nast Publications Inc.: *Vogue,* Copyright © 1976 by The Condé Nast Publications Inc.), 243. *Country Miss:* 60, 61 top, *Denim Council:* 214. *Denson-Frey & Affiliates:* 115 bottom. *di Sant'Angelo, Inc.:* 10 right. *Walt Disney Productions, Character Merchandising Division, California International Apparel, Kennington:* 90 top left, 91, 217. *Doyle, Dane, Bernbach, Inc.:* 194. *E. I. du Pont de Nemours & Co.:* 5 bottom center (Dacron), 10 left (Orlon), 25 (Antron), 85 top left and bottom right (Orlon), top right (Dacron), 100 bottom left and right (Qiana), 128 (Dacron), 138 top (Antron and Lycra), 146 (Orlon), 241 (Lycra), 255 bottom left (Dacron, Orlon, and Lycra), bottom right (Dacron), 262 bottom (Qiana). *Eastman Kodak:* 70 top right, 262 top, 115 top. *EMBA (Eastern Mink Breeders Assn.):* 40. *Emporium;* 203. *Esquire Inc.:* 198. *Essie Pinsker Associates, Inc.:* 54, 57, 59 left and right, 263, 267. *Fairchild Publications, Inc.:* 140, 195. *Fashion Institute of Technology:* 139, 141, 215, 269 top. *Fortune Magazine:* 105 bottom left. *Franklin Simon:* 178. *Gimbel's, Phila.:* 212. *Hagstrom Co., Inc.:* 133. *Harcour Publications:* 196 (*Body Fashions*). *Hattie Carnegie:* 240. *The Hearst Corp.:* 126 right. *Herald House:* 210. *International Ladies' Garment Workers' Union:* 13 right, 14 bottom, 21 and 22 bottom ("What They Wore," 1973), 132 top and bottom (Justice Photo, Jerry Soalt), 154, 155 top (Photo by Brown Bros., N.Y.C.), 156, 157 (Photo by Lewis Hine), 158 (Photoworld, Inc.), 162, 165 (Photo by Jerry Soalt), 166, 167. *Johnston, Inc.:* 88 right. *Levi Strauss & Co.:* 83 top, 205. *Lord & Taylor:* 118 top. *McCall Pattern Co.:* 224, 225, 229, 233, 234 left and right, 235 top. *R. H. Macy:* 85 bottom left, 111 (January Furniture Show—Macy's New York), 172 and 216 (Macy's Annual Thanksgiving Day Parade in New York), 181 left (Macy's Herald Square, New York—The World's Largest Store), 188 left, 203, 216. *Man-Made Fiber Producers Assn, Inc.:* 46. *Market Previews Inc.:* 196 (*Textile Directions*). *Marshall Field & Co.:* 181. *Martin's, Brooklyn, N.Y.:* 183. *Terry Mayer:* 214. *Merchandise Mart, Chicago:* 113. *Monsanto Textiles Co.:* 9. *New Yorker Inc.:* 199. *New York Public Library, Picture Collection:* 2, 3, 4, 5 top and bottom right, 6, 7, 8, 12, 14 top, 15, 16, 17, 18, 19, 20, 22 top, 23 top, 24, 26, 27, 28, 29, 30, 31, 34, 35, 36, 37, 39, 55, 56, 65, 66, 69, 70 bottom, 71 bottom, 72 bottom, 73, 74, 75, 76 top and left, 77, 78, 80, 81, 82, 83 right, 84, 87, 88 left, 90 right, 94, 95, 96, 97, 98, 99, 100 top, 102 left, 103, 109, 110, 112 ("The Chairmaker" by Stanley Anderson), 114, 116, 117, 121 bottom, 123 bottom, 129, 130, 131, 135, 142, 174, 177, 180, 183, 184, 188 bottom, 221, 222, 223, 232, 239, 240, 241 top right, 269 bottom, 274, 275, 276. *Ohrbach's:* 194. *Mary Quant;* 144 top. *Retail Reporting Bureau, N.Y.C.:* 183, 269 bottom. *Leonard Rubin Collection:* 23 bottom, 71 left, 72 top, 104, 222 bottom. *Saks Fifth Avenue:* 143, 206, 240, 269 bottom. *Sanger-Harris:* 86 left. *Schiffli Embroidery Promotion Board:* 266. *Sears Roebuck & Co.:* 175, 176, 182, 187. *Simplicity Pattern Co.:* 226, 230. *Swedish Trade Commission:* 144 right. *Time Inc.:* 199 (*Sports Illustrated* and *Time*). *F. R. Tripler & Co.:* 206. *Vogue-Butterick Pattern Co.:* 61 right. *Wamsutta Mills, Division of M. Lowenstein & Sons, Inc.:* 122 top, 124 left. *Warner Bros., Inc.:* 238 photo of George C. Scott. *Watt & Shand:* 86 right. *Woolworth's:* 184. *World Publishing Co.; Leonard Vosburgh, artist:* 173 top.